Excellent

BOOKS
FOR EARLY
and EAGER
Readers

Excellent

BOOKS
FOR EARLY
and EAGER
Readers

KATHLEEN T. ISAACS

An imprint of the American Library Association
Chicago | 2016

Longtime teacher and occasional librarian **KATHLEEN T. ISAACS** has worked with young people of all ages at schools and colleges in Maryland, Washington, D.C., British Hong Kong, and China as well as the Enoch Pratt Free Library in Baltimore. Primarily a middle-school humanities teacher, she also taught children's and young adult literature at Towson University and geography to highly able elementary-school students for the Center for Talented Youth at Johns Hopkins University. She served on the Citizen's Advisory Committee for the Baltimore County Office of Gifted Education and on numerous ALA book award committees, including Newbery, Batchelder, and Best Books for Young Adults. She has chaired the ALSC Notable Children's Books, the ALSC Sibert Award, and the USBBY Outstanding International Books Committees. She writes and reviews books for *Kirkus Reviews, Booklist,* and other professional journals. She is an active participant in the Capitol Choices book discussion group. She is the author of *Picturing the World* (ALA Editions) and *Bugs, Bogs, Bats, and Books* (Huron Street Press). She is the parent of three early able readers and the grandparent of seven.

© 2016 by the American Library Association

Extensive effort has gone into ensuring the reliability of the information in this book; however, the publisher makes no warranty, express or implied, with respect to the material contained herein.

ISBN: 978-0-8389-1344-4 (paper)

Library of Congress Cataloging-in-Publication Data
Isaacs, Kathleen T., author.
  Excellent books for early and eager readers / Kathleen T. Isaacs.
    pages cm
  Includes bibliographical references and indexes.
  ISBN 978-0-8389-1344-4 (paper)
  1. Gifted children—Books and reading—United States.
  2. Children's literature—Bibliography. 3. Best books—United States.
  4. Reading—Parent participation—United States. I. Title.
Z1039.G55I83 2015
028.5'5—dc23
                                          2015020059

Book design by Kim Thornton in the Charis SIL and Aleo typefaces.
Cover illustrations by bluelela/Shutterstock, Inc.

♾ This paper meets the requirements of ANSI/NISO Z39.48–1992 (Permanence of Paper).

Printed in the United States of America

20 19 18 17 16   5 4 3 2 1

To Jenny, Katy, and Robert

Contents

Acknowledgments | *ix*

1 Early Eager Readers and Their Books.................1

2 What Makes a Good Children's Book and
What Makes a Good Book for a Young Reader?...7

3 Early Reader Transitional Books.....................17

4 Poetry...33

5 Families 47

6 Friends and School 65

7 Talking Animals and Tiny People....................79

8 Witches and Wizards and Magic 95

9 Quests and Adventures...............................111

10 Traditional Tales......................................127

11 Living Long Ago.......................................145

12 Real Places and People..............................163

13 Humor...183

14 Compelling Characters...............................197

15 Complicated Plots.....................................213

16 Finding Books for the Eager Reader 227

Subject Index | *231*

Author & Title Index | *239*

Acknowledgments

I am most grateful for the advice and support of numerous librarians, teachers, booksellers, parents, and young readers who helped and encouraged me with this project. I would especially like to thank

Miriam Lang Budin, Chappaqua Library, Chappaqua, New York

Margaret Chang, formerly of the Massachusetts College of Liberal Arts

Lisa von Drasek, University of Minnesota Libraries

Roxanne Hsu Feldman, The Dalton School, New York, New York

Lisa Field

Joann Fruchtman, The Children's Bookstore, Baltimore, Maryland

Twig George, The Park School, Brooklandville, Maryland

Jane Gerson

Gina Hirschorn

Amy Palmer Laster

Melissa Kaplan

Kym Martelly

Karen McPherson, Takoma Park Library, Takoma Park, Maryland

Dan Pier

Heidi Powell, Politics & Prose, Washington, D.C.

John Peters, formerly of the New York Public Library

Deena Raja

Robin Smith, The Ensworth School, Nashville, Tennessee

Shae Uden

Shoba and Mira Vanchiswar

Caroline Ward, Ferguson Library, Stamford, Connecticut

Elisabeth Willers

As well as my own children and grandchildren, who cheerfully shared their personal experiences.

Early Eager Readers and Their Books

 TWO-YEAR-OLD IN A CAR SEAT ENTERTAINS herself with hand-me-down copies of *Babybug* magazine, looking at the pictures and reciting the words. Probably she's memorized them, possibly she's reading. A five-year-old in a school library quietly whispers each word in a favorite picture book, following the text with his finger and matching it to the sounds of the story he knows by heart; another reads her favorite picture book to a friend. Bored with listening to her classmates read the class assignment aloud, a third grader reads her own book under her desk. A boy, perhaps in fourth grade, whose goal is to read all the Doctor Doolittle stories, comes day after day to the New York Public Library Central Children's Room's historical collection because there are no circulating

copies of most of the sequels. In a public library in Connecticut, a young patron arrives every week with two empty cloth shopping bags. After asking the librarians to recommend titles she hasn't read yet, she fills them with more books than she can lift. What do these children have in common? They're all early able, eager readers.

Some years ago a blogger called The Book Whisperer listed some identifying characteristics of children she calls "underground readers," perhaps because they often seem to live more in the world of their reading than in the classroom. Such children, she says, may "read constantly, often covertly, and choose reading as a pastime." She describes them as follows:

- They read at an early age.
- They may have taught themselves to read.
- They require less drill to master the reading process.
- They synthesize multiple reading strategies.
- They possess advanced vocabulary knowledge and usage.
- They read three to four times more than most children their age.
- They will continue to read voraciously after the peak reading years (fourth to eighth grades) and into adulthood.
- They may prefer abstract genres like fantasy, read deeply in one genre or topic, or prefer nonfiction to fiction.[1]

Librarians in school and public libraries are often asked to provide suggestions for these children and their parents. So are teachers and caregivers. I asked some librarians and teachers I know to connect me with parents who might be willing to talk about their children's early, eager reading. These parents were clear about their children's enthusiasm. One parent said that her daughter "seemed to be born wired for words." Another described her son, already reading early chapter books in kindergarten: "He would pick up a book and sit down and read for over an hour." A third told me her daughter "devoured anything she could find."

But early eager readers are as different from one another as are any other young people. Their reading depends far more on their interest in the text than on their skills or chronological age. If they care, they will make enormous efforts. The range of their choices is surprising. They look for highly interesting and challenging books, but they also look for books that are simply fun. They may choose to read everything written by a particular author, or involving a specific character, or about a certain subject. One reads every title in a series; another is satisfied after only two or three.

Many eager readers are quite articulate about their preferences, though they may change from week to week or year to year. Some children realize very early on that they read for character; others like action or a well-constructed plot. One parent told me her daughter enjoyed rewriting and adding to the stories, as older writers of fan fiction do. Others prolong their involvement in the story by dramatizing it, reciting the dialog, imagining what characters would do in a different situation, writing sequels, or writing to the author. They don't do these things because an adult told them to; they do them spontaneously, extending the enjoyment of the reading experience.

In my research for this book, I had conversations with numerous parents, booksellers, teachers, and librarians who serve such children, and with young people who had been early, eager readers themselves. I looked at lists of suggested titles compiled by libraries that often have such requests, and at lists of good books, and book reviews. Not surprisingly, I found that some of the books that young, eager readers enjoy reading and rereading are classics, books that have been popular for years, even generations, and books that have won awards. But even more often, they are books that meet their personal needs, books on subjects that interest them, and books that are readily available. (Several parents told me that they had been more successful in leading their young readers to a particular title by leaving it around than by suggesting it.)

It is tempting to want to offer an eager reader a book we loved as a child. It can be hard to remember how old we were when we read it, and many of us underestimate the difficulty of books we particularly enjoyed, especially for children living in a different era and with different reading experiences. It's also tempting to steer these readers to "good" books—award winners, or books that affirm positive values or that will improve their vocabulary and their understanding of the world. Most adult readers don't limit themselves to books that are good for them. In fact, most adults who read in their leisure time read for entertainment, not improvement. To develop a lifetime love of reading, children need to read for pleasure.

I read or reread every book I've annotated in this bibliography and many of the mentioned sequels. This list of suggestions includes plenty of "good" books, but it also includes numerous titles that are, frankly, forgettable, especially titles introducing popular early chapter book series. These titles may not stretch vocabulary and broaden horizons, but they build reading comfort and reading fluency.

Readers' advisors expect to see recommended age levels attached to titles. These suggestions take into account a book's appearance, its subject, the approach, the presentation, and the difficulty of the text. They appear in reviews, on book jackets, in library and store catalogs, and in various rating systems used in schools. As a reviewer, I provide them for readers of book review journals. But for these early readers, a book can't really be prescribed for a given age. Their appeal and the child's ability to read them depend far more on the child's reading and life experiences and on the child's interests and determination.

Conventional wisdom says that beginning readers look for books with just a few words on each page, without complex sentences or challenging vocabulary. But a five-year-old I know resolutely made her way through the fairy poems of Mary Barker, one poem a night, first choosing the illustration she liked, from a complete collection, and then working out the accompanying words. Another first grader who had barely mastered phonics laboriously sounded out the words from titles that interested him in Scholastic's Insider books, a nonfiction series designed for much older readers but which had been for several years his favorite bedtime listening.

For the purposes of this bibliography I have offered general interest levels (younger, middle, older) that might suggest when (within the limits of ages four to ten) a book might be of interest to a child who reads a lot. These are advisory rather than prescriptive. Books about kindergartners with simple sentences and few words on a page are not likely to appeal to a third- or fourth-grade reader unless they are very humorous. Suspenseful books with three hundred pages won't work for most second graders—but there is the *Harry Potter* exception. Books you could read aloud to a preschooler, like Kipling's *Just So Stories,* can be quite a challenge for them to read on their own. So, take my suggestions with a large grain of salt. The bibliographic entries include one company's measure of text complexity, The Lexile® Framework for Reading. These measures may be particularly helpful in comparing books you don't know to books you do. An explanation of the system and the ratings from the company's website follows:

> Teachers and parents can best serve a student's literacy needs when they treat him or her as a unique individual, rather than as a test score or a grade-level norm or average. The reading abilities of young people in the same grade at school can vary just as much as their shoe sizes. However, grade-leveling methods commonly are used to match students with books.
>
> When a Lexile text measure matches a Lexile reader measure, this is called a "targeted" reading experience. The reader will likely encounter some level of difficulty with the text, but not enough to get frustrated. This is the best way to grow as a reader—with text that's not too hard but not too easy.[2]

Many librarians use Lexile® measures to connect young readers with books they not only can read but will enjoy, and to help parents, grandparents, caregivers, and even teachers find appropriate reading material for their early, eager readers.

I included original copyright dates. In some cases, I have suggested particular editions, especially of classics presented particularly well and of books that have been revised in some way. Where possible, I've given the dates of recent hardcover editions. Many of these titles have even more recent paperback, prebound, or e-book versions for those who prefer those formats. Books go in and out of print so quickly that book buyers will need to check to see what's currently available.

Finally, although I had a great deal of help along the way, this is just one person's idiosyncratic selection of what public librarian Karen McPherson jokingly calls "lo-high books": books for children in lower grades with high reading skills. Another writer might make very different choices. I have tried to make my scope broad, though I've left out the whole genre of graphic fiction and nonfiction usually lumped under the heading of graphic novels. I've made a point of including authors whose works children might want to explore beyond the titles listed. I've had to leave out many titles that would, and do, also appeal to these young, enthusiastic readers. Knowing the child you have in mind is the first consideration in any attempt to find the right book for him or her. This should not be your only guide. The final chapter includes suggestions for other places to seek suggestions of titles and authors that might engage the child you know.

NOTES

1. Donalyn Miller, "Mind the Gap: Engaging Gifted Readers," *The Book Whisperer* (blog), March 7, 2009, http://blogs.edweek.org/teachers/book_whisperer/2009/03/mind_the_gap_engaging_gifted_r.html.

2. "What is a Lexile Measure?" https://lexile.com/about-lexile/lexile-overview.

Chapter 2

What Makes a Good Children's Book and What Makes a Good Book for a Young Reader?

ICTURE BOOKS—TRADITIONALLY DESIGNED TO be a shared experience between adult and child—are the books most children encounter first. These books serve as an introduction to how a book is read: the flow of information from left to right, the magic of page turns, the progression of a story from beginning to end. In the best picture books, words and pictures work together to make the whole greater than the sum of its parts. The pictures may be what readers see first, but the text is also vital and often challenging. The best picture books also have grand words. Think about the "wild rumpus" in *Where the Wild Things Are,* or the matador, picadores, and bandilleros in *Ferdinand,* or how Peter Rabbit "scuttered

7

underneath the bushes." These words build vocabulary long before children are able to use them on their own.

Many children memorize the text of picture books that are repeatedly read to them, reciting the words that go with each picture as they turn the pages. But most who are beginning to read on their own will spend some time with the kinds of books considered for the Geisel Award, given each year to the "most distinguished American book for beginning readers published in English in the United States." Named for Theodor Seuss Geisel, better known as Dr. Seuss, this award honors books that provide "a stimulating and successful reading experience for the beginning reader" and have "the kind of plot, sensibility, and rhythm that can carry a child along from start to finish."[1] The Geisel committee is one of several award committees sponsored by the Association for Library Service to Children division of the American Library Association. In comparison to other ALSC awards, the criteria for these early readers are quite detailed:

- Subject matter must be intriguing enough to motivate the child to read.
- The book may or may not include short "chapters."
- New words should be added slowly enough to make learning them a positive experience.
- Words should be repeated to ensure knowledge retention.
- Sentences must be simple and straightforward.
- There must be a minimum of twenty-four pages.
- Books may not be longer than ninety-six pages.
- The illustrations must demonstrate the story being told.
- The book creates a successful reading experience, from start to finish.
- The plot advances from one page to the next and creates a "page-turning" dynamic.[2]

Even within the tight framework of these very specific criteria—illustrations that demonstrate, as opposed to the illustrations in a picture book, which might provide a whole separate story line; and the need for word repetition, simple sentences, and so on—the range of books whose authors and illustrators have been honored by this committee since its establishment in 2006 has been quite wide. Winners and honor books include titles in series by Mo Willems, Kevin Henkes, Grace Lin, Cynthia Rylant, and Kate DiCamillo and Alison McGhee. There are graphic novels such as *Benny and Penny in the Big No-No!* (Hayes, 2009), picture books such as *I Want My Hat Back* (Klassen, 2011), and nonfiction such as *Wolfsnail: A Backyard Predator* (Campbell, 2008) and *Hello, Bumblebee Bat* (Lunde, 2007). The Geisel website offers a solid list of reading suggestions.

Beginning readers do like stories where structures are predictable. Series are especially popular because the story pattern, setting, and characters quickly become familiar. Series have long been a staple of early reading diets. They make the young reader feel more confident and competent by allowing them to digest new material within a recognizable framework. Every title annotated in the next chapter, "Early Reader Transitional Books," has at least one sequel or companion book, and most have many. Series also work for older readers and provide a comfortable follow-up for author and publisher. (Indeed, series make up a good portion of adult readers' diets as well.) In this bibliography I've attempted to note series, and I list their titles if there are five or fewer. Other good places to look for sequel titles are authors' websites and even Wikipedia.

Children who catch on to the magic of decoding early may quickly move on to the magic of making a story come to life in their imaginations—the movie in their heads, so to speak. At this point they prefer books that have the look and heft of chapter books. Even though picture books often have more difficult vocabulary and more interesting subjects, these children see themselves as readers and want to be seen that way. Let them choose to be seen reading chapter books and use the fantastic range of picture books as bedtime stories. Maybe your reader will be willing to try reading one of them on his or her own, in privacy.

It used to be a given that children's stories were told in a straightforward, chronological fashion. There might be a flashback early on, or possibly a framing story, but more complicated narrative structures were reserved for an older intended audience. This is no longer the case except in the transitional books. There are children's stories with several narrative strands, stories that follow several different characters, and stories told in multiple formats, including cartoons. First-person stories have unreliable narrators and plot threads are left dangling. Young readers seem to manage them all, and the more experience they have with narrative complexity, the better readers they become. Children also enjoy rereading; they do it often. Things they didn't get the first time come clear when they're encountered again, or the third or fifth or seventeenth time.

It also used to be a given that children's books were short. *Harry Potter* changed all that. Many of the young readers I encountered in the course of my teaching and my research had read the first titles in that series before they were eight years old. Some read and reread the first 309-page volume obsessively. Some continued with the series, either until a parent or teacher gently suggested that perhaps they'd like to wait to read the final, darker stories or until they'd finished the last 784-page tome. After being immersed in the boarding school world and the familiar fantasy tropes for a period of weeks or months or years, they emerge ready for nearly anything. In a telephone conversation, one parent expressed surprise at her sixth grader's reading sophistication: "She doesn't miss anything. . . . The Harry Potter books and Rick Riordan touched on archetypal themes, so she's understanding them."

When people talk about children's books beyond picture books, they're usually thinking of fiction, the kinds of stories made into movies and television shows. Most books that win the general children's book awards best known in this country—the Newbery award, and the National Book Award for Young People's Literature—are fiction. Every year, the ALA/ALSC Newbery award committee chooses the most distinguished book published for children in the Unites States the previous year and may also highlight some honor books. The criteria are remarkably general. Committee members are asked to consider the following:

interpretation of the theme or concept

presentation of information, including accuracy, clarity,
    and organization

development of a plot

delineation of characters

delineation of a setting

appropriateness of style[3]

The award winners and honor books sometimes surprise people. But they are usually fiction and usually aimed at readers at the upper end of the age group that ALSC serves, children from zero to fourteen years old.

The National Book Award for Young People's Literature is chosen annually by five judges, usually writers, but sometimes librarians, educators, and bookstore owners. Finalists are named, but no criteria are published. These books also tend to be for readers at the upper end of childhood. These award-winning books can be very good choices for early able readers, but there is no guarantee that they will have themes and content that are right for four- to ten-year old readers.

Almost all the parents I talked to said their young readers had a favorite subject or subjects. They want to know about trucks and soccer players, or space exploration and dolphins, or the environment and Greek mythology. And fiction is not the only form they choose to read. Many young readers look for true stories. They want to learn facts. Many adults remember reading countless biographies in the venerable Childhood of Famous Americans series. Librarians and bookstore owners say that titles in the *Who Was?* biography series are circulating and selling well today. In the chapter called "Real Places and People," I barely scratch the surface of the possibilities of nonfiction; I've annotated many more informational titles in previous bibliographies: *Picturing the World* (ALA Editions, 2013) and *Bugs, Bogs, Bats, and Books* (Huron Street Press, 2014). This is an area where a child's particular interest tends to trump any consideration of reading level.

There are criteria for good nonfiction books as well. Another ALA/ALSC Committee, the Sibert Award Committee, annually chooses the most distinguished informational book published in English in this country. Committee members look for titles with these qualities:

> excellent, engaging, and distinctive use of language
> excellent, engaging, and distinctive visual presentation
> appropriate organization and documentation
> clear, accurate, and stimulating presentation of facts, concepts, and ideas
> appropriate style of presentation for subject and for intended audience
> supportive features (index, table of contents, maps, time lines, etc.)
> respectful and of interest to children[4]

More and more, publishers are providing back matter or a second level of information in nonfiction books so that what appears to be a picture book is also a good source for the elementary student's exploration of a subject.

Some early readers have a special interest in language, perhaps reflecting the way language is used and talked about in their homes. The National Council of Teachers of English has an award for fiction, the Charlotte Huck Award; one for nonfiction, the Orbis Pictus Award; and an Excellence in Poetry award that goes to a poet for his or her body of work for young people. Their honorees tend to reflect an emphasis on distinctive use of language. Poetry can be particularly appealing, both for the introduction of new vocabulary and interesting connections, and for the apparent accessibility of its short lines and ample white space on a page. Every family should own at least one general collection of poetry to go along with its collections of nursery tales and myths. Libraries should be offering many more. When poetry collections are included in themed book talks, they circulate.

When children move past simple decoding and start looking for meaning in their reading, it has become commonplace to say that they are looking for both mirrors and windows. This apt metaphor was coined by education professor Rudine Sims Bishop. Her original image, as expressed in a 1990 essay, was even more complex:

> Books are sometimes windows, offering views of worlds that may be real or imagined, familiar or strange. These windows are also sliding glass doors, and readers have only to walk through in imagination to become part of whatever world has been created or recreated by the author. When lighting conditions are just right, however, a window can also be a mirror. Literature transforms human experience and reflects it back to us, and in that reflection we can see our own lives and experiences as part of the larger human experience. Reading, then, becomes a means of self-affirmation, and readers often seek their mirrors in books.[5]

Bishop was writing particularly about African American children, arguing that they needed to see themselves specifically in some of their reading. The same can surely be said for many other racial, ethnic, and cultural groups, for children from less common or less privileged backgrounds, and children with disabilities. All children deserve books in which they easily see themselves as well as books that connect them to others' lives.

But what happens when the reflection children see of themselves is a negative one? Many of the stories that adults remember most fondly from their own childhood reading and listening include stereotypes and prejudices that twenty-first-century readers would and should find troubling and likely offensive. African Americans speak in dialect and are caricatured in illustrations. They serve and support; they're not the principal players. Native Americans wear paint and feathers and engage in massacres. Women, if pictured at all, are homemakers. Derogatory names and phrases that reflect the prejudices of time gone by are part of the narrative.

Some popular books have been reissued with appropriate editorial changes. P. L. Travers herself removed a chapter in *Mary Poppins* in which the children travel around the world meeting Eskimos, near-naked Negroes, Red Indians, and a pigtailed Mandarin[6] and replaced it with a chapter in which the children meet animals from different parts of the world. Newer editions of Edward Eager's *Magic by the Lake,* originally published in 1957, have eliminated an offensive illustration and slightly changed some words in the children's cannibal adventure.[7] But in *Caddie Woodlawn* (1935), although Caddie and her father support Indian John, their friend, the language Carol Ryrie Brink uses to describe her Native characters and details she chooses to include throughout the book are so shaped by prejudices still current in the 1930s that it would be difficult to redact the text without destroying the story. I didn't include this Newbery Medal winner in this selection, though it makes me sad to let go of one of my childhood favorites. Similarly, the most recent editions of the often-recommended *Homer Price* (McCloskey, 1943) still include a chapter describing a Centerburg pageant celebrating an episode in which Indians were said to have sold land to the town founders for a jug of cough syrup and then become addicted, with an illustration showing Homer and a friend in loincloths and two feathers in their hair.[8]

We cannot expect authors from the past to have present-day sensibilities. And there is an argument to be made for presenting their words without editorial correction. They tell us how it was in those times and places, how they or the people they chose to write about saw their world. It is easy to make an author's prejudices the opportunity for conversation with a child who is listening to a text, or in a classroom discussion of a book. It is much harder to do this when children are reading on their own. It takes maturity and considerable reading experience to understand phrases such as "Indian giver" or "half-breed" as representative of the author's times; younger children may incorporate them into their own language. I don't advocate keeping children from their own reading choices, for the most part, but I do think that parents need to be aware of what their children are reading and must be prepared to counteract outdated assumptions about other people and places. Parents of children of color have been particularly sensitive to these upsetting portrayals; all parents need to be paying attention.

Similarly, books may include subject matter that parents feel their children are not ready for. Many children's classics include the death of a child; it happened more often in the past, but it still happens today.

No one who has read, heard, or watched Alcott's *Little Women* or Paterson's *Bridge to Terabithia* can forget Beth or Leslie; these are part of our culture's shared literary experience. Some parents, though, prefer to postpone that experience for their children, or to make it one they share, through reading aloud, rather than one their young child encounters on his or her own. Some children's classics include pieces of history that involve upsetting violence: the Holocaust in Europe, for example, or slavery, or the Native American experience in the United States. Again, it's important for adults to know the child and the child's reading experience, and to be ready and able to continue discussion.

One reason parents of early able readers look for guidance on their children's reading is the increasing edginess of books published for middle graders and teens. Sexual subjects that were once taboo are now openly addressed. In six books, published between 1908 and 1938, Montgomery's Anne of Green Gables grows up, marries, and has children, but nothing in the narrative touches on how that actually happened. A child who begins a more modern series, like Naylor's Alice McKinley (1985–2013) books, may find the sexual and emotional content of the later books surprising, or beyond their ken. But children have a way of ignoring what they don't understand. For several years I read George's *Julie of the Wolves* with my fifth-grade students. In their nightly reading journal entries and daily class discussions, none showed any awareness that there was a sexual assault in that book. When one of my granddaughters was seven, she insisted on taking *Julie of the Wolves* home with her to read in spite of my efforts to substitute *My Side of the Mountain*. She did notice what happened between Julie and her childlike husband. As she explained to her mother, "They were laughing at him because he couldn't mate with her." She interpreted the scene in terms of her experience with cats and dogs and ducks.

Many of the parents I talked with work hard to keep up with their young child's reading. A parent of an eight-year-old commented: "When we discuss the books, he sticks to the themes in the stories that are relevant for his age, and he tends not to ponder on the mature themes, which I believe is because he doesn't fully understand them. I tend to discuss the topics he brings up and not 'force' additional topics that may be addressed in the book."

NOTES

1. Association for Library Service to Children, "Theodor Seuss Geisel Award," www.ala.org/alsc/awardsgrants/bookmedia/geiselaward/geiselabout.

2. Association for Library Service to Children, "Theodor Seuss Geisel Award Terms and Criteria," www.ala.org/alsc/awardsgrants/bookmedia/ geiselaward/geiselawardtermscriteria/geiselawardtermscriter.

3. Association for Library Service to Children, "Newbery Award Terms and Criteria," www.ala.org/alsc/awardsgrants/bookmedia/newberymedal/ newberyterms/newberyterms.

4. Association for Library Service to Children, "(Robert F.) Sibert Informational Book Award Terms and Criteria," www.ala.org/alsc/awardsgrants/ bookmedia/sibertmedal/sibertterms/sibertmedaltrms.

5. Reading Is Fundamental, "Mirrors, Windows, and Sliding Glass Doors," www.rif.org/us/literacy-resources/multicultural/mirrors-windows-and -sliding-glass-doors.htm.

6. P. L. Travers, "Bad Tuesday," chapter 6 in *Mary Poppins* (New York: Harcourt, Brace, 1934).

7. Edward Eager, *Magic by the Lake* (San Diego: Harcourt Brace Young Classics edition, 1999).

8. Robert McCloskey, *Homer Price* (New York: Puffin, 1943), 143.

Chapter 3

Early Reader Transitional Books

THESE ARE TRULY "TRANSITIONAL BOOKS"— the chapter books children are likely to read as soon as they are reading on their own. Some children stick with these early readers for some time; others will graduate to more complicated texts quite quickly. These books have relatively simple sentences and vocabulary; their illustrations provide textual clues. These are stories with familiar subjects, most often families, friends, and pets, or appealing nonfiction topics. The successful ones spawn sequels and series that allow young readers to tackle new titles with confidence because they have enough experience with the structure, characters, and, usually, the setting they will be reading about. Some of the titles listed in this section are packaged as part of publishers' early reader series; others are not explicitly labeled but are still appropriate. Readers who have gone on to more challenging books sometimes enjoy returning to old friends from this group, as well.

Fly Guy Presents: Space

By Tedd Arnold. Illustrated by Tedd Arnold. Scholastic, 2013.

Interest level: **Younger** • Lexile measure: **590L**
Early reader; Nonfiction

Buzz and his pet, Fly Guy, visit a space museum and learn facts about the universe. This is the second in a very easy informational series spun off from Arnold's original Fly Guy titles for beginning readers. Arnold uses simple sentences and appropriate words, offers pronunciation in context, and combines photographs with cartoon illustrations of the googly-eyed boy and his pet. The facts are intriguing, the kind of information young readers want to know. They're generally accurate, although there are issues. (The picture of the space-traveling monkey, for example, is not Albert II, but the later-flying Ham, a chimp.) This series began in 2013 with *Sharks* and has already covered dinosaurs, firefighters, and insects. Fly Guy and Buzz's enthusiasm make these especially appealing for children who love facts.

Anna Hibiscus

By Atinuke. Illustrated by Lauren Tobia. Kane Miller, 2010.

Interest level: **Younger** • Lexile measure: **670L**
Fiction; Short stories

Interconnected short stories introduce the world of Anna Hibiscus in "amazing Africa." Anna lives in a compound with her father; Canadian-born mother; twin brothers, Double and Trouble; and her father's extended family. In this first title, Anna vacations at the seaside and sells oranges from the family tree. She gets an invitation to visit her Canadian grandmother, setting the stage for sequels including *Hooray for Anna Hibiscus!* (2010), *Good Luck Anna Hibiscus!* (2011), *Have Fun Anna Hibiscus!* (2011), and *Welcome Home Anna Hibiscus!* (2012). In these, Anna goes to school, experiments with not braiding her hair, copes with the dry season, and enjoys Christmas and snow in Canada before returning. These warm biracial family stories celebrate both traditional ways and the conveniences of the modern world. They stand out among series for early readers not only for their unusual setting, but for smooth story telling and deft handling of issues of poverty, race, and class.

Ivy + Bean

By Annie Barrows. Illustrated by Sophie Blackall. Chronicle Books, 2006.

Interest level: **Younger** • Lexile measure: **510L**
Fiction

Resentful of their mothers' insistence that they might be friends, seven-year-old neighbors Ivy and Bean discover that they have much in common, including enjoyment of bugging Bean's sixth-grade sister. Bean is a girl who lives on the edge. She'll play with anyone. She loves action and being part of a large group. Ivy, on the other hand, always wears a dress and has her nose in a book. But it turns out she's teaching herself to be a witch. Not so boring after all! This friendship story is illustrated with gray-scale drawings that bring the girls to life. (Ivy is particularly appealing tricked out in a turban, white face paint with tears of red blood, and black-rimmed eyes.) Funny and realistic at the same time, this modern friendship series already has nine popular sequels.

The Stories Julian Tells

By Ann Cameron. Illustrated by Ann Strugnell.
Random House, 2006 (orig. 1981).

Interest level: **Younger** • Lexile measure: **520L**
Early reader; Short stories

Six stories introduce Julian Bates; his little brother, Huey; and his new neighbor, Gloria, describing family activities and experiences common to six- and seven-year-olds. Julian loses a tooth. When the boys get into trouble, their father helps them find a way out of it. When Gloria moves in, Julian likes her immediately because she doesn't laugh at his first attempt at a cartwheel. Gentle humor, realistic situations, and warm family relationships make this an excellent chapter book series for young readers ready for the dialog-rich writing style. Occasional black-and-white illustrations show Julian's African American family and scenes from his imagination as well as his real life. Julian is a boy who can imagine a catalog of gardening cats; his father makes a pudding "that tastes like a night on the sea." Nine sequels feature both Julian and Huey's stories as well as Gloria's. (See next entry.)

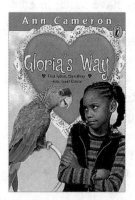

Gloria's Way

By Ann Cameron. Illustrated by Lis Toft.
Farrar, Straus, Giroux, 2000.

Interest level: **Younger** • Lexile measure: **410L**
Fiction; Short stories

Six stories from the life of Gloria Jones, friend of Julian and Huey Bates, and their new neighbor, Latisha, show the youngster dealing with common problems of family relationships, balancing friendships, and encountering new subjects at school. Like the books in the Julian series, this is gentle and positive. Gloria makes a valentine for her mother and has a slightly scary encounter with a parrot. She struggles with fractions and has a serious conversation with her father. She gets good advice from Mr. Bates about more than one problem. The adults are sometimes busy but unfailingly reassuring, and the children have realistic issues. For young readers who prefer to read about girls, this might be a good entry point into the series. Occasional soft pencil illustrations can help readers visualize these African American children and Huey's dog, Spunky, star of the most recent series title, *Spunky Tells All* (2011).

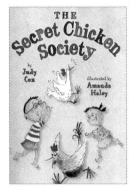

The Secret Chicken Society

By Judy Cox. Illustrated by Amanda Haley.
Holiday House, 2012.

Interest level: **Younger** • Lexile measure: **450L**
Fiction

Daniel is excited when his third-grade class hatches chicken eggs, and thrilled when he gets to bring home the five chicks, but when Peepers, his favorite, turns out to be a rooster, illegal in the city, he has a big problem. This fast-moving, funny story weaves in some environmental messages. (Daniel's stay-at-home father is making an eco-website.) Daniel's enthusiasm for animals will be shared by readers, and cheerful gray-scale illustrations offer support. There's even helpful back matter about raising chickens, for readers who live in a city like Daniel's Portland, where they are now legal. Other pleasing stories about third graders from this author-illustrator pair include *Ukelele Hayley* (2013) and *Nora and the Texas Terror* (2010).

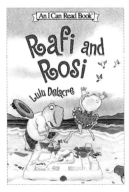

Rafi and Rosi

By Lulu Delacre. Illustrated by Lulu Delacre.
HarperCollins, 2004.

Interest level: **Younger** • Lexile measure: **440L**
Early reader; Animal fantasy; Short stories

Three short stories star a pair of Puerto Rican tree frogs: Rafi and his younger sister, Rosi. In this beach science-oriented early reader, they magically separate sand particles with a magnet, learn about luminescent algae, find a mangrove seedling, and watch a hermit crab change shells. For children in Florida and Puerto Rico, these activities would not seem unusual; others around the country may find their semitropical world unfamiliar. The book begins with a glossary of Spanish words and phrases that appear occasionally in the text, adding to the reading challenge and the cultural interest. The publisher labels this book level 3 "for confident readers"; it's complex enough to be engaging and challenging though it looks relatively simple. In this and a sequel, *Rafi and Rosi: Carnival* (2006), appended information supplements and extends the story.

Bink & Gollie

By Kate DiCamillo and Alison McGhee. Illustrated by Tony Fucile. Candlewick Press, 2010.

Interest level: **Younger**
Fiction; Short stories

Three humorous interconnected stories star unlikely best friends, short Bink and tall Gollie, in a winning combination of early reader, graphic novel, and picture book. Some spreads are wordless, and others have simple text suitable for beginning readers, who will find the cartoon-like illustrations supporting and appealing. Bink is enthusiastic and messy, while Gollie is more sophisticated, stylish, and cool. In these first three episodes, Bink buys colorful socks that Gollie finds outrageous; Gollie adventures in her imagination but invites Bink to join her; and, finally, Bink buys a fish, a special pet, and Gollie gets jealous. This Geisel Award–winning title is the first in a series describing bumps in a firm friendship. In *Two for One* (2012), they go to a state fair, and in *Best Friends Forever* (2013), they unsuccessfully pursue dreams of glory separately and together.

Leroy Ninker Saddles Up

By Kate DiCamillo. Illustrated by Chris Van Dusen. Candlewick Press, 2014.

Interest level: **Younger** • Lexile measure: **500L**
Fiction

Cowboy wannabe Leroy Ninker acquires a horse named Maybelline who loves spaghetti and compliments. In this first of a promising new series, Ninker buys his horse, feeds and compliments her as instructed, but leaves her alone too long. She wanders off and gets lost in a terrible storm. They are reunited on Deckawoo Drive, where they join the Watsons and their pig, Mercy, in a breakfast of Mercy's favorite buttered toast. (See next entry.) Maybelline may only have four teeth, but she is certainly the horse of the reformed robber's dreams. Van Dusen's grayscale caricatures emphasize the horse's cheerful mouth and Ninker's lengthy nose and cowboy hat. DiCamillo's text is full of interesting vocabulary and old-fashioned exclamations that will challenge and appeal to early readers. Aspiring cowboys don't need to have read the Mercy Watson books to enjoy these humorous chapters.

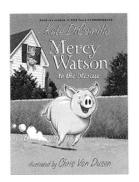

Mercy Watson to the Rescue

By Kate DiCamillo. Illustrated by Chris Van Dusen. Candlewick Press, 2005.

Interest level: **Younger** • Lexile measure: **450L**
Fiction

When the floor under their bed cracks under the combined weight of Mr. and Mrs. Watson and their pet pig, Mercy, the pig accidentally saves them by going next door in search of a snack. This very funny chapter book is the first of a series of six about an overenthusiastic pig who loves generously buttered toast. Mercy is not a talking animal, but a beloved and indulged member of the household. Lively, full-color gouache illustrations emphasize her energy and enthusiasm. The first sequel, *Mercy Watson Goes for a*

Ride (2006), was a Geisel honor book, but any would be a joy for a newly independent reader. Mercy's tastes broaden to hot buttered popcorn and a neighbor's pansies, but the interesting language, appealing action, and humor never flag as the series continues with *Mercy Watson Fights Crime* (2006), *Mercy Watson: Princess in Disguise* (2007), *Mercy Watson Thinks Like a Pig* (2008), and *Mercy Watson: Something Wonky This Way Comes* (2009).

Runaway Radish

By Jessie Haas. Illustrated by Margot Apple.
Greenwillow Books, 2001.

Interest level: **Younger** • Lexile measure: **340L**
Fiction

Radish is a pony who thinks for himself and knows what he likes. Like all ponies, he stays small while his owners outgrow him. Luckily, Judy and Nina find him a home in a horse camp, where he can teach many children. Haas has been writing, mostly about horses, for over thirty years. Parents who were once horse-crazy children are sure to have encountered one of her books, and probably went on to read all they could find. This is the first of her pony series, just right for a young reader who dreams of having a horse of her own and is ready to step up to chapter books. Apple's pencil drawings add appeal, giving personality to this bouncy, roly-poly pony. Full of details about riding technique and horse care, this is a perfect introduction to a popular genre.

Dory Fantasmagory

By Abby Hanlon. Illustrated by Abby Hanlon.
Dial Books, 2014.

Interest level: **Younger** • Lexile measure: **550L**
Fiction

Six-year-old Dory, called Rascal by her family, can never convince her older brother and sister to play with her. Tired of her endless pestering, they tell her that Mrs. Gobble Gracker, a kidnapping witch, is after her. Rascal's efforts to avoid the witch make up the bulk of this charming, true-to-life story. Accompanied by her imaginary friend, Mary—a monster out of Sendak—and helped by a make-believe fairy godparent, Mr. Nuggy, she temporarily becomes a dog, concocts a poison soup, and builds a giant hiding place in the living room. Her day's antics exhaust her parents but will thoroughly entertain readers, who will recognize her underlying need for attention and celebrate the final act of bravery that earns her a place in her brother and sister's games. Told in words, childlike pictures, and words with pictures, this is laugh-out-loud funny. *Dory and the Real True Friend* appears in 2015.

Uh-oh, Cleo

By Jessica Harper. Illustrated by Jon Berkeley.
G. P. Putnam's Sons, 2008.

Interest level: **Younger** • Lexile measure: **710L**
Fiction

Saturday started out normally for eight-year-old Cleo until the toy house fell down and she had to go to the hospital to get nine stitches in her head. The resilient middle child in her not-so-Small family tells the story of her day in considerable detail, just as a real child might. With realistic sibling relationships (she has 5 siblings) and considerable humor, this is a strong beginning for a chapter book series. Little songs made up by her mother and sister and plenty of gray-scale illustrations break up the text. Cleo's adventures continue in two sequels: in *Underpants on My Head* (2009) the family takes a vacation in Colorado; having eaten too much, Cleo gets carsick in *I Barfed on Mrs. Kenley* (2010). These stories from the author's own childhood in a large family work well for even the youngest readers.

Busybody Nora

By Johanna Hurwitz. Illustrated by Debbie Tilley.
HarperCollins, 2001 (orig. 1976).

Interest level: **Younger** • Lexile measure: **630L**
Fiction

Nora wants to know everyone who lives in her large New York City apartment house. More than that, she works to get them to know each other. This first of the Riverside Kids chapter book series introduces kindergartner Nora; her three-year-old brother, Teddy; a younger neighbor, Russell; Mrs. W., a surrogate grandmother; and a grumpy neighbor, Mrs. Mind-Your-Own-Business. Each of the four chapters is a stand-alone adventure. Nora, Teddy, Russell, and Elisa, Russell's younger sister, are all featured in individual sets of titles in the fourteen-volume series, now in a uniform edition with this illustrator. (*Nora* was originally illustrated by Susan Jeschke and others in this series were illustrated by Lillian Hoban.) The main characters grow only a bit, ranging in age from four to seven—not far from the age of the early able readers who continue to identify with them today.

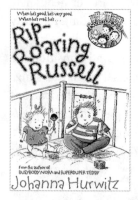

Rip-Roaring Russell

By Johanna Hurwitz. Illustrated by Debbie Tilley.
HarperCollins, 2001 (orig. 1983).

Interest level: **Younger** • Lexile measure: **600L**
Fiction

At four, Russell Michaels, one of the Riverside Apartment House kids, goes off to nursery school, where he loses some favorite things as well as his two front teeth, makes new friends, and learns to appreciate being a big brother. Russell enjoys playing with blocks and small cars, he likes parades and loud noises, but he also envies his baby sister. Chapter by chapter, in six self-contained episodes, Russell grows up a bit, learning to control his temper and find ways to get what he wants without having a tantrum. He also discovers that a baby's life isn't very interesting. This is the first of the Riverside Kids series to focus on Russell's family. Three more books follow Russell to the age of seven and then six conclude the series as Russell's sister, Elisa, grows from age four to nearly eight. Earlier editions were illustrated by Lillian Hoban.

Ling & Ting: Not Exactly the Same!

By Grace Lin. Illustrated by Grace Lin. Little, Brown, 2010.

Interest level: **Younger** • Lexile measure: **390L**
Fiction; Early reader; Short stories

Ling and Ting, Chinese American twins, look alike until an accident during a haircut gives wiggly Ting uneven bangs in the first story in this engaging, easy chapter book. For the reader, the haircut reveals which twin is which, and their different personalities unfold in the incidents that follow. They do magic tricks, make and eat dumplings together but differently, and read books. The sixth chapter, a story told by Ting, reviews all that went before and reaffirms their sisterly bond. The text is straightforward, but each story has a surprising and usually humorous conclusion. Lin's framed gouache illustrations support the text and help the reader visualize both the characters and the action. There are two sequels, so far, to this welcome series: *Ling and Ting Share a Birthday* (2013) and *Ling and Ting: Twice as Silly* (2014).

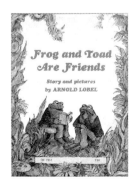

Frog and Toad Are Friends

By Arnold Lobel. Illustrated by Arnold Lobel. Harper & Row, 1970.

Interest level: **Younger** • Lexile measure: **400L**
Early reader; Short stories

Five short stories star Frog and Toad, talking animal friends who enjoy doing simple things together. These episodes demonstrate how well characters can develop and how complex feelings can be conveyed even in the controlled vocabulary of the I Can Read beginning readers. Frog tricks Toad into coming out of hibernation to enjoy spring; Toad tries to tell a story; Toad and Frog together look for Toad's lost button; they go for a swim (with Toad wearing a funny-looking bathing suit); and Frog writes Toad a letter. In Lobel's illustrations, Frog is green and a little taller than stout Toad. Both wear clothes. This title won a Caldecott honor. *Frog and Toad Together* (1972) won a Newbery honor. There are two more sequels in the original series: *Frog and Toad All Year* (1976) and *Days with Frog and Toad* (1979), now packaged in a four-title *Frog and Toad Storybook Treasury* (2013).

Lulu and the Dog from the Sea

By Hilary McKay. Illustrated by Priscilla Lamont. Albert Whitman, 2013.

Interest level: **Younger** • Lexile measure: **770L**
Fiction

On a seaside vacation, seven-year-old cousins Lulu and Mellie befriend a stray dog who has eluded the dogcatchers and survived by stealing from townspeople and vacationers alike. The dog from the sea becomes a hero when Mellie hurts her foot and the two girls are lost and stranded in the dunes. Funny and endearing, the story is enlivened further by cheerful gray-scale illustrations which reveal that Lulu and Mellie are biracial. This is the second in a series that began with *Lulu and the Duck in the Park* (2012). The most recent published here are *Lulu and the Cat in the Bag* (2013) and *Lulu and the Rabbit Next Door* (2014), but more have appeared in England. Lulu's love of animals is the connecting thread. McKay's English families are always original, and Lulu's is no exception. Chapter book readers will be delighted to meet them.

Duck for a Day

By Meg McKinlay. Illustrated by Leila Rudge.
Candlewick Press, 2012.

Interest level: **Younger**
Fiction

Pets are too messy, say Abby's parents, but they are willing to make an exception for one that visits temporarily. The second grader manages to satisfy her teacher's many requirements and brings Max, the class duck, home, but it escapes and she needs the help of her neighbor and competitor, Noah, to find and recapture it. This gentle chapter book is surprisingly suspenseful and will keep young readers alternately on edge and smiling. There's an interesting contrast between Abby's tidy home and Noah's sloppy one, and the children are believable. Plentiful gray-scale illustrations show kids in uniforms, play clothes, and night clothes and a frizzy-haired teacher as well as the duck and plenty of duck feathers. A grand school pet story from Australia.

Dinosaurs Before Dark

By Mary Pope Osborne. Illustrated by Sal Murdocca.
Random House, 2012 (orig. 1992).

Interest level: **Younger**
Fantasy; Adventure

This is a full-color anniversary edition of the first title in a beloved series that serves as a metaphor for the magic of reading. Near their Pennsylvania home, eight-year-old Jack and his little sister, Annie, find a magic treehouse filled with books that can take them anywhere. Here, they're transported into the age of dinosaurs. Annie befriends them; Jack takes notes. When they return, they bring with them a medallion that might be a clue about their sponsor. In later books they learn it's librarian Morgan Le Fay who sends them on missions to times and places as disparate as ancient Australia, Pompeii, and the Titanic's last voyage. They encounter dolphins, gorillas, Vikings, and ninja. Each book comfortably presents and defines interesting vocabulary while introducing facts and traditional stories. These are perfect for the child who, having mastered decoding, is ready to use it to explore the world.

Amelia Bedelia

By Peggy Parish. Illustrated by Fritz Siebel. Greenwillow Books, 2013 (orig. 1963).

Interest level: **Younger** • Lexile measure: **140L**
Fantasy; Adventure; Picture book

This is an anniversary edition of the classic picture book about the maid who interprets all her instructions literally. Although this was published as a picture book, the text, with all its wordplay, is just right for a precociously verbal child. Amelia draws the drapes, dresses the chicken, changes the towels by cutting them up, and dusts the furniture disastrously, but she makes a terrific lemon pie. This longtime favorite has spawned a lengthy series (twelve by Peggy Parish and sixteen more by her nephew, Herman Parish): titles about Amelia Bedelia as a young girl, titles in the I Can Read series, picture books, chapter books, and several special editions, including the facsimile of the original text and pictures annotated here. This edition also includes a lengthy afterword in pictures and text describing the story's creation and providing information about the author and original illustrator.

Junie B. Jones and the Stupid Smelly Bus

By Barbara Park. Illustrated by Denise Brunkus. Random House, 2012 (orig. 1992).

Interest level: **Younger** • Lexile measure: **380L**
Early reader

Kindergartner Junie B. Jones tells about her first school day, when she feared the school bus so much she stayed in school rather than taking it home. This is genuinely funny, but told in a breathless young voice that includes grammatical misconstructions ("I never rided on the bus before.") and some observations that might be funnier to older readers looking back on their kindergarten years. The series continues through twenty-eight titles (so far) taking Junie B. most of the way though first grade. She never loses her baby talk. Black-and-white line drawings (fully colored in this anniversary edition)—in which Junie B. has a distinctly Eloise look—interrupt the text from time to time. This series is advertised as a First Stepping Stone Book—a bit more daunting in appearance than the usual easy reader, but the difference is more in the number of words.

The Absent Author

By Ron Roy. Illustrated by John Gurney. Random House, 1997.

Interest level: **Younger** • Lexile measure: **510L**
Mystery

Third-grade friends Dink, Josh, and Ruth rush to a bookstore author signing only to find the author missing. Has he been kidnapped? They set right out to look for him. This is the first of a twenty-six-book series with relatively simple texts and plots, plenty of clues, humorous pencil illustrations, and predictable resolutions. The protagonists are logical in their problem solving and the pace of story telling is leisurely enough to include interesting detail. There's an old-fashioned flavor to these mysteries, set in a small Connecticut town. A map precedes the first chapter so that readers can locate each adventure. They don't have to be read in order. Roy has followed these with other series: Calendar Mysteries, Capital Mysteries, and Super Edition A to Z Mysteries that are slightly longer. None of these titles is notable for literary quality, language, character development, or originality, but they're fine fuel for the road to reading mastery.

Henry and Mudge: The First Book of Their Adventures

By Cynthia Rylant. Illustrated by Suçie Stevenson. Bradbury Press, 1987.

Interest level: **Younger** • Lexile measure: **460L**
Early reader

In this first of a beloved series, Henry, a boy with no brothers and sisters, acquires an English mastiff. Mudge grows quickly into a dog who's considerably taller and heavier than his boy. Mudge accompanies Henry to school and sleeps on his bed. Just once, he wanders off and gets lost, which teaches him to stay close to his friend. The language is simple, the chapters are short, and the topics familiar—just right for beginning readers. Stevenson's cheerful watercolor illustrations are reasonably realistic and demonstrate the story. There are twenty-eight dog-and-boy titles in all, plus five even simpler books about Mudge's puppyhood. Book 26, *Henry and Mudge and the Great Grandpas* (2005), won the very first Geisel medal for the most distinguished book for beginning readers.

Chapter 4

Poetry

....

POETRY IS BOTH A GENRE AND A FORM. IT'S ONE of the most ancient ways humans have organized words and ideas, perhaps the most ancient. A poem distills a thought or an experience. It is this very succinctness that makes poems attractive to young readers. Indeed, today, many books for children and teens are presented in a form referred to as novels in verse though they rarely rhyme and aren't necessarily fiction. They have short lines, with carefully crafted language and, often, evocative imagery. Most of the titles in this section, though, are collections of actual poems that appeal to young readers as well as adults. Several are large collections appropriate for families to own.

The Complete Book of the Flower Fairies: Poems and Pictures by Cicely Mary Barker

By Cicely Mary Barker. Illustrated by Cicely Mary Barker. Frederick Warne, 2002 (orig. 1923–1985).

Interest level: **Younger**
Poetry

This large volume is a compilation of eight much-loved books about flower fairies, published first in England long ago but still popular. This poetry uses varying rhyme schemes and some surprising imagery. Young fairy fans will pore over the illustrations: realistic images from the natural world inhabited by tiny fairies whose costumes match appropriately. The sweet-faced fairies were modeled on English children the author knew; the flowers and trees are also English, but most can be found in this country as well. This compendium, ideal for the child still willing to believe, comes in varying editions. The most recent includes fairies of the four seasons, as well as of the garden, trees, and wayside, and an alphabet book, all indexed. An earlier edition (Warne, 1996) has no index but also includes some short stories and a short collection of poetry by other authors.

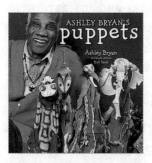

Ashley Bryan's Puppets: Making Something from Everything

By Ashley Bryan. Photographs by Ken Hannon. Atheneum, 2014.

Interest level: **Middle** • Lexile measure: **NP**
Poetry

An oversized album of photographs of hand puppets Bryan has made from sea treasures and brought to life in his accompanying poems. These figures have intriguing faces, arms, and legs, as well as elaborate costumes. Each has an African name and a personality. Each of the three sections begins with a lineup of puppets on a double-page spread, followed by spreads with a poem and two photos. The cover image of the smiling puppeteer and four of his creations shows a representative sampling: a string-nosed frog, an elephant, a queen with a wine-glass crown, and a bird with a lobster claw beak. The characters describe themselves in the poems. "We are born of cast-off pieces / And, like magic, brought alive / By your own imagination." Readers are invited to write more poems and might even be inspired to look at their own collections of found objects in a new light.

Love That Dog

By Sharon Creech. HarperCollins, 2001.

Interest level: **Middle** • Lexile measure: **1010L**
Poetry; Novels in verse

When his teacher makes Jack hear and write poetry, he resists: ". . . boys / don't write poetry. // Girls do." But she persists, and he begins to experiment, finding his own voice, a subject in his beloved pet, and a model in Walter Dean Myers. Creech includes both Jack's poems and some of the poetry Miss Stretchberry read to her fourth-grade class, including works by numerous well-known poets (William Carlos Williams, Robert Frost, etc.) as well as Myers. Readers gradually learn that the titular dog has died—hit by a car—and the boy's grief comes through clearly. But so does his appreciation for the act of writing and, even better, for author Myers, who visits his school. In a sequel, *Hate That Cat* (2008), Jack reveals more about his family life and signs for his deaf mother at go-to-school night.

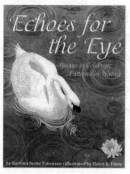

Echoes for the Eye: Poems to Celebrate Patterns in Nature

By Barbara Juster Esbensen. Illustrated by Helen K. Davie. HarperCollins, 1996.

Interest level: **Middle**
Poetry

Distinct mathematical patterns in the natural world—spirals, branches, polygons, meanders, and circles—form the underlying organization for this collection of twenty-four poems designed for a child's bedtime reading. Combining math, environmental studies, and literature, this is an interesting title for reading or browsing at any time of day. The concept is intriguing, and the illustrations, soft watercolors, also filled with patterns, support each poem perfectly. A vast spiral sky over an angry sea is the background for this unforgettable image of a hurricane: "High in some empty place / warm and cold collide / and spin / their terrible / winds / around a moving / unblinking / eye." There are wonderful words such as lapidary, medallions, and compass rose. This is a delight for both eye and mind.

Mathematickles!

By Betsy Franco. Illustrated by Steven Salerno. Margaret K. McElderry Books, 2003.

Interest level: **Middle**
Poetry

This brain-tickling poetry collection combines mathematical symbols and words to make meaning. From a late fall morning through winter, spring, and a summer night, these clever poem-puzzles make use of math concepts in a surprising and pleasing way. Most of the notation will be familiar to early elementary-school students: plus, minus, multiplication, division, and equal signs ("cold air ÷ breath = tiny cloud"). There are graphs and simple fractions ("tadpole = 2/3 frog") and vectors. These "problems" have poetic imagery but not the sounds of poems. Readers need to combine the word meanings with the mathematical idea. The exercise should be particularly appealing to a child who enjoys thinking out of the box. Salerno's lively, colorful illustrations, done in watercolor and gouache, give this the look of a picture book but also reinforce the idea of the passage of time by following a girl and her cat through the seasons.

Emma Dilemma: Big Sister Poems

By Kristine O'Connell George. Illustrated by Nancy Carpenter. Clarion Books, 2011.

Interest level: **Younger**
Poetry

This sequence of poems, presented in the voice of a fourth-grade girl, describes the difficulties and occasional joys of having a little sister. There's a slim plot thread: after all the annoying things her little sister does (embarrassing her in public, messing up her room, leaving her marker tops off, and making her late to school), when Emma breaks her arm trying to climb up in a tree where the narrator is hiding with a friend, Jessica feels terrible. The free verse poems are illustrated with pen and ink and digital media vignettes that look like they were colored with watercolor. Emma's joyful play and her love of costume come through; she's a recognizable child. Numbered pages make it easy to return to a favorite poem.

Hip Hop Speaks to Children: A Celebration of Poetry with a Beat

Edited by Nikki Giovanni; advisory editors, Tony Medina, Willie Perdomo, and Michele Scott. Illustrated by Michele Noiset, Kristen Balouch, Jeremy Tugeau, Alicia Vergel de Dios, and Damian Ward. Sourcebooks Jabberwocky, 2008.

Interest level: **Middle** • Lexile measure: **NP**
Poetry

Fifty poems and a selection from King's "I Have a Dream" speech celebrate the rhythms of poetry and of African American life. Whether originally written as poems or lyrics, the works Giovanni has chosen have a strong, compelling beat. These are attractively presented in an oversized volume and illustrated by a variety of artists. Forty of the selections can be heard on the accompanying CD, sometimes read or performed by the original artists, and sometimes by talented interpreters. From Langston Hughes and James Weldon Johnson to Eloise Greenfield and Lucille Clifton to Queen Latifah and Tupac Shakur, the variety of forms and styles is astounding and the collective impact very pleasing. This is a perfect companion to *Poetry Speaks to Children,* annotated later in this chapter.

A Pocketful of Poems

By Nikki Grimes. Illustrated by Javaka Steptoe. Clarion Books, 2001.

Interest level: **Younger** • Lexile measure: **390L**
Poetry

Playing with words and poetic forms, Grimes offers thirteen poem pairs describing city life. The poet is Tiana, a brown, paper-doll child who enjoys playing with her "pocketful of words." She's pictured in playful collage illustrations with cut-paper outline features in different colors representing her activities and mood. Steptoe uses everyday materials as well as plenty of cut, torn, and painted papers. There's a slim narrative thread. Life in the city, as Tiana describes it, extends through a year from spring to Christmas. Almost every spread includes two poems describing a word: one poem looks traditional and has rhyme, alliteration, and interesting imagery, and one is in haiku, often printed in lines that wander on the page. Young readers can relate to Tiana's words, like "spring," "pigeon," "hot," "Harlem," "pumpkin," "angels," and "gift." Beginning with the gingerbread letters on the endpapers, this is appropriately child centered, a tasty treat.

Firefly July: A Year of Very Short Poems

Selected by Paul B. Janeczko. Illustrated by Melissa Sweet. Candlewick Press, 2014.

Interest level: **Younger** • Lexile measure: **NP**
Poetry

A short poem can be surprisingly evocative, as this splendidly chosen collection demonstrates. Janeczko has arranged thirty-six poems into four seasons, beginning with daybreak in spring and ending in a winter's night. These come from a broad range of poets and times: poems written originally for adults by poets like Emily Dickinson and Richard Wright and poems written for children by authors such as Alice Schertle and X. J. Kennedy. What they share is evocative imagery, perhaps the heart of poetry. Sweet's illustrations make the most of these images. Using gouache, watercolor, and what she terms mixed media—lots of collage—she grounds the images in reality (sandpipers "hemming the ocean," a cat drinking from a moon-shaped puddle, and so forth) and adds her own imagination. Readers can do that, too. This collection is a fine, accessible introduction to some grand poets and poetry's possibilities.

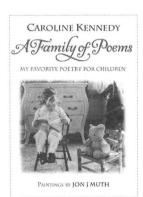

A Family of Poems: My Favorite Poetry for Children

Selected by Caroline Kennedy. Illustrated by Jon J. Muth. Hyperion, 2005.

Interest level: **Younger**
Poetry

This handsomely produced album presents more than a hundred poems, mostly written for adults but quite accessible to children. Organized into seven sections—About Me, That's So Silly!, Animals, The Seasons, The Seashore, Adventure, Bedtime—they range widely in their sources and style. Some are old and familiar, others relatively new. Muth's soft watercolors reflect and build on the words on the page. The array of poets is gratifying: Robert Louis Stevenson, Sandra Cisneros, Langston Hughes, William Blake, and the writer of the King James Bible, to name just a few. The ten translated poems have been reproduced in their original languages in the end matter. In her introduction, Kennedy describes her family's custom of writing or choosing and illustrating a favorite poem to serve as presents. A family of readers might be tempted to do the same. An ideal selection for an early able reader.

Poetry Speaks to Children

Edited by Elise Paschen; advisory editors, Billy Collins, Nikki Giovanni, X. J. Kennedy. Illustrated by Judith DuFour Love, Wendy Rasmussen, and Paula Zinngrabe Wendland. Sourcebooks MediaFusion, 2005.

Interest level: **Younger** • Lexile measure: **NP**
Poetry

From seventy-three poets, old and relatively new, here are ninety-five poems, all with child appeal. Fifty are also read aloud, often by the poet, on an accompanying CD. Chosen with an eye to children's interests, there are selections from famous names such as William Shakespeare, W. B. Yeats, and Edgar Allan Poe and from both well- and lesser-known children's poets; from authors known more for their prose, and even from anonymous Inuit and Osage poets. Some poems are humorous; others quiet and serious. The three illustrators use distinctive styles that emphasize the variety of subjects and approaches and yet seem to go together. These illustrations show children of many races, in many settings and situations. With or without the accompanying CD, with its pleasing range of voices and accents, this is a collection that can grow with readers and will please their parents, too.

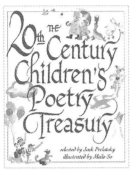

The 20th Century Children's Poetry Treasury

Selected by Jack Prelutsky. Illustrated by Meilo So. Knopf, 1999.

Interest level: **Middle** • Lexile measure: **NP**
Poetry

A selection of more than two hundred poems accessible to young readers, chosen by a noted children's poet, arranged and presented in small, related groups, and illustrated with impressionistic watercolors. These poems were all written in the twentieth century by a diverse range of poets, both men and women, mostly American. Some are better known as poets for adults, others star in the children's poetry world, and still others are less familiar. There are selections from most of the NCTE children's poetry winners and from popular children's poets, including Silverstein and Prelutsky himself. These poems are relatively short, upbeat, and memorable. The wordplay is intriguing, and the use of rhythm and rhyme varies. The gentle illustrations support the arrangement that is the strength of this volume. The poems on each spread are connected, but Prelutsky's choices require readers to think about both themes and subject matter.

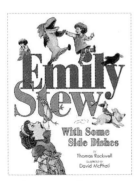

Emily Stew: With Some Side Dishes

By Thomas Rockwell. Illustrated by David McPhail. Roaring Brook Press, 2010.

Interest level: **Middle**
Poetry

Two dozen poems starring various children named Emily mix nonsense and strong feelings. Largely unrhymed but carefully crafted, these combine silliness with some real insight into a child's imagination. There is appealing grossness ("Emily Pemily ate a fat toad") and rebellion ("Emily Rose / wouldn't wear clothes"), an understanding of childhood feelings ("Emily Tears was so sad and bored / that when it rained, she thought the summer was weeping . . .") and some grand vocabulary (both "erstwhile" and "egregious" pigs). Some of the Emilies are young, others may be older, and in McPhail's accompanying pen sketches they look different, too. Or maybe it's all the same Emily in wildly different moods. (There's also a raven and a small boy named Ned with no front teeth.) This is quite sophisticated silliness bordering on the surreal.

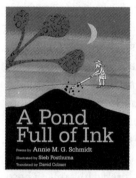

A Pond Full of Ink

By Annie M. G. Schmidt. Illustrated by Sieb Posthuma. Translated by David Colmer. Eerdmans, 2014.

Interest level: **Middle** • Lexile measure: **NP**
Poetry

Sophisticated, humorous illustrations form the perfect accompaniment for twelve whimsical poems by a beloved Dutch writer, winner of the Hans Christian Andersen Award for her lasting contributions to children's literature. Irreverent and original, these poems are longer and meatier than those of Silverstein, but they have a similarly mischievous sensibility. The drawings add to the fun. For example, the page opposite the poem "Nice and Naughty" shows just the lower halves of two aunts and (presumably) an uncle with their shoelaces tied together. The little girl described wears a devilish expression. Some poems get an extra wordless spread: the treehouse home of "Aunt Sue and Uncle Steve" is full of intriguing details. This collection was illustrated and published posthumously in Holland in 2011 and has been ably translated (with both rhythm and rhyme) from the Dutch. This U.S. edition should bring them a wide new audience.

Winter Bees & Other Poems of the Cold

By Joyce Sidman. Illustrated by Rick Allen. Houghton Mifflin, 2014.

Interest level: **Younger** • Lexile measure: **NP**
Poetry; Informational picture book

Twelve poems and accompanying text describe the cold winter world. Well crafted in a variety of forms, Sidman's poetry is both accessible and appealing. Her information is solid and her subjects surprising. The juxtaposition of the familiar (chickadees and snakes) with the less familiar (skunk cabbage and springtails) helps keep readers engaged. The imagery is interesting and the vocabulary rich. Both kinds of text are set on Allen's digitally manipulated but hand-colored linoleum block prints that show wintry scenes and the poems' subjects in subdued colors, appropriate to the weather. Snow is everywhere. This gorgeous informational picture book is another in a series of pleasing combinations of facts and imagination by Sidman and various illustrators, including *Swirl by Swirl: Spirals in Nature* (2011), *Dark Emperor and Other Poems of the Night* (2010), and *Ubiquitous* (also 2010). All four demonstrate the wonder of the natural world and the power of words.

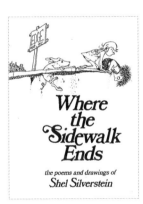

Where the Sidewalk Ends: The Poems and Drawings of Shel Silverstein

By Shel Silverstein. Illustrated by Shel Silverstein. HarperCollins, 2004 (orig. 1974).

Interest level: **Younger** • Lexile measure: **NP**
Poetry

Elementary school-aged readers have gloried in Silverstein's exploration of "the place where the sidewalk ends" for forty years. This is a place of nonsense, humor, and wild imagination, often with an underlying, thought-provoking idea. The original collection contained 127 poems. Twelve new poems were included in this thirtieth anniversary and subsequent editions. The poet's own line drawings, gracing almost every spread, add to the humor. Later collections—*A Light in the Attic* (1981), *Falling Up* (1996), and the posthumously published *Everything on It* (2011) —have cemented the best-selling poet's reputation. With varied styles, rhythm and rhyme schemes, and a wide range of subjects, he offers something for everyone. His poetry alludes to familiar nursery tales, makes occasional use of bathroom humor, and is often irreverent. He plays with words and ideas. There's no apparent organization, but each volume is indexed so that favorite poems can be easily found.

Mirror Mirror: A Book of Reversible Verse

By Marilyn Singer. Illustrated by Josée Masse. Dutton, 2010.

Interest level: **Middle** • Lexile measure: **NP**
Poetry

Fourteen poem pairs use the same lines but reverse their order to reveal two sides of familiar fairy tales. This demonstrates both the power of word arrangement and the importance of point of view in story telling. For readers already familiar with these tales, it is a treat to look at the world through the eyes of the hard-working prince, a beast, or Snow White's stepmother. The Ugly Duckling can be optimistic or pessimistic. And do you suppose Cinderella thinks about her stepsisters while she dances at the ball? The poems are set opposite vibrant acrylic paintings split with a vertical line down the middle of the page to transform the image and hint at the changes in point of view. A short endnote encourages readers to write their own reversos, a poetic form the author invented. Singer's *Follow, Follow* (2013) makes a nice companion to this collection.

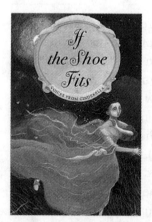

If the Shoe Fits: Voices from Cinderella

By Laura Whipple. Illustrated by Laura Beingessner. Margaret K. McElderry Books, 2002.

Interest level: **Middle** • Lexile measure: **NP**
Poetry

The traditional story, complete with scurvy stepsisters and charming prince, is retold here in thirty-three poems that suggest a happily ever after in the palace family. Whipple presents the tale from some surprising points of view, fleshing out characters and exploring motivations. We hear from the stepmother and stepsisters, the ghost of Cinderella's father, the godmother, the rat coachman, the king, queen, and, of course, Ella and her prince. Even the glass slippers have their say. The cat provides links along the way. Gouache illustrations show scenes from the story in vignettes and full-spread paintings that suggest the story's French origins. Both the language and the ideas expressed in these varied, lengthy poems are better suited to the older, more experienced reader. Funny and fresh, this slim book adds surprising depth to a familiar nursery tale.

Families

··

TEACHERS KNOW THAT CHILDREN LEARN BEST when they begin with something they know. There is nothing young readers know better than family life. Stories about families are particularly and perennially popular. The titles in this section reflect a wide range of times, places, and cultures, and they also reflect a wide but familiar range of family relationships—with siblings, parents, steps, cousins, grandparents, and other relatives. Young readers are likely to see themselves reflected in one or another of these families even though the time and place and situation may be quite different from their own. And, they can begin to see how other families are unlike as well as like their own.

How Tía Lola Came to ~~Visit~~ Stay

By Julia Alvarez. Knopf, 2001.

Interest level: **Middle** • Lexile measure: **740L**
Fiction

When Tía Lola comes from the Dominican Republic to Miguel's new home in Vermont, she seems totally out of place. Despite being wildly colorful, practicing magic, and knowing almost no English, she somehow makes friends with everyone in town. Moving to a different part of the country, making friends, fitting in, living in a bicultural world, and adjusting to divorce are all strands of this tale. Miguel celebrates his tenth birthday, loves baseball, argues with his little sister, and misses his friends. But, during a visit with his extended family in the Dominican Republic, he comes to realize how much he loves his exuberant great-aunt. The narrative includes plenty of Spanglish and immediate translation. Common immigration issues are concerns in *How Tía Lola Learned to Teach* (2010), and the series concludes with *How Tía Lola Saved the Summer* (2011), and *How Tía Lola Ended Up Starting Over* (2011).

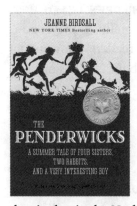

The Penderwicks: A Summer Tale of Four Sisters, Two Rabbits, and a Very Interesting Boy

By Jeanne Birdsall. Knopf, 2005.

Interest level: **Middle** • Lexile measure: **800L**
Fiction

The four motherless Penderwick girls spend an enchanting three-week holiday in a cottage in the Berkshires and find a new friend, Jeffrey. Like children's classics by Nesbit and Ransome, this is a story of children playing on their own, but more modern and with some helpful adults in the background. Rosalind, twelve, falls in love with Cagney, the gardener, who's just a bit too old for her; Skye and Jane, eleven and ten, play soccer, shoot bows and arrows, and climb a rope ladder to be with Jeffrey; while four-year-old Batty befriends Cagney's rabbits. Sequels in this funny and immensely satisfying series include *The Penderwicks on Gardam Street* (2008), in which the girls work to keep their widowed father from providing them a stepmother, until the right one is discovered; *The Penderwicks at Point Mouette* (2011), in which the three younger girls and Jeffrey holiday in Maine; and *The Penderwicks in Spring* (2015), which deals with the blended family.

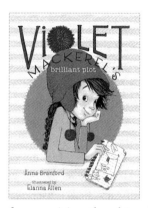

Violet Mackerel's Brilliant Plot

By Anna Branford. Illustrated by Elanna Allen. Atheneum, 2012.

Interest level: **Younger** • Lexile measure: **960L**
Fiction

Seven-year-old Violet Mackerel is imaginative and determined, an engaging heroine for a series of quiet, family-focused chapter books from Australia. In this first title, Violet makes various plans for acquiring the china bird she's admired for weeks at the Saturday market where her mother sells knitted things. Her theory of the importance of small things mirrors the series of small moments that make up this gentle story in which Violet finally succeeds through an act of generosity. Violet's theories adapt to fit the circumstances as she undergoes a tonsillectomy in *Violet Mackerel's Remarkable Recovery* (2013), helps her sister with a science project in *Violet Mackerel's Natural Habitat* (2013), copes with change (her mother's remarriage and a move) in *Violet Mackerel's Personal Space* (2013), makes a new friend in *Violet Mackerel's Possible Friend* (2014), and saves a tree in *Violet Mackerel's Possible Protest* (2014).

The Not-Just-Anybody Family

By Betsy Cromer Byars. Illustrated by Jacqueline Rogers. Delacorte Press, 1986.

Interest level: **Middle** • Lexile measure: **690L**
Fiction

With their mother off traveling with the rodeo, it's up to Vern and Maggie to put the family back together after Pap gets arrested and Junior breaks his legs trying to fly off the barn. This warm story is the first of a series of fast-paced, funny books about the Blossom family and their dog, Mud. Self-contained chapters focus alternately on different characters, making this a more complicated reading experience than it first appears. There are some moderately scary moments (especially for the dog as he tries to make his way back home alone, and for Vern, breaking into jail), but all ends very satisfyingly. The rural, hardscrabble setting and the children's independence give this an old-fashioned feel, but the adventure will carry modern readers along. Sequels include *The Blossoms Meet the Vulture Lady* (1986), *The Blossoms and the Green Phantom* (1987), *A Blossom Promise* (1987), and *Wanted . . . Mud Blossom* (1991).

Beezus and Ramona

By Beverly Cleary. Illustrated by Jacqueline Rogers. HarperCollins, 2013 (orig. 1955).

Interest level: **Younger** • Lexile measure: **780L**
Fiction

Four-year-old Ramona Quimby has an incredible imagination, but her antics annoy and embarrass her older sister, Beezus. In this first of a beloved series, the irrepressible Ramona writes in a library book, invites all her friends to a party without telling her mother, and bakes her doll in the oven. Ramona is a surprisingly complex character. She's seldom well behaved, but her actions always make sense, from her point of view. The family's love of reading and fairy tales will hearten parents, but it's Ramona's spirited self that has made her a favorite of young readers since she first appeared in her own series sixty years ago, following the popular Henry Huggins books in which she was a secondary character. The humor continues in seven books that grow up with her through fourth grade. Louis Darling did the original illustrations, but this title has been reillustrated several times.

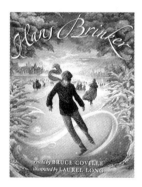

Hans Brinker

By Bruce Coville. Illustrated by Laurel Long.
Dial Books, 2007.

Interest level: **Middle** • Lexile measure: **AD690L**
Classics

After their father was injured at work, Hans and Gretel Brinker's family struggled for ten years, until Hans's carving earned them both new silver skates and a fortunate encounter with a famous doctor provides a cure for his father and the solution of two mysteries. Coville has smoothly adapted Mary Mapes Dodge's 1865 story, removing pages and pages of encyclopedia-style information about nineteenth-century Holland and leaving the heartwarming story of a good son and brother who, through steady purpose, finds the family's lost fortune. Since the original is almost unreadable, this is an excellent way to introduce this unselfish hero and that wintry Dutch world. Long's oil paintings recall classic art, with rosy-cheeked people arranged against the snow-covered countryside. The endpapers and text pages opposite the illustrations look like crackled Delft pottery. Vignettes point up important plot points—the wooden chain, the silver watch, the stump.

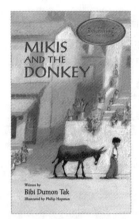

Mikis and the Donkey

By Bibi Dumon Tak. Illustrated by Philip Hopman.
Translated by Laura Watkinson. Eerdmans, 2014.

Interest level: **Middle** • Lexile measure: **640L**
Fiction

When his grandfather gets a donkey to help carry firewood down from the olive groves on the heights of their Greek island, Mikis falls in love with her immediately. He and the donkey choose her name, Tsaki, together. He accompanies his grandfather on wood-gathering expeditions and soon can do it on his own. When Tsaki gets sores on her sides, he takes her to the human doctor, and when he thinks she's lonely, he finds her a friend. A sympathetic teacher allows him to share his donkey news, and his classmates are enthusiastic, especially his good friend Elena. This lovely depiction of Greek island life seems timeless—it's both modern (his teacher's boyfriend has a motor scooter) and traditional (old men gather under the sycamore in the center of town). The plentiful illustrations, pencil drawings, are perfectly suited. A surprise provides a delightful ending to this gentle, satisfying story.

The Saturdays

By Elizabeth Enright. Illustrated by Elizabeth Enright.
Square Fish, 2008 (orig. 1941).

Interest level: **Middle** • Lexile measure: **820L**
Fiction; Short stories

Mona, Rush, Randy, and Oliver, the four Melendy children, decide to pool their allowances to give each one a special Saturday outing. These interconnected short stories are set in New York City in the early 1940s and feature trips to the opera, circus, and Central Park, as well as Mona's unauthorized haircut and manicure. Rush finds a stray dog that saves them from near suffocation by coal gas. There's even a fire. This family story hasn't lost its charm, though the world it describes has radically changed. Today's readers will be surprised by the children's freedom and will envy their adventures. This book and three sequels have been reissued as a boxed set. In *The Four-Story Mistake* (1942), the family moves to a house in the country with a secret room. The children befriend an orphan in *Then There Were Five* (1944), and Randy and Oliver solve a mystery in *Spiderweb for Two* (1951).

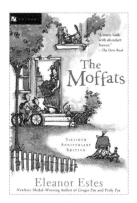

The Moffats

By Eleanor Estes. Illustrated by Louis Slobodkin. Harcourt, 2001 (orig. 1941).

Interest level: **Middle** • Lexile measure: **800L**
Historical fiction

When a "for sale" sign goes up in front of the yellow house they've been renting for years, the Moffat family worry through a year of everyday family events. In a time of coal stoves and oil lamps, in their small town outside New Haven in the early twentieth century, Sylvie, Joey, Jane, and Rufus have surprising freedom. When they hitch a ride to church on a buggy, twelve-year-old Joey drives the horses. Sent to the grocer's for sugar, nine-year-old Jane hides and falls asleep in the store breadbox. On his first day of first grade, Rufus hops into a freight car and rides all the way to New Haven. The four work together, and with the help of the family cat, construct a ghost that terrifies a bullying neighbor. Their experiences and feelings are described with humor and pleasing detail. Sequels include Newbery honor–winning *The Middle Moffat* (1942), *Rufus M* (1943), and *The Moffat Museum* (1983).

Ginger Pye

By Eleanor Estes. Illustrated by Eleanor Estes. Harcourt, 2000 (orig. 1951).

Interest level: **Middle** • Lexile measure: **990L**
Fiction

When Rachel and Jerry Pye's new puppy, Ginger, disappeared at Thanksgiving, they spent most of the year searching unsuccessfully. Sure that their dog was taken by an "unsavory character," a man in a yellow-mustard-colored hat, the nine- and ten-year-olds never suspect the real perpetrator. At the end of May, Ginger returns, full grown and even cleverer than before. Fairly early in the book, the third-person narration slips into the dog's point of view for a while, as he tracks Jerry to school, climbs a fire escape, and appears on the windowsill with Jerry's pencil in his mouth. The author's own sketches illustrate this and other scenes. Set in a small Connecticut town in an unidentified past time, probably years before World War II, this Newbery Medal–winning title from the 1950s still has appeal today. In a sequel, *Pinky Pye* (1958), the family summers at Fire Island and acquires a kitten.

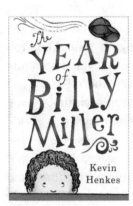

The Year of Billy Miller

By Kevin Henkes. Greenwillow Books, 2013.

Interest level: **Younger** • Lexile measure: **620L**
Fiction

Worried that he might not be able to meet the challenge of second grade, Billy Miller gets low-keyed but important support from his teacher and from his father, sister, and mother. Billy has reasonable worries and sometimes gets himself into situations he doesn't know how to handle—as when he convinces himself there's a monster under his bed while trying to keep himself awake all night, or when he accidently seems to make fun of the teacher. Billy's family is clearly described; these are very specific characters and yet recognizable. Billy's teacher makes a big deal of family, too, while allowing the word to have many different meanings. This episodic story is divided into manageable sections, each with its own conflict. The chronological organization and straightforward narrative are very accessible for young readers, though the language can be sophisticated at times. A spot-on reflection of common children's concerns.

Emma Dilemma and the New Nanny

By Patricia Hermes. Marshall Cavendish, 2006.

Interest level: **Middle** • Lexile measure: **470L**
Fiction

Eight-year-old Emma has several dilemmas. Can she keep her troublesome pet ferret? Can she join the travel soccer team? Can she convince her busy parents that new nanny Annie, whom Emma and her four siblings love, is responsible enough to stay? This is a rollicking story of a large and rather chaotic family and the development of responsibility. There are six books in the series, all featuring the large family, some important pets (and a horse next door), Nanny Annie, and, usually, soccer: *Emma Dilemma and the Two Nannies* (2007), *Emma Dilemma and the Soccer Nanny* (2008), *Emma Dilemma and the Camping Nanny* (2009), *Emma Dilemma, the Nanny, and the Secret Ferret* (2010), and *Emma Dilemma, the Nanny, and the Best Horse Ever* (2011). These are a nice step up from Junie B. Jones, young in approach but relatively challenging to read, with no illustrations.

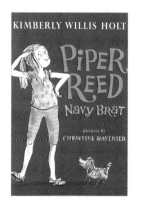

Piper Reed, Navy Brat

By Kimberly Willis Holt. Illustrated by Christine Davenier. Henry Holt, 2007.

Interest level: **Middle** • Lexile measure: **610L**
Fiction

When fourth grader Piper Reed and her family move to Pensacola, Florida, she misses her old home in San Diego, but there are good things, too. In short, first-person chapters, dyslexic Piper describes the disruption of moving, the anxiety of a first day of school that isn't the first day for anyone else, choosing a puppy, watching the Blue Angels perform overhead, and sharing a purple popsicle moment with her sisters. Gray-scale illustrations break up the text. Piper is good at making friends and manages this major change well, in spite of difficult moments. This solid contemporary family story has just enough tension to keep readers going. Sequels, *Piper Reed, the Great Gypsy* (2008), *Piper Reed Gets a Job (or . . . Party Planner)* (2009), *Piper Reed, Campfire Girl* (2010), *Piper Reed, Rodeo Star* (2011), and *Piper Reed, Forever Friend* (2012), take this Navy brat through fifth grade and into yet another state.

The Misadventures of the Family Fletcher

By Dana Alison Levy. Delacorte Press, 2014.

Interest level: **Middle** • Lexile measure: **750L**
Fiction

This old-fashioned story with a modern twist is the tale of four adopted boys, two dads, a dog, a cat, an imaginary cheetah, and a grouchy neighbor. Over the course of a school year, soccer-playing sixth grader Sam participates in a school musical; fourth grader Eli discovers he doesn't like the school for academically gifted students he desperately wanted to attend; his same-age brother, Jax, has to interview the neighbor for a school report and loses his best friend; and kindergartner Frog (Jeremiah) can't convince anyone that his new school friend isn't as imaginary as his cheetah. This very funny title is notable for its matter-of-fact depiction of an atypical and multiracial family. Two boys are white, one African American, and one adopted from India. They're very different from one another, but closely tied with strong family bonds. Their banter is realistic, and the disorder of their everyday lives is convincing.

The Year of the Dog: A Novel

By Grace Lin. Illustrated by Grace Lin. Little, Brown, 2006.

Interest level: **Middle** • Lexile measure: **690L**
Fiction

The Year of the Dog means a year of finding friends and finding yourself, according to Pacy Lin's Taiwanese American family. That's just what it is for Pacy. The Lins are the only Asian American children in their elementary school until Melody Ling joins Pacy's class and becomes her best friend. Pacy's description of her year includes Chinese meals and family celebrations, performing in a play, the agony of writing a story for a national contest, and a visit to Chinatown in New York City. This first of a series fits perfectly into a long tradition of family-friendship-and-school narratives, but it has a cultural twist. Lin weaves in stories from her parents' and grandparents' lives, and there are mouth-watering food descriptions. In *The Year of the Rat* (2007), Melody moves away. In *Dumpling Days* (2012), the family visits Taiwan. All three are illustrated with Lin's own pen-and-ink sketches.

Ruby Lu, Brave and True

By Lenore Look. Illustrated by Anne Wilsdorf. Atheneum, 2004.

Interest level: **Younger** • Lexile measure: **640L**
Fiction

Almost every day is a good day for seven-year-old Ruby Lu—even Saturdays, when she has to go to Chinese school (where she makes a best friend); even when her baby brother gives away her magician secrets; and even when immigrant relatives arrive to live in her house. She has a flair for fashion (especially using capes and reflective tape), but not so much for learning the Chinese language. Stand-alone chapters chronicle adventures that will amuse a beginning reader, including Ruby's driving the family car and her dealings with a bullying neighbor. This warm, family story includes details about Chinese American life and a glossary. Sequels include *Ruby Lu, Empress of Everything* (2006), in which she helps her deaf cousin get used to second grade, and *Ruby Lu, Star of the Show* (2011), in which she becomes a third grader and the family experiences some hard times when her father loses his job.

Anastasia Krupnik

By Lois Lowry. Houghton Mifflin, 1979.

Interest level: **Middle** • Lexile measure: **700L**
Fiction

Anastasia Krupnik has a pretty significant year, coming to appreciate her grandmother, her teacher, and the expected new baby. In this first title, readers meet her family: her English professor father, her painter mother, and her senile grandmother who doesn't recognize her. Visiting one of her father's classes, where he attempts to teach a Wordsworth poem, she realizes that memories still make her grandmother's life worthwhile. Although her teacher doesn't understand that poetry doesn't have to rhyme, she does understand how the ten-year-old feels when her grandmother dies. Anastasia decides that her new baby brother deserves her grandfather's name. The dialog and family relationships are believable. By book 4 of this series, Anastasia is thirteen; she stays that age for five more titles. The series is a great favorite for its combination of serious topics with humor.

All About Sam

By Lois Lowry. Illustrated by Diane deGroat.
Houghton Mifflin, 1988.

Interest level: **Younger** • Lexile measure: **670L**
Fiction

From birth into his nursery school years, Sam Krupnik has always had very clear ideas about what he wants and solid, if not always sensible, plans to get it. After seven stories about Anastasia Krupnik and her family, Lowry switches to the point of view of their new baby, Sam. From learning to communicate in cries and words to learning Morse Code, he turns out to be diligent and determined. He hides foods he doesn't like, flushes his sister's fish down the toilet, makes a pet of an earthworm, and gives himself a haircut. Elementary-school readers will enjoy the humor and the superior feeling of seeing the world through the eyes of a preschooler. If they've read earlier stories, they may recognize some of his adventures. The series continues with *Attaboy, Sam!* (1992), *See You Around, Sam!* (1996), and *Zooman Sam* (1999), which takes Sam to kindergarten.

Fly Away

By Patricia MacLachlan. Margaret K. McElderry Books, 2014.

Interest level: **Younger** • Lexile measure: **490L**
Fiction

Everyone in Lucy's family loves music, but Lucy doesn't sing. Lucy, who writes poems, has words but no tunes. Her brother Teddy, not yet two, has tunes but no words. Secretly, at night he sings to her. When Lucy and her family visit an elderly relative's farm in North Dakota, the flooding Red River threatens the farmhouse and Teddy wanders off. Lucy bravely sings to find him. This gentle, lyrical, perfectly paced story is a collection of family moments—a shared admiration for a spectacular breed of cow, a stubborn elderly aunt accepting help, and Teddy's first words (including "cow," "Dutch Belted," and "Mama"). There is tension and satisfying relief as the river rises to the level of the porch and stops, and even more tension while Teddy is lost. His return prompts Lucy's beautiful cow poem and reestablishment of their peaceful, loving nighttime ritual. Enchanting.

Saffy's Angel

By Hilary McKay. Margaret K. McElderry Books, 2002.

Interest level: **Middle** • Lexile measure: **630L**
Fiction

Feeling herself an outsider as an adopted cousin in the Casson family, thirteen-year-old Saffron longs to find a way to prove that she belongs by finding the angel that once graced her mother's Italian garden.

This is the first of a grand series about a delightful, if wacky, British family, all named for paint colors. This is a happy story of inclusion, not only of the cousin, but also of Sarah, a neighbor who uses a wheelchair, whose family's willingness to spoil her extends to their taking her to Siena, Italy, where she and Saffy search for the angel. Each of the four children gets star billing in sequels including *Indigo's Star* (2004), *Permanent Rose* (2005) (beware the Santa Claus revelation), and *Caddy Ever After* (2006). The last is *Forever Rose* (2008). There's a prequel, too, *Caddy's World* (2012). All have moving moments and are laugh-out-loud funny.

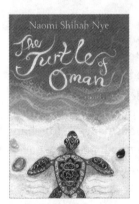

The Turtle of Oman: A Novel

By Naomi Shihab Nye. Illustrated by Betsy Peterschmidt. Greenwillow Books, 2014.

Interest level: **Middle** • Lexile measure: **700L**
Fiction

Third grader Aref Al-Amri spends a week exploring Oman with his grandfather, gearing himself up to facing his family's big move to Michigan in America for three years. What makes this tour of an unfamiliar country so attractive is the loving relationship between the boy and the old man. Sidi takes him camping in the desert; they have an overnight at Sidi's house, where they sleep on the flat roof and look at the stars. They admire sea turtles on the beach and collect some stones Aref can take with him to remind him of home. This is especially good for early readers because the book is hefty and substantive, dealing with the real issue of facing change, but the boy is young. Nye's language is poetic, and the depth of feeling—both Aref's fears and his love for his grandfather, his country, and his cat—is strong.

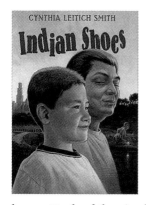

Indian Shoes

By Cynthia Leitich Smith. Illustrated by Jim Madsen. HarperCollins, 2002.

Interest level: **Younger** • Lexile measure: **820L**
Fiction

Native Americans Ray Halfmoon and his grandfather find surprising ways to solve problems as they go about their daily lives in urban Chicago and vacation with Cherokee relatives in Oklahoma. Each of the six chapters in this transitional reader is a self-contained episode. Ray manages to trade his hightops for a pair of moccasins for his homesick grandfather. At a wedding, when Ray's rented finery comes without the bottom half, his grandfather lends him his own pants. When the power goes off during a Christmas storm, they bring all the animals they are pet sitting into their own apartment, where they can be warmed by a fire. Ray enters an art contest, plays Little League baseball, and goes fishing with his grandfather. This is notable both for its urban setting and Native American connections, but also for the family composition—just the grandparent and the child.

Ballet Shoes

By Noel Streatfeild. Illustrated by Diane Goode. Random House, 1991 (orig. 1937).

Interest level: **Older** • Lexile measure: **930L**
Historical fiction

Adopted by Great-Uncle Matthew, who promptly disappears, Pauline, Petrova, and Posy Fossil are enrolled in the Academy of Dancing and Stage Training, where they learn the skills necessary for a career on stage and screen. This satisfying story from the 1930s stands up surprisingly well. It's full of interesting details about their instruction. The girls are distinct, so there's someone for every reader to identify with. The style is reasonably natural, and while their world is long gone, it seems less distant than some, since it's focused on the children's experiences. The girls themselves contribute to their upkeep. The money is all a foreign currency; you don't really sense how different it is. There's quite a bit about learning Shakespeare bits and plenty about the ballet for enthusiasts. Numerous companion books about working children are still available in paperback, including *Dancing Shoes* (1957), *Theater Shoes* (1945), and *Skating Shoes* (1951).

The Boxcar Children
GERTRUDE CHANDLER WARNER

The Boxcar Children

By Gertrude Chandler Warner. Illustrated by L. Kate Deal. Albert Whitman, 2002 (orig. 1924; 1942).

Interest level: **Younger** • Lexile measure: **490L**
Historical fiction

Orphaned and hiding from a grandfather they don't know, Henry, Jessie, Violet, and Benny find and fix up an abandoned boxcar in the woods, industriously furnishing it from a dump and supporting themselves through Henry's odd jobs. Warner, a teacher, revised her 1924 story to make it accessible to less able readers; there's additional material in this anniversary edition. This survival story has long been a favorite first independent reading book. It's relatively lengthy, but the sentences are short, the vocabulary simple, and the suspense keeps readers engaged. Silhouette illustrations head every chapter. In the sequel, *Surprise Island* (1949), the four children, now happily reunited with their grandfather, go on to solve a mystery, as they do in all the subsequent titles in this popular series (137 so far by various writers). The original books are set in a pre–World War II world, but current titles are usually set in the present day.

Amber Was Brave, Essie Was Smart: The Story of Amber and Essie Told Here in Poems and Pictures

By Vera B. Williams. Illustrated by Vera B. Williams. Greenwillow Books, 2001.

Interest level: **Younger** • Lexile measure: **NP**
Poetry

A series of poems show how sisters Amber and Essie support each other in the scary time while their father is in jail and their mother works long hours. Sometimes the girls tell their story; sometimes there's an outside narrator. The poems and pictures (occasional black-and-white sketches and an album of images done with colored pencil) emphasize the girls' warm relationship. Brave Amber goes to meet the new neighbor, Nata-Lee. Essie is smart enough to call her uncle after their jumping broke their bed. It's Essie who straightens Amber's haircut after Amber cuts off her braids to send her father. The two plus a stuffed bear make a "Best Sandwich" for warmth and comfort. The punctuation is unconventional. Without periods, narrative pauses are provided by line spacing, commas, and ellipses. This is moving and unusual in its matter-of-fact depiction of a hard-pressed family in an appealing, accessible way.

Chapter 6

Friends
and School

....

AFTER FAMILY, CHILDREN'S LIVES REVOLVE around friends and school. The need to get along with other people provides the conflict necessary for a good plot and, often, some impetus for character growth and change. Most readers are happy to read story after story about finding friends, keeping friends, losing friends, and juggling competing friendships. The school setting is almost as familiar as the home setting, although the schools described in these titles may seem quite different from one another. Friends and school go together in most books for young readers just as they do in their lives. Some books in this section are particularly easy to read; with their recognizable settings and situations, they could also be classed with the transitional books.

Jasper John Dooley: Star of the Week

By Caroline Adderson. Illustrated by Ben Clanton. Kids Can Press, 2012.

Interest level: **Younger** • Lexile measure: **570L**
Fiction

Jasper John Dooley can't wait to be his classroom's star of the week, to show and tell, share his family tree, perform a science experiment, share his talent, and bring a snack, but his plans and projects have unexpected results. Jasper has difficulty getting his classmates excited about his lint collection. Jasper would like a baby, like his best friend Ori's new sister, to enlarge his family tree. He constructs a wooden brother who has the advantage of being much quieter than Ori's constantly crying sister. This gentle, episodic story is full of humor, the excitement of school, and the mystery of babies. The children are believable, the situations realistic. Occasional black-and-white illustrations depict the characters with large heads, small bodies, and plenty of smiles. Sequels *Left Behind* (2013) and *Not in Love* (2014) continue Jasper's primary-grade adventures.

The Year of the Book

By Andrea Cheng. Illustrated by Abigail Halpin. Houghton Mifflin, 2012.

Interest level: **Younger** • Lexile measure: **590L**
Fiction

Making and keeping friends can be difficult. For ten-year-old Anna Wang, like many other good readers, books can be a comfort when navigating friendships proves difficult. Fourth grade is not turning out well for this likeable Chinese American child. She's become self-conscious about her mother's accent and her family's status, and her best friend, Laura, has found other friends. But books, a new friend from Chinese school, and a growing empathy for others help Anna through her year. Good readers will particularly enjoy the frequent references to familiar book titles and may find some new suggestions as well. In a sequel, *The Year of the Baby* (2013), Anna and her friends use Kaylee, her newly adopted baby sister, as the subject of a successful fifth-grade science fair project. Both books include some simple Chinese words, translated in an opening pronunciation guide.

Henry Huggins

By Beverly Cleary. Illustrated by Jacqueline Rogers. HarperCollins, 2014 (orig. 1950).

Interest level: **Middle** • Lexile measure: **670L**
Fiction

Third grader Henry Huggins brings home a stray dog he names Ribsy and has a series of small adventures, each in a self-contained chapter. He even meets the dog's original owner. This humorous story has stood the test of time. Both boy and dog have charmed generations of readers who have gone on to read many more titles about the children on Klickitat Street. Things cost a lot less in 1950, and the children of Portland, Oregon, had more freedom in those days, but their relationships and their feelings for their pets haven't changed. This title and its sequels were originally illustrated by Louis Darling, reillustrated by Tracy Dockray in 2007, and reillustrated again for the current edition. Other stories starring Henry include *Henry and Beezus* (1952), *Henry and Ribsy* (1954), *Henry and the Paper Route* (1957), *Henry and the Clubhouse* (1962), and *Ribsy* (1964).

Frindle

By Andrew Clements. Illustrated by Brian Selznick. Simon & Schuster, 1996.

Interest level: **Middle** • Lexile measure: **830L**
Fiction

When Mrs. Granger, his dictionary-loving fifth-grade teacher, tells independent thinker Nicholas Allen that words were invented by people, he decides to test this out, inventing the word "frindle" to mean pen. Though his schoolmates' eager adoption of his new word disrupts school routine and eventually makes national news, it also demonstrates the teacher's point about the power of words. Indeed, Nick's invention makes a fortune, which he puts to good use, endowing college scholarships for other students in Westfield, New Hampshire. This cheerful school story has a simple and understandable moral and a positive outcome. Each chapter includes Selznick's gray-scale illustrations. Clements has gone on to write numerous funny and thought-provoking stories about fifth and sixth graders, but this one has long been a particular favorite.

Nikki & Deja

By Karen English. Illustrated by Laura Freeman. Clarion Books, 2007.

Interest level: **Younger** • Lexile measure: **670L**
Fiction

Third graders Nikki and Deja, next-door neighbors and best friends, weather strains in their relationship when new neighbor Antonia's standoffishness prompts them to form an exclusive drill team, but Nikki can't do the dance moves. This easy-to-grasp story is the first of a successful series of books chronicling a third-grade friendship. These lively African American girls have different strengths and realistic weaknesses. Their emotional ups and downs, described in the present tense by an omniscient narrator, will be familiar to readers. Frequent gray-scale drawings depict the girls, their classmates, and other important details. So far, in five sequels, still solidly set in a third-grade world, the girls show little character growth, but the author, a former teacher, has not run out of good examples of how small things can loom large in a young person's life: *Birthday Blues* (2009), *The Newsy News Newsletter* (2010), *Election Madness* (2011), *Wedding Drama* (2012), and *Substitute Trouble* (2013).

Make Way for Dyamonde Daniel

By Nikki Grimes. Illustrated by R. Gregory Christie.
G. P. Putnam's Sons, 2009.

Interest level: **Younger** • Lexile measure: **620L**
Early reader

Feeling alone in her new school, Dyamonde Daniel has some sympathy with the even newer Free, even though he is taller than any other third grader and something of a bully. She secretly names him Rude Boy, but later he becomes her best friend. They share a dislike for their new, small apartments, and Dyamonde introduces him to people in her lively Harlem neighborhood. She encourages him not to be so touchy about his real name, Reed. Though the story is told from the point of view of this strong, smart African American girl, the author gives readers a glimpse into Free's thinking as well, making this a more complicated and probably more rewarding reading experience than is usual for books at this level. Dyamonde's third-grade year continues in three sequels: *Rich* (2009), *Almost Zero* (2010), and *Halfway to Perfect* (2012), which explore other issues, including homelessness and healthy eating.

Just Grace

By Charise Mericle Harper. Illustrated by Charise Mericle Harper. Houghton Mifflin, 2007.

Interest level: **Younger** • Lexile measure: **NC1060L**
Fiction

Just Grace, so called to distinguish her from the three other Graces in her third-grade classroom, has a small superpower: the ability to see when someone else is unhappy and the need to do something about it. In this first of a series that has already stretched to twelve titles, Grace and her best friend, Mimi, devise a way to cheer up their neighbor, Ms. Luther, by sending her postcards from her cat, Crinkles, from around town. The plan backfires when the cat disappears and Grace has to work with her least favorite person, Sammy Stringer, to find it. Illustrated with Grace's own drawings and "Not So Super" comic book heroes, these first-person narratives have an engaging, believable voice. Grace's thinking is appropriate to her age, and throughout the series the author shows her growth as she comes to understand and appreciate people she didn't originally like.

Toys Go Out: Being the Adventures of a Knowledgeable Stingray, a Toughy Little Buffalo, and Someone Called Plastic

By Emily Jenkins. Illustrated by Paul O. Zelinsky. Schwartz & Wade Books, 2006.

Interest level: **Younger** • Lexile measure: **730L**
Fantasy; Short stories

Six interconnected adventures in which three of Little Girl's toys venture outside their comfort areas, going to school, the park, beach, and even a birthday party, and experiencing occasional near disasters. In this first of a charming series of chapter books, we meet these unlikely friends: not-so-knowledgeable StingRay, who loves to answer questions; Lumphy, an often-sticky buffalo; and Plastic, who doesn't know what he is. These toys have familiar childhood yearnings and face familiar fears. They're young enough in their sensibilities to give the child reader a pleasing sense of sophistication. In *Toy Dance Party* (2008), their owner has grown, becoming less interested in the toys of her childhood and more in sleepovers and her silent Barbies. Finally, *Toys Come Home* (2011) looks back a few years to the toys' arrivals. These humorous and insightful revelations about the secret life of toys are charmingly illustrated in shaded pencil drawings.

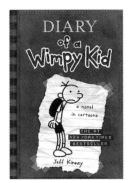

Diary of a Wimpy Kid: Greg Heffley's Journal

By Jeff Kinney. Illustrated by Jeff Kinney.
Amulet Books, 2007.

Interest level: **Middle** • Lexile measure: **950L**
Fiction

In words and cartoons, middle schooler Greg Heff-ley chronicles a year in which he plays a tree in the school musical, considers weight lifting as a hobby, and nearly loses his best friend. Greg portrays himself as a loser, but he is clearly a winner in the eyes of readers who have eagerly followed him through eight best-selling sequels and visited his website at www.poptropica.com. The design is attractive: it's presented as a journal with hand-lettered text on lined paper and cartoons. Although this story takes place in middle school, these books are eagerly read by much younger students who often comment in their reviews about the speed at which they finished them. Greg's voice is convincing, and Kinney's simple cartoons grace every page. Episodic short chapters and laugh-out-loud humor add to the reading appeal.

Alvin Ho: Allergic to Girls, School, and Other Scary Things

By Lenore Look. Illustrated by LeUyen Pham.
Schwartz & Wade Books, 2008.

Interest level: **Younger** • Lexile measure: **600L**
Fiction

Though he's Firecracker Man at home, fearful seven-year-old, superhero wannabe Alvin Ho shuts down at school. Luckily, neighbor Flea insists on being his friend and translator. In his Concord, Massachusetts, hometown, kids play Revolutionary War on the playground and Thoreau appears in the second-grade curriculum. Alvin's understanding of the world is believably naïve, but even very young readers can predict the likely consequences of his mistakes and will sympathize. Plentiful line drawings add to the humor. Four sequels continue to focus on Alvin's second-grade year; in the fifth, the family visits relatives in China: *Allergic to Camping, Hiking, and Other Natural Disasters* (2009), *Allergic to Birthday Parties, Science Projects, and Other Man-Made Catastrophes* (2010), *Allergic to Dead Bodies, Funerals, and Other Fatal Circumstances* (2011), and *Allergic to the Great Wall, the Forbidden Palace, and Other Tourist Attractions* (2014).

Betsy-Tacy

By Maud Hart Lovelace. Illustrated by Lois Lenski. HarperCollins, 1995 (orig. 1940).

Interest level: **Younger** • Lexile measure: **650L**
Historical fiction

Just before Betsy Ray's fifth birthday, Tacy Kelly moves in across the street and becomes the perfect friend. Published in 1940, this is the first of a long series of books based on the author's own pre–World War I childhood. These five-year-olds have problems that still resonate today. On their first day in kindergarten, Tacy is too shy to stay at school; Betsy runs away with her. Tacy's littlest sister dies; Betsy helps her by describing heaven. Betsy feels displaced by her new baby sister; Tacy sympathizes. They play dress-up, go calling, and find another friend, Tib. The ten-book series ends with Betsy's wedding. The later books are a bit more difficult and probably less interesting to elementary-school readers, but the first four—this title, *Betsy Tacy and Tib* (1941), *Betsy and Tacy Go over the Big Hill* (1942), and *Betsy and Tacy Go Downtown* (1943) —are appropriate and sometimes packaged together.

The Great Cake Mystery: Precious Ramotswe's Very First Case

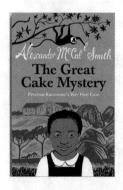

By Alexander McCall Smith. Illustrated by Iain McIntosh. Anchor Books, 2012.

Interest level: **Middle** • Lexile measure: **720L**
Mystery

In this series for young readers, mystery writer McCall Smith shows us how a good detective develops. As a child, Precious Ramotswe, the star of his popular adult series, No. 1 Ladies' Detective Agency, always notices things, asks questions, and never stops at the first easy answer. Here, when snacks disappear at her school, the eight-year-old is uncomfortable when her schoolmates call their "rather round" classmate Poloko a thief. She identifies the actual thieves and traps them in the act. These stories celebrate the landscape and reveal something of the culture of Botswana, but most of all, they introduce a remarkable character. Stylized illustrations in red, black, and gray appear on nearly every page. Two sequels describe other cases: *The Mystery of Meerkat Hill* (2013) and *The Mystery of the Missing Lion* (2014). These books conclude with reader's guides, curricular connections, and a relevant recipe. They make a fine introduction to the genre.

Judy Moody

By Megan McDonald. Illustrated by Peter Reynolds. Candlewick Press, 2000.

Interest level: **Younger** • Lexile measure: **530L**
Fiction

Third grade turns out to be better than Judy Moody had expected after Mr. Todd assigns a Me collage. She gets to share her new favorite pet, a carnivorous plant, and paste-eating Frank Pearl becomes a new friend. This first of an extended series is lighthearted, engaging, and spot-on about the moods and interests of second and third graders. There's a rubber hand in the toilet, a toad pee club, and a shark T-shirt with dripping jaws. Most importantly, there's a likeable protagonist who sometimes feels very grumpy, just as real children do. Judy and her little brother, Stink, have gone on to twelve more titles in this series, but Judy remains in or just finishing third grade. Gray-scale, cartoon-like drawings add appeal and there are occasional double-page spreads—the best showing Judy's completed Me collage, something readers may well want to imitate.

Kelsey Green, Reading Queen

By Claudia Mills. Illustrated by Rob Shepperson. Farrar, Straus, Giroux, 2013.

Interest level: **Younger** • Lexile measure: **750L**
Fiction

Third grader Kelsey Green is the best reader in her class—except maybe for classmate Simon Ellis. Kelsey's efforts to win the class title and the school-wide contest have some interesting results. In spite of her suspicions, she discovers that Simon really is reading all the books he claims, and better, they share a love for *The Secret Garden*. She helps another classmate find books he can enjoy by insisting that he read to her, and she discovers new genres in her search for short books that are still reading level appropriate as her teacher requires. She turns to biography (lots of pictures) and poetry (lots of white space). But everyone is happier when the contest is over and she can get back to the long books she loves. This title is part of a series about friends with different talents, including *Annika Riz, Math Whiz* (2014) and *Izzy Barr, Running Star* (2015).

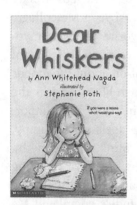

Dear Whiskers

By Ann Whitehead Nagda. Illustrated by Stephanie Roth. Holiday House, 2000.

Interest level: **Younger** • Lexile measure: **400L**
Fiction

When the fourth graders are assigned to write letters to second graders, Jenny has a problem: her pen pal doesn't have enough English to write back. Sameera has no interest in going along with the pretense that she's receiving letters from a mouse named Whiskers. Sameera comes from Saudi Arabia, where even today's date is different. Jenny finds other ways to communicate—reading some of her favorite picture books to the unhappy immigrant, drawing, and acting out stories with mice cookies she makes. Her example draws some of Sameera's classmates into helping her, too. This gentle school story nicely points out that a harder job can be a gift. For young readers, this interesting chapter book is a realistic window into the difficulty of attending school in a language that's not your own. A companion title, *Meow Means Mischief* (2003), stars Indian American Rana, also new in Jenny's school.

Project Mulberry: A Novel

By Linda Sue Park. Clarion Books, 2005.

Interest level: **Middle** • Lexile measure: **690L**
Fiction

Julia Song has always done projects with her friend Patrick, but she's not so happy with the animal husbandry project they've come up with for an afterschool club. Raising silkworms doesn't sound very American, and the seventh grader is already uncomfortable about her Korean American background. In a departure from usual story-telling practice, the author lets her readers in on her writing process by having conversations with Julia between the chapters of the silkworm project narrative. But it's Julia's experience that readers will remember: her discovery that farming, even silk farming, involves some killing; her reflections on racism, prompted by her mother's discomfort with kind Mr. Dixon, an African American who provides leaves from his mulberry tree to feed their worms and his mistaken assumptions about her ethnicity; and her increased appreciation for her pesky little brother. A complex, rewarding read.

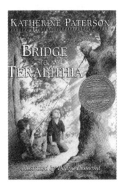

Bridge to Terabithia

By Katherine Paterson. Illustrated by Donna Diamond. HarperCollins, 1977.

Interest level: **Older** • Lexile measure: **810L**
Fiction

Ten-year-old Jess Aarons's life expands far beyond his Virginia farm world when a new neighbor, Leslie Burke, helps him create the magical kingdom of

Terabithia. Their imaginary game makes use of Jess's fears of the woods behind their homes to recreate it as a mystical place. Then, tragically, she's drowned there, leaving him to pass on the "beauty and caring" she had left him. As moving and as real nearly forty years after it was first written, this has a special place in most readers' hearts as the first truly sad book they ever read, and loved, and reread again and again. References to hippies and the farm community's outdated ideas about gendered behavior and clothing set this story in the past, but this is still an outstanding story of friendship with characters you'll never forget.

Calvin Coconut: Trouble Magnet

By Graham Salisbury. Illustrated by Jacqueline Rogers. Wendy Lamb Books, 2009.

Interest level: **Younger** • Lexile measure: **410L**
Fiction

Fourth graders Calvin Coconut and his friends live on the island of Oahu, where the food is different, the beach is nearby, and trouble is easy to find. In this series beginner, Calvin starts fourth grade badly. He brings a centipede to class; accidentally incurs the wrath of an older boy, a bully he calls Sinbad; and has to give up his bedroom to a family friend, a teenager from Texas who has come to live with them and be a "big sister" or babysitter. Calvin's boisterous behavior provides the opportunity for plenty of humor. His friends (both boys and girls) are Hawaii-diverse; his parents are divorced; he wants a dog; his teacher is strict but highly admired—there are many avenues for young readers to connect with this popular series. So far, eight sequels have appeared, but Calvin and his friends are still engaging fourth graders.

Like Pickle Juice on a Cookie

By Julie Sternberg. Illustrated by Matthew Cordell.
Amulet Books, 2011.

Interest level: **Younger** • Lexile measure: **440L**
Novels in verse

Eight-year-old Eleanor Abigail Kane has a very bad August after her first and only babysitter moves away. In short lines, Eleanor describes her sad feelings, the difficult adjustment to a new nanny (with beautiful hair), and her worries about starting third grade. All turns out well in this first of a series of stories for young readers that deal sensitively with difficult times in a child's life. In *Like Bug Juice on a Burger* (2013), Eleanor, now nine, goes to sleepaway camp, and in *Like Carrot Juice on a Cupcake* (2014), she responds to the threat of losing a best friend by saying something mean, and has to make amends. In all three, Cordell's gray-scale line drawings reflect the story line and help break up the text for readers ready for a step beyond beginning chapter books.

Keena Ford and the Second-Grade Mix-Up

By Melissa Thomson. Illustrated by Frank Morrison.
Dial Books, 2009.

Interest level: **Younger** • Lexile measure: **620L**
Fiction

Talented second-grade writer Keena Ford keeps a diary reflecting the rapid mood changes and daily dilemmas of her first week in second grade. A disappointing but ultimately satisfying class placement, lying accidentally and continuing the deception until she's caught, and friendship struggles are a few of the issues here. The particulars of this African American girl's life are clear; she lives in a Washington, D.C., apartment and spends weekends with her father. But this realistic story is more focused on school life and changing friendship patterns. Impulsive Keena thinks like a second grader, but her writing is far older; the chapters are relatively lengthy, more appropriate for a very good reader. Keena continues to chronicle her second-grade life in two sequels, *Keena Ford and the Field Trip Mix-Up* (2009) and *Keena Ford and the Secret Journal Mix-Up* (2010), also illustrated with occasional full-page, gray-scale drawings showing Keena and her friends in action.

Chapter 7

Talking Animals and Tiny People

· ·

T HERE IS A LONG TRADITION IN CHILDREN'S LIT-
erature of portraying characters as talking animals or tiny people. Set outside the realistic
human world, these characters may allow
young readers to identify with traits and situations, instead of with appearances. Readers also
enjoy the adventures of childlike or child-sized adults. These stories are usually called fantasy (animal fantasy, if the characters
are animals), but they are a distinct subset of that broader genre.
The stories in this section star characters with recognizable human
personalities and issues. They're often set in a realistic world but
usually involve a somewhat unbelievable adventure. Many have
been beloved by generations of children and have been retold,
usually less effectively, in movies and videos, comics, and abridg-

ments. In most cases, eager readers will find it worthwhile to seek out the richer original versions even if it means waiting a few years for a first encounter.

The True Blue Scouts of Sugar Man Swamp

By Kathi Appelt. Atheneum, 2013.

Interest level: **Middle** • Lexile measure: **810L**
Animal fantasy

When the delicious muscovado sugar of Sugar Man Swamp is threatened by a family of wild boars, it's up to raccoon scouts Bingo and J'miah to wake the yeti-like swamp guardian to come to the rescue. Similarly, with his grandfather gone, it's up to twelve-year-old Chap Brayburn to save his family's sugar pie business, as well as the swamp, from developer Sonny Boy Beaucoup. In 104 short chapters, the folksy narrator switches back and forth from the raccoons, now living in Chap's grandfather's lost 1949 DeSoto, to the Sugar Man's history with the Brayburn and Beaucoup families, to the journey of the marauding hogs, to Chap and his mother's efforts to raise "a boat-load of money." There are several scenes of alligator wrestling and the tantalizing possibility of ivory-billed woodpecker sightings. This is a complex and entertaining tall tale with an ecological message.

Jenny and the Cat Club: A Collection of Favorite Stories About Jenny Linsky

By Esther Averill. Illustrated by Esther Averill. New York Review of Books, 2003 (orig. 1944–53).

Interest level: **Younger**
Animal fantasy; Short stories

Shy Jenny Linsky, outfitted with a red scarf, gets up her nerve to join the neighborhood cat club, goes to a party, gets her scarf rescued by Pickles, the Fire Cat, and adopts two more strays as brothers, bringing them along to the club. These five simple stories, featuring talking animals with distinct, catlike personalities, were brought together as a collection in 1973. Reissued in this edition, they're reaching a third generation of readers. Said to be Averill's favorites, the stories include "The Cat Club," "First Party," "Adopted Brothers," and "How the Brothers Joined The Cat Club." For many young readers, Cat Club books were the first real chapter books they read on their own. Six more stories (all the titles in the series with the exception of the I Can Read title, *The Fire Cat*) have been reissued by the same publisher.

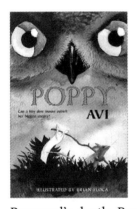

Poppy

By Avi. Illustrated by Brian Floca. Orchard Books, 1995.

Interest level: **Middle** • Lexile measure: **670L**
Animal fantasy

Because deer mouse Poppy and her friend Ragweed went to dance on Bannock Hill without the permission of Mr. Ocax, the ruling owl, he denies her large family's request to move to the New House. After Ragweed's death, Poppy determines to journey to New House to find out what it is Mr. Ocax fears there. For readers who can get past a stomach-churning beginning, when the owl eats Ragweed, this old-fashioned adventure has grand suspense, as Poppy makes her way through Dimwood Forest, and a highly satisfactory ending. This award-winning lesson in speaking truth to power was the first to be published of the Tales of Dimwood Forest although it is second in chronological time. It makes sense for younger readers to start with this title rather than the prequel, *Ragweed* (1999), which would make his death harder to take. Sequels include *Poppy and Rye* (1998), *Ereth's Birthday* (2000), *Poppy's Return* (2005), and *Poppy and Ereth* (2009).

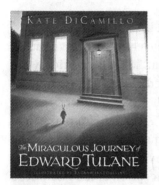

The Miraculous Journey of Edward Tulane

By Kate DiCamillo. Illustrated by Bagram Ibatoulline. Candlewick Press, 2006.

Interest level: **Middle** • Lexile measure: **700L**
Animal fantasy

Edward Tulane, a fashionably dressed china rabbit, leads a privileged life in Abilene's home. Rather than returning his young owner's love, though, he cares only for himself. Over the course of a series of adventures, beginning with being lost at sea, both his heart and his head get broken, but he develops the ability to love. This sad but ultimately hopeful story takes place in an unspecified past that's probably the 1930s. One of the rabbit's owners is a hobo, another an elderly couple still missing a son who died young, a third, a fatally ill girl. This beautifully presented book is decorated with sepia-toned vignettes at the beginning of each chapter and occasional tipped-in full-color paintings. With a thick, creamy paper and generous leading, it has the look of a classic from the mid-twentieth century. Perfect for any doll lover who doesn't mind some tragedy, this is a good adventure, too.

My Father's Dragon

By Ruth Stiles Gannett. Illustrated by Ruth Chrisman Gannett. Random House, 2008 (orig. 1948).

Interest level: **Younger** • Lexile measure: **990L**
Animal fantasy

At the suggestion of an alley cat he's befriended, Elmer Elevator travels to Tangerine Island to free a young dragon trapped by a group of lazy and hungry wild animals. The narrator of this popular early chapter book tells the whole story as if it were something that had happened to his father. Provisioned with a variety of useful objects, including chewing gum, a toothbrush, magnifying glasses, and lollipops, Elmer outwits seven tigers, a rhinoceros, a gorilla, and a large number of crocodiles and flies off in triumph on the dragon's back. Black-and-white drawings (with lots of stripes!)

include a detailed map and appealing animals. Sequels *Elmer and the Dragon* (1950) and *The Dragons of Blueland* (1951) follow both Elmer and the dragon (Boris) to a second island and to Boris's Blueland home. An anniversary edition includes all three stories.

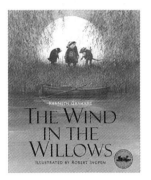

The Wind in the Willows

By Kenneth Grahame. Illustrated by Robert Ingpen. Sterling, 2012 (orig. 1908).

Interest level: **Middle** • Lexile measure: **1140L**
Classics; Animal fantasy

For more than a hundred years, children have enjoyed the language and the adventures of Mole and Rat, their Wild Wood friend Badger, and the impulsive Toad. Mole learns there is nothing half so much worth doing as simply messing about in boats. When Toad develops a passion for motor-cars, his friends try, and fail, to bring him to his senses, but when he escapes from jail they help him regain his beloved home, Toad Hall. Home matters to all of these characters, and their world is lyrically described. Young readers may well skip the description—and maybe whole chapters—in their first pass through this classic, but they will return over and over. Although the book was originally published without illustrations, numerous artists have since brought these characters to life including Ernest Shepard and Arthur Rackham. A remarkably successful sequel, *Return to the Willows* (Jacqueline Kelly, 2012), continues the adventures.

The Reluctant Dragon

By Kenneth Grahame. Illustrated by Ernest H. Shepard. Holiday House, 2013 (orig. 1938).

Interest level: **Middle** • Lexile measure: **1070L**
Classics; Fantasy

In a misty, long-ago time when dragons still survived in England, Boy, who loved reading and therefore knew all about dragons, becomes friends with the dragon who turned up in a cave in the downs above his family home. They share a love for poetry and pass pleasant evenings together. When St. George turns up in the village, summoned to slay the animal, Boy looks forward to a fight but doesn't want anyone to get hurt. He gets the reluctant dragon to agree to fighting, provided there are no real injuries. The dragon's reward will be a big banquet and a larger audience for his poems. This near-perfect story is a grand read-aloud, but also a joy for the child reader willing to tackle a text full of interesting vocabulary and pleasing imagery. This anniversary edition, with the Shepard illustrations, fits neatly in the hand.

The Bat-Poet

By Randall Jarrell. Illustrated by Maurice Sendak. Macmillan, 1964.

Interest level: **Middle** • Lexile measure: **660L**
Fiction; Poetry

THE BAT-POET
By Randall Jarrell
Pictures by Maurice Sendak

Left behind when his bat friends moved to the barn, a little brown bat begins to notice the daytime world. He admires the mockingbird's song so much that he starts composing his own poems. The chipmunk provides an appreciative audience. This charming fable is really about poetry—writing poetry and listening to it. What is it in a poem that appeals to an audience? Is it the subject (especially if the subject is yourself)? Is it how it makes you feel? Is it the construction? The story also points up how much there is to see in the natural world if you stop to look. The bat's poems are beautiful, but they are also filled with details reflecting his careful observation. The bats and the other woodland creatures are beautifully delineated in Sendak's drawings. Reflective rather than active, this is for a thoughtful child, and a writer.

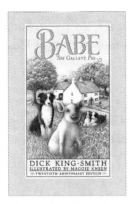

Babe: The Gallant Pig

By Dick King-Smith. Illustrated by Mary Rayner. Knopf, 2005 (orig. 1985).

Interest level: **Middle** • Lexile measure: **1040L**
Animal fantasy

Adopted by the sheepdog, Fly, when he first arrived at Farmer Hoggett's, piglet Babe learns good manners and sheep training. His natural courtesy and respect for the sheep make him a star. Babe is clever, kind, and considerate, a pig in the class of Wilbur. Fly is not only a good mother, but an excellent trainer. She gets him to slim down and exercise so that he is also a very fit pig, fast enough to challenge the stars at the Grand Challenge Sheepdog Trials. There's some dialect here, but not so much as to make the reading difficult, and the sheepherding details are fascinating. Parents may need to explain to children that female dogs are correctly termed bitches, a word that has nearly lost that meaning in this country. Occasional pen-and-ink drawings will help readers visualize the setting and the inhabitants of this very English farm.

A Mouse Called Wolf

By Dick King-Smith. Illustrated by Jon Goodell. Crown, 1997.

Interest level: **Middle** • Lexile measure: **950L**
Animal fantasy

Worried about his small size, Mary Mouse gives her youngest child an important name, Wolfgang Amadeus Mouse. Young Wolf, though much teased for his short stature by his larger, older siblings, turns out to be a musical genius himself. He sings with and later composes for elderly Jane Honeybee, a former concert pianist, whose home he shares. This straightforward story has some slight suspense: an encounter with a cat, entrapment inside the closed piano, and Mrs. Honeybee's broken ankle. It's young Wolf's determination that is the big appeal. He has to work up to being an accomplished musician, and Mrs. Honeybee trains him slowly. The pace of the story will appeal more to a reflective reader than one who looks for action. Occasional pen-and-ink illustrations of Mrs. Honeybee and her animals add to the charm.

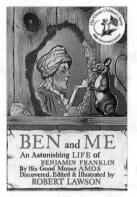

Ben and Me: A New and Astonishing Life of Benjamin Franklin as Written by His Good Mouse, Amos

By Robert Lawson. Illustrated by Robert Lawson. Little, Brown, 1939.

Interest level: **Middle** • Lexile measure: **1010L**
Historical fiction; Animal fantasy; Biography

Amos, a onetime church mouse, takes credit for Ben Franklin's many accomplishments in a long and productive life as inventor, experimenter, Revolutionary War patriot, and diplomat. Narrated by the mouse, this amusing look at Franklin's life and times has been popular for more than seventy years. Amos describes the invention of the Franklin stove; the trouble he caused by editing *Poor Richard's Almanack*; several experiments with electricity, including an unpleasant kite ride; the writing of the Declaration of Independence; Franklin's time in France; and a rodent battle at Versailles. The humor is infectious; no child could forget the mice hiding in French ladies' towering hair arrangements. Lawson's illustrations add appeal. The text is challenging but not too much for a child with a good vocabulary who enjoys learning new words and something about history. *Mr. Revere and I* (1953), told by his horse, provides similar fun.

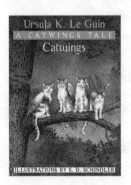

Catwings

By Ursula K. Le Guin. Illustrated by S. D. Schindler. Orchard Books, 1988.

Interest level: **Younger** • Lexile measure: **700L**
Animal fantasy

Alley cat Mrs. Jane Tabby sends her four winged children off to find their place in the world, and

Roger, Thelma, Harriet, and James have various adventures in the woods before they find some Hands and a new home. This is a short, slight, and very sweet story beautifully told by an accomplished writer and illustrated with old-fashioned, delicately tinted pen-and-ink drawings. The similarities between the gritty city neighborhood and the equally dangerous forest are interesting, and the ultimate fate of the young cats is very satisfying. In a sequel, *Catwings Return* (1989), James and Harriet return to the city and rescue another winged kitten. Two more titles, *Wonderful Alexander and the Catwings* (1994) and *Jane on Her Own* (1999), describe further adventures. These chapter books, just right for transitional readers, also introduce an author they will surely rediscover in later years.

The Doll People

By Ann M. Martin and Laura Godwin.
Illustrated by Brian Selznick. Hyperion, 2000.

Interest level: **Middle** • Lexile measure: **570L**
Fantasy

For more than a hundred years, little changed in eight-year-old Annabelle's life, except for the disappearance of her Auntie Sarah. But when her current owner gets a modern set of dolls, Annabelle and new friend Tiffany Funcraft go searching for Annabelle's missing aunt. The mystery of the older doll's disappearance is enough to keep readers going, and the danger of encountering the cat provides plenty of suspense. The contrast between the plastic Funcrafts and the more formal Dolls offers plenty of humor, in both the text and Selznick's delightful drawings. Told from Annabelle's point of view, this is hefty but relatively easy to read. Progressively more challenging sequels include *The Meanest Doll in the World* (2003), in which Annabelle and Tiffany get carried off to school; *The Runaway Dolls* (2008), in which the two end up in a toy store; and *The Doll People Set Sail* (2014), in which the families take a transatlantic voyage.

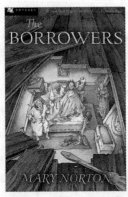

The Borrowers

By Mary Norton. Illustrated by Diana Stanley.
Harcourt, 2003 (orig. 1953).

Interest level: **Middle** • Lexile measure: **780L**
Fantasy

The Clock family, six-inch people who lived hidden for generations, find they have to move when young Arrietty talks to a visiting boy, revealing their presence. In four sequels, *The Borrowers Afield* (1955), *The Borrowers Afloat* (1959), *The Borrowers Aloft* (1961), and *The Borrowers Avenged* (1982), available as a boxed set, they flee to a farmer's field, take a boat downriver to a model village, get captured by humans who keep them in over winter, and finally settle in a rectory near some relatives. Arrietty's parents, Pod and Homily, do their best to protect her from "human beans," but the fourteen-year-old does like to explore. The first three books have a great deal of setting and character development; the last two are more plot-based. The details of Borrower lives are fascinating. The language is a treat, with many new, unusual words that are clear in context. Beth and Joe Krush drew the original illustrations.

Secrets at Sea

By Richard Peck. Illustrated by Kelly Murphy.
Dial Books, 2011.

Interest level: **Middle** • Lexile measure: **600L**
Animal fantasy

When the social-climbing Upstairs Cranstons sail to England to find a husband for daughter Olive, the mice downstairs go along for an eventful ocean voyage that results in happy endings for all the eligible young ladies, both human and mouse. Set at the time of Queen Victoria's Jubilee, this humorous story has all the trappings of a nineteenth-century romance: dashing young gentlemen, daring daughters, unruly brothers, and plenty of royalty to spice things up. Sensible Helena, forced to take charge of her siblings after her parents' death by drowning, tells the story. The mice are afraid of water, of course, but courageous. The narrative is fast paced and full of suspense, especially as the mice attempt to avoid the ship's cat. Peck uses vocabulary and phrases that evoke the period and will intrigue young readers who enjoy new words. A companion title, with new characters and new problems, is *The Mouse with the Question Mark Tail* (2013).

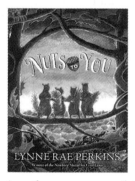

Nuts to You

By Lynne Rae Perkins. Illustrated by Lynne Rae Perkins. Greenwillow Books, 2014.

Interest level: **Middle**
Animal fantasy

The gray squirrel Jed had a harrowing experience in his youth when he was captured by a hawk, escaped, and discovered that humans were clearing the area around "buzzpaths" (utility wires) and would soon destroy his neighborhood. Jed and the friends who followed him have to find their way back home and then convince the other squirrels (realistically distractible and parochial) to move. Their adventure is framed by the much-older Jed's encounter with a human who offers a bit of a peanut butter sandwich and hears his story. The author's voice appears, too, in side comments and chapter-ending footnotes, and her drawings are a treat. In this humorous tale of friendship and the power of story, the natural history and environmental concerns are true to life. There are real dangers in Jed's world, but his third-person narrative is warm and reassuring in the tradition of classic animal adventures.

The Complete Adventures of Peter Rabbit

By Beatrix Potter. Illustrated by Beatrix Potter. Frederick Warne, 2007 (orig. 1902–1912).

Interest level: **Younger**
Classics; Animal fantasy; Short stories

Here's a lovely edition of four tales starring Peter Rabbit and his family, complete and authorized by the original publisher. It includes *The Tale of Peter Rabbit* (1902), *The Tale of Benjamin Bunny* (1904), *The Tale of the Flopsy Bunnies* (1909), and *The Tale of Mr. Tod* (1912), all with the original illustrations. These were first published as tiny books for tiny hands, but each oversized page of this edition includes two or three original pages, with their accompanying illustrations. For each adventure, one illustration is enlarged so that readers can admire its amazing detail. The images in Mr. Tod may surprise. Along with the traditional watercolor pen-and-ink scenes, there are many in black and white with a coarser line that recalls woodcuts. This collection represents some of the best of Potter's work, a good introduction to her pleasing animal families and her love of the natural and pastoral world of England's Lake District.

Gully's Travels

By Tor Seidler. Illustrated by Brock Cole. Michael Di Capua Books, 2008.

Interest level: **Middle** • Lexile measure: **890L**
Animal fantasy

Pampered and privileged, Gulliver has often traveled from Manhattan to Paris with his professor, but when the man gives the Lhasa Apso away to his building's doorman, whose boisterous family lives in Queens and calls him "Gully," he runs away, becoming a transatlantic traveler on his own. This story of the relative importance of a loving home versus fancy things is told with gentle humor and plenty of drama (including the dog's suicide attempt). Arrogant and superior at first, Gully learns tolerance and appreciation for others through his travels. Charmingly told in third person from the dog's point of view, the emphasis is on other animals, but also on the contrast between Professor Rattigan's betrayal and Roberto Montoya's loyalty. Expressive sketches on nearly every page document Gully's travels and the characters (animal and human) he meets.

The Cricket in Times Square
By George Selden. Illustrated by Garth Williams. Yearling, 2005 (orig. 1960).

Interest level: **Middle** • Lexile measure: **780L**
Animal fantasy

After accidentally journeying from the country, Chester Cricket finds a new home, with Mario Bellini in his family's newsstand in a Times Square subway station, and new friends in Tucker Mouse and Harry Cat. This sweet friendship story stars the three talking animals, a hardworking Italian American boy, and an elderly Chinese gentleman. The original edition of this 1961 Newbery honor book included a stereotyped representation of Chinese grammatical errors and mispronunciations. In recent printings and paperback editions much of the difficult, offensive dialect has been removed, leaving the Chinese shopkeeper's remarkable generosity and the boy's appreciation for his different culture. The story itself is appealing, and the cricket's perfect musical memory is a delight. Five sequels and a prequel follow Chester back home to Connecticut, and explain Harry and Tucker's friendship.

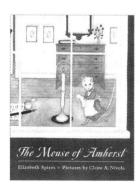

The Mouse of Amherst
By Elizabeth Spires. Illustrated by Claire A. Nivola. Farrar, Straus, Giroux, 1999.

Interest level: **Younger** • Lexile measure: **900L**
Animal fantasy; Poetry

When Emmaline mouse moves into the Dickinson family home in Amherst, Massachusetts, she finds a kindred spirit in Emily, a reclusive young poet.

The mouse so enjoys Dickinson's poetry that she writes some of her own. The premise is sweet and immediately engaging to readers charmed by talking animals. Even the book is small. Not much happens. Emily has a visit from an editor who turns down her work and Emmaline has some run-ins with the cat. Emily makes gingerbread, sending it down to the neighborhood children in a basket from the window, and the mouse takes a ride. Mostly this is a vehicle to introduce some of Dickinson's most famous poetry. Spires's choices are good, and her own Dickinson imitations are well done. The short poems have interesting language and thought-provoking sentiments. Nivola's pen-and-ink sketches add to the delicate humor.

ABEL'S ISLAND • *William Steig*

FARRAR/STRAUS/GIROUX

Abel's Island

By William Steig. Illustrated by William Steig. Farrar, Straus, Giroux, 1976.

Interest level: **Middle** • Lexile measure: **920L**
Animal fantasy

In 1907, while newlyweds Abel and Amanda are happily picnicking, a storm blows up. They take shelter in a cave, but her scarf blows away. He tries chivalrously to retrieve it, falls into a river, and is swept away to an island. Here the once-privileged mouse lives by his wits and his penknife for a year before he's able to make his way back to civilization and his wife. This charming tongue-in-cheek animal fantasy and exceptionally well-told survival tale won a Newbery honor. Steig's language is unforgettable. Young readers will encounter plenty of new and wonderfully useful words. *The New Yorker* cartoonist illustrates his story with gray-scale images of the Abel's transformation from well-dressed gentleman to ragged but determined survivor with a potentially more useful life ahead. Suspenseful and rewarding, especially for *Stuart Little* fans.

The Trumpet of the Swan

By E. B. White. Illustrated by Fred Marcellino.
Harper & Row, 2000 (orig. 1970).

Interest level: **Middle** • Lexile measure: **750L**
Animal fantasy

In this third of a beloved author's talking animal
tales, a trumpet gives voice to a swan with a speech
problem, and music gives him a full life. In the
idyllic opening, eleven-year-old Sam Beaver, camp-
ing in the Canadian wilderness, finds a nesting pair of trumpeter swans.
Later, in Montana, where the swans winter, the voiceless fifth cygnet,
Louis, encounters Sam again and enlists him in his quest to find a way to
communicate. The swan attends school, steals a trumpet, and earns money
as a musician. Finally, after he's repaid the music store, Louis's true love,
Serena, turns up in Philadelphia. The mute swan communicates his passion
through his playing, and they live happily ever after. Full of details from
the natural world and sly commentary on human behavior, this is another
all-time favorite, originally illustrated by Edward Frascino and attractively
reillustrated in this Collector's Edition.

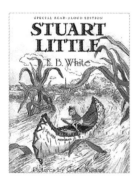

Stuart Little

By E. B. White. Illustrated by Garth Williams.
Harper & Row, 2005 (orig. 1945).

Interest level: **Middle** • Lexile measure: **920L**
Animal fantasy

Mr. and Mrs. Little's second son, a mouse, adventures in New York City and then ventures north-
ward in search of his bird friend, Margalo. Sophis-
ticated in its humor but clear enough in its story line for young readers
willing to accept the unlikely premise, this classic from 1945 is dated in its
details but still has charm. Stuart gets rolled up in a window shade, helms
a sailboat in Central Park, spends a day as a substitute teacher, and drives
away in a classic car. Readers enjoy the particulars of his miniature life,

the exertions necessary to turn the faucet to brush his teeth, and his doll-sized clothes and equipment. The bittersweet end encourages continued imagination. Williams's engaging drawings show him in action—shooting an arrow at the menacing cat, for example—and in his dreams of a romantic canoe outing. This anniversary edition has been colorized by Rosemary Wells.

Chapter 8

Witches and Wizards and Magic

···

PERHAPS IT'S EASIER FOR YOUNG READERS TO suspend disbelief, or, since so much of their world is mysterious and strange, perhaps they're just more open to stories that adults might find impossible to believe. Fantasies allow young readers to stretch their imaginations while learning some important truths. Often they offer humor as well. The titles in this section involve magic talismans, magic wielders, and magical creatures, from a wish-granting hamster to a tiny fairy. Their main characters might be ordinary or extraordinary, with magical backgrounds and powers. There are also witches (both good and bad), magical books, magical cars, and creatures from various European folklore traditions. Though many of these titles could be listed in the following chapter on quests and adventures, they were grouped together here because of the important role of magic.

Jinx

By Sage Blackwood. HarperCollins, 2013.

Interest level: **Older** • Lexile measure: **HL620L**
Fantasy

This fresh and original fantasy has familiar elements; it's a good suggestion for someone looking for a follow-up to *Harry Potter*. Abandoned by his stepfather in Urwald's dangerous forest and with part of his magic stolen by his rescuer, wizard Simon Magus, Jinx sets out to explore his world. With new friends Elfwyn and Regen, he braves the island of the Bonemaster, hoping to find antidotes to their individual curses. Jinx, when he has all his powers, can see people's moods as colors and listen to the forest through the soil on his bare feet. Readers will recognize the girl with the red hood and her grandmother, the witch; the haunted forest and wizard's workroom are familiar places. In the trilogy's middle volume, *Jinx's Magic* (2014), Jinx goes to Samara to learn more about his magic powers while the forest becomes increasingly endangered. *Jinx's Fire* will appear in 2015.

Chitty Chitty Bang Bang Flies Again

By Frank Cottrell Boyce. Illustrated by Joe Berger. Candlewick Press, 2012.

Interest level: **Middle** • Lexile measure: **710L**
Fantasy

The Tooting family's new car, rebuilt from an old camper van, has its own agenda. It's determined to collect its missing parts, from an airplane engine to its original bodywork, and provides adventure all along the way. Authorized by Fleming's heirs, this first of a trilogy of companions to *Chitty Chitty Bang Bang* (annotated later in this chapter) follows the adventures of a more modern, biracial family and their rebuilt car, but it has much of the same flavor and humor. This car, too, has a mind of its own, taking the family to France, Egypt, and Madagascar. Two sequels, *Chitty Chitty Bang Bang and the Race Against Time* (2013) and *Chitty Chitty Bang Bang Over the Moon* (2014), take the family through time and space, pit them against new criminals, and even reunite them with Fleming's Pott family before winding up. Fresh, fast paced, and entertaining, these are fine journeys.

The Boggart

By Susan Cooper. Margaret K. McElderry Books, 1993.

Interest level: **Middle** • Lexile measure: **1030L**
Fiction

Emily and Jess Volnik's family accidentally ships a mischievous boggart from a castle in Scotland to their home in Toronto, where it encounters the modern world with some disastrous results. It takes considerable computer programming to get him home again. This shape-shifter is not scary, like boggarts in *Harry Potter*, but charmingly naughty. Like a small child, he doesn't think about consequences. Twelve-year-old Emily breaks her leg. It's ten-year-old Jess and his friends who figure out how to return the homesick sprite to Port Appin. The parallels between the Old Magic of this boggart, the magic of the theater, and the magic of electrons—whether in electric wires or in computers—are interesting to think about. This book is dated in its computer details but is still an engaging read. In *The Boggart and the Monster* (1997), the boggart meets up with its cousin, the Loch Ness monster.

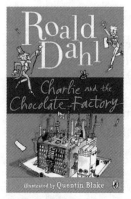

Charlie and the Chocolate Factory

By Roald Dahl. Illustrated by Quentin Blake.
Knopf, 2001 (orig. 1964; rev. 1973).

Interest level: **Middle** • Lexile measure: **810L**
Fantasy

Desperately poor and hungry, Charlie Bucket is thrilled to find the golden ticket that earns him a tour of Willy Wonka's Chocolate Factory. For ten years, marvelously inventive candy treats have been made by Wonka's tiny employees, hidden inside. Now the owner has opened his doors to five lucky young people. The faults of Charlie's companions on the tour lead them to deserving misfortunes, and Charlie emerges the winner. This humorous classic was revised by the author to remove the Oompa-Loompas' connection to Africa. The text was originally illustrated by Joseph Schindelman and later by Michael Foreman, but it is Blake's illustrations, from the 1998 edition, that are most familiar today. Blake has also reillustrated Dahl's sequel, *Charlie and the Great Glass Elevator* (1972), which moves from the realm of fantasy to science fiction, taking Charlie and his family into space for a while. A conclusion to the planned trilogy was never written.

The Witches

By Roald Dahl. Illustrated by Quentin Blake.
Farrar, Straus, Giroux, 2013 (orig. 1983).

Interest level: **Middle** • Lexile measure: **740L**
Fantasy

Introduced to witches by his Norwegian grandmother, the narrator accidentally eavesdrops on a meeting of witches planning the eradication of all English children. With only a little help, he turns them all into mice even though he has been turned into a mouse-appearing human himself. This has all of Dahl's characteristic macabre humor, too exaggerated to be truly scary. At seven, the narrator loses his parents in an automobile accident, but luckily his flexible, tolerant, and loving grand-mother is an expert on witches. Much of the suspense is created as the never-named narrator hides from witches and later, after his transformation, invades the Grand High Witch's hotel room and creeps through the hotel kitchen to place a potion in their food. In the 1990 film, the narrator regains his human form, but Dahl's preference was to have him remain a mouse, living out his short life with his aging grandmother.

The Field Guide

By Tony DiTerlizzi and Holly Black. Illustrated by Tony DiTerlizzi. Simon & Schuster, 2003.

Interest level: **Middle** • Lexile measure: **600L**
Fantasy

An old house with secrets and an angry boggart is the new home for nine-year-old twins Jared and Simon and their thirteen-year-old sister, Mallory, stars of this series featuring creatures from the fairy world. In the first episode, the three children explore their new home, finding *Arthur Spiderwick's Field Guide to the Fantastical World Around You.* This was designed as a five-book series. In sequels *The Seeing Stone* (2003), *Lucinda's Secret* (2003), *The Ironwood Tree* (2004), and *The Wrath Of Mulgarath* (2004) the children encounter ever more hostile creatures. The tone grows considerably darker, making these better for readers who seek suspense and won't mind some animal gore. Beautifully presented, with plentiful gothic-style illustrations, these books have physical appeal. The five have been published together in a six hundred-plus page *Completely Fantastical Edition* (2009), which also includes further information and sketches.

Half Magic

By Edward Eager. Illustrated by N. M. Bodecker. Harcourt, 2004 (orig. 1954).

Interest level: **Middle** • Lexile measure: **830L**
Fantasy; Adventure

For children who love reading, Jane, Mark, Katharine, and Martha are characters who share that passion. They love E. Nesbit's stories and wish that their lives were like that: ordinary children having extraordinary adventures. Then Jane finds a magic talisman in a crack in the sidewalk. Unfortunately, it only grants half of each wish. There's considerable humor in their initial attempts to use their wishing coin effectively, but after they learn, it not only takes them to King Arthur's Camelot, it provides them with a book-loving new stepfather. Published sixty years ago and set thirty years earlier, this story has worn well. Three sequels (available as a quartet called *Edward Eager's Tales of Magic*) feel more dated. Look for revised editions of *Magic by the Lake* (1957, 1999), *Knight's Castle* (1956, 1999), and *The Time Garden* (1958, 1999). The last title still has some outdated stereotypes about Indians.

Chitty Chitty Bang Bang: The Magical Car

By Ian Fleming. Illustrated by Joe Berger. Candlewick Press, 2013 (orig. 1964).

Interest level: **Middle** • Lexile measure: **NC1370L**
Fantasy

Commander Caractacus Pott (Commander Crackpot) refurbishes an old car for his family and then discovers its extraordinary qualities and its habit of taking them on adventures. Fleming's spoof on his adult thrillers is funny, fast paced, and full of interesting language. With the magical car the family nearly gets marooned by a rising tide, flies from England to France, and finds and destroys the munitions of a gang of criminals who retaliate by kidnapping the children. This story is quite different from the movie version and a delight to read. The original illustrations by John Burningham are grand, but somewhat smudged in the Buccaneer Books reprint. This 2013 reissue has Berger's lively new ones. Readers enchanted by the idea of a car with a mind of its own will appreciate the companion titles written by Frank Cottrell Boyce annotated earlier in this chapter.

Igraine the Brave

By Cornelia Funke. Illustrated by Cornelia Funke. Translated by Anthea Bell. Scholastic, 2007.

Interest level: **Middle** • Lexile measure: **900L**
Fantasy

While making the suit of armor that will be a present for Igraine's twelfth birthday, her magician parents accidentally turn themselves into pigs. To undo this spell and save the family castle, besieged by Osmund the Greedy, who wants the family's *Singing Books of Magic,* Igraine must fetch hairs from a redheaded giant, while her older brother defends the castle with his fledgling magic skills. Igraine succeeds and returns with a helpful Sorrowful Knight. Though they quarrel, brother Albert obviously cares for her. He's getting to be a pretty good magician as well, except that the only food he can make is dry biscuits and blue eggs. Igraine, who dreams of becoming a knight, can't remember spells, but she's practiced swordplay a lot. Becoming the Sorrowful Knight's squire, she gets the training she needs. This gender-reversing tale has humor, fast-paced action, and plenty of reader appeal.

Operation Bunny: The Fairy Detective Agency's First Case

By Sally Gardner. Illustrated by David Roberts. Henry Holt, 2014.

Interest level: **Middle** • Lexile measure: **700L**
Fantasy

Emily Vole, whose adoptive parents treat her like Cinderella, is freed by a neighbor with a talking cat; becomes Keeper of the Keys; temporarily outwits wicked witch Harpella, who's been turning people into rabbits; and reopens the fairy detective agency, Wings & Co. First of a new series from Great Britain, this has the appropriate ingredients: orphans, cruel stepparents, witches, fairies, and plenty of humor. Emily is resourceful and determined, and, while this first volume is more stage setting than mystery, the series promises much adventure to come. This is grandly illustrated with detailed line drawings, funny in themselves. There are references to fairy tales and snide comments about the materialism of the Dasherwoods, who adopted the child, found in a basket at Stansted Airport, and whose own triplets get zombified. There's already a sequel, *The Three Pickled Herrings* (2014).

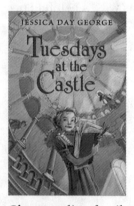

Tuesdays at the Castle

By Jessica Day George. Bloomsbury, 2011.

Interest level: **Middle** • Lexile measure: **860L**
Fantasy

Eleven-year-old Princess Celie has been trying to map her castle for years. But Glower Castle has a mind of its own. It changes regularly, sometimes to meet its inhabitants' needs but mostly for inscrutable reasons of its own. But the castle's love for the Glower ruling family helps Celie and her siblings, Lilah and Crown Prince Rolf, overcome a usurper who attempts to assassinate her parents and take over the country. This charming fantasy should have particular appeal for young readers who fell in love with the inventiveness of J. K. Rowling.

There's genuine grief, plenty of giggles, and all ends well. Best of all, there are sequels. *Wednesdays in the Tower* (2013) is a darker story that leaves readers hanging at the end. *Thursdays with the Crown* (2014) winds up more satisfactorily, and there's Friday to come.

Samuel Blink and the Forbidden Forest

By Matt Haig. G. P. Putnam's Sons, 2007.

Interest level: **Middle** • Lexile measure: **770L**
Fantasy

After their parents' accident, Samuel and Martha Blink are sent to live with an aunt in Norway, near a forbidden forest into which Martha, now mute, wanders away. Samuel follows, hoping to rescue her, and meets trolls, truth pixies, huldres, and worse—creatures he's read about in a book (also forbidden). Commanded by the Changemaker, Professor Horatio Tanglewood, these creatures have become evil. Drawing on Scandinavian legends, Haig has concocted a humorous fantasy with short chapters full of fast-paced action and humor. Intriguing chapter names and occasional authorial warnings add atmosphere. This won a Nestlé prize in Great Britain. It would appeal to readers who don't mind dark and scary stories and aren't put off by the parents' untimely death. In *Samuel Blink and the Runaway Troll* (2008), one of the forest creatures comes to live with his idol, Samuel, and the forest is threatened with development.

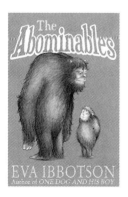

The Abominables

By Eva Ibbotson. Illustrated by Fiona Robinson. Abrams, 2013.

Interest level: **Older** • Lexile measure: **1010L**
Fantasy

A furry family of yetis will win your heart in this charming last novel by a beloved fantasy and historical fiction writer. Needing a parent for his motherless brood, Father yeti abducts an English girl, Lady Agatha, who falls in love with the kind creatures and raises them in her best Victorian manner. A century later, when development threatens their idyllic Himalayan valley, two other children and a long-distance truck driver smuggle five yetis and a baby yak to Europe and across to England and safety in Agatha's stately home. But times have changed; Farley Towers' new occupants are members of a hunting club who whisk the yetis away into further danger. Just suspenseful enough to keep readers engaged, this imaginative story is also very funny. Far from abominable, the yetis, who believe the best about everyone, apologize to their (vegetable) food, and love to hear stories, are irresistible.

The Secret of Platform 13

By Eva Ibbotson. Illustrated by Sue Porter. Dutton, 1998.

Interest level: **Older** • Lexile measure: **910L**
Fantasy

Through a portal that only opens once every nine years, a nine-year-old hag named Odge and other residents of a hidden kingdom journey back to London to rescue their kidnapped prince. Unfortunately, the boy they find is not the heir they'd hoped for. Three years before Harry Potter first took a train, Ibbotson described this railway platform hiding a passage to a magical world. This island kingdom is inhabited by friendly wizards, giants, and ogres; horrid harpies and sky yelpers; and a thoroughly nice, human, royal family whose child was accidentally taken to London and kidnapped by a wealthy woman wanting a baby of her own. Today's readers are likely to come to this after meeting Harry. It's a fine follow-up, both an adventure and an attempt to right a wrong. The magical characters are endearing, the wealthy family exaggeratedly obnoxious, and the human ghosts helpful at just the right times. Predictable but pleasing.

How to Catch a Bogle

By Catherine Jinks. Illustrated by Sarah Watts. Houghton Mifflin, 2013.

Interest level: **Older** • Lexile measure: **790L**
Fantasy

Named for her beautiful voice, ten-year-old Birdie McAdam is bogle bait. Apprentice to Alfred Bunce, a man who makes his living killing these child-eating demons in Victorian London, she lures them from their dark places. When posh folklorist Miss Eames offers to sponsor and educate Birdie, Alfred takes her seriously. He's fond of the child, who is street-smart, quick-witted, and endearing. Birdie herself, though tempted, likes her important work. A bogler's job is risky, but Birdie and Alfred are even more threatened by necromancer wannabe Dr. Morton, who kidnaps Birdie to get the bogler to do his bidding. Dr. Morton's menace and the question of Birdie's future intertwine in this compelling story, first in a series that promises plenty more scary moments and spectacularly gory explosions. The first sequel to appear in this country is *A Plague of Bogles* (2015); another has been published in Australia.

Hamster Magic

By Lynne Jonell. Illustrated by Brandon Dorman. Random House, 2010.

Interest level: **Younger** • Lexile measure: **620L**
Fantasy

Hammy the Third, the hamster the four Willow children found in their new house, turns out to be no ordinary pet. He can grant wishes—or at least one wish. But Abner, Tate, and Derek spend so much time discussing what their one wish might be that Celia, the youngest, impatiently blurts out that she wishes she were big. Transformed into a giant hamster, she presents a big problem to the others, who spend the rest of the night trying to get her back to her normal shape and size. Jonell's series of magic-gone-awry chapter books continues with *Lawnmower Magic* (2012), in which an old-fashioned reel mower develops an insatiable appetite; *Grasshopper Magic* (2013), in which Abner and Tate become surprisingly bouncy after eating baked grasshoppers; and the promised *Deep Water Magic* (not yet published). Family teamwork is a connecting thread, though each title stars a different child.

A Wrinkle in Time

By Madeleine L'Engle. Farrar, Straus, Giroux, 1962.

Interest level: **Older** • Lexile measure: **740L**
Fantasy

With the help of Mrs. Who, Mrs. Whatsit, and Mrs. Which, Meg and Charles Wallace Murry and their friend Calvin O'Keefe travel through a wrinkle in time and face hatred, unbearable cold, and the loss of free will to save Mr. Murry from the dark cloud and disembodied brain that had captured him. This classic quest adventure won a Newbery Medal in 1963. Current readers' parents may be surprised at Meg's age (fourteen), the many religious references, and dated details. But the adventure is appropriately suspenseful, and younger readers will particularly appreciate Charles Wallace, only five years old but competent and frighteningly knowing. The frightening IT almost swallows Charles Wallace before his sister's love rescues him. There are three direct sequels: *A Wind in the Door* (1973), *Many Waters* (1986), and *A Swiftly Tilting Planet* (1978), and a prequel, *An Acceptable Time* (1989), and other titles connected by the characters.

The Lion, the Witch and the Wardrobe: A Story for Children

By C. S. Lewis. Illustrated by Pauline Baynes. HarperCollins, 2009 (orig. 1950).

Interest level: **Middle** • Lexile measure: **940L**
Fantasy; Adventure

Through the back of a wardrobe in the old professor's house where they've come to wait out the Battle of Britain, Peter, Susan, Edmund, and Lucy Pevensie travel to Narnia. There they're caught up in the effort to end the rule of the White Queen and her endless winter. They learn forgiveness and become kings and queens thanks to the sacrifice of the lion, Aslan. This is probably the most well known of the Chronicles of Narnia, the first to be written (1950). It's a classic children's adventure, reminding some readers of Andersen's "The Snow Queen" and others of Christian themes of death and redemption. Younger, less analytic readers appreciate the solid story telling, the believable characters, and the wonderfully imaginative world Lewis has created. Baynes's illustrations have been retained in most editions of the books in the series, though color has been added to some.

The Magician's Nephew

By C. S. Lewis. Illustrated by Pauline Baynes. HarperCollins, 2007 (orig. 1955).

Interest level: **Middle** • Lexile measure: **790L**
Fantasy

Traveling through alternate worlds through the use of magic rings Digory's mad magician uncle has given them, Digory and his next-door neighbor Poll witness the creation of Narnia, setting for the long and successful series. Though sixth in the writing, this title is often presented first in the series; it might be enjoyed even more when read after *The Lion, the Witch, and the Wardrobe*. Full of Christian symbolism, the story is also a grand adventure that is just as satisfying for readers unfamiliar with the biblical parallels. Sequels in the series' time sequence are *The Horse and His Boy*

(1954), *Prince Caspian* (1951), *The Voyage of the Dawn Treader* (1952), The *Silver Chair* (1953), and *The Last Battle* (1956). In this last, a Carnegie Medal winner, the Calormenes are called "Darkies," a reflection of the racism of the times that will shock and sadden modern readers.

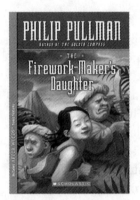

The Firework-Maker's Daughter

By Philip Pullman. Illustrated by S. Saelig Gallagher. Arthur A. Levine Books, 1999.

Interest level: **Middle** • Lexile measure: **870L**
Fantasy; Adventure

In a faraway Asian country, Lila's quest to become a firework maker like her father includes a journey to the heart of a volcano, kidnapping by would-be pirates, help from a talking elephant and its trainer, and the creation of a splendid fireworks display that saves her father's life. Like his heroine, Pullman uses magical ingredients to create a colorful, convincing setting, memorable characters, fast-paced action, and a thought-provoking message—all with humor and charm. The book is attractively designed. Each chapter begins with a gray-scale drawing of the major characters, including the elephant; each page is decorated, and there are some further soft-focused images. The fireworks are especially grand, and worth the read. This Nestlé prize winner is a good introduction to quest pattern adventures and an internationally beloved author.

Harry Potter and the Sorcerer's Stone

By J. K. Rowling. Illustrated by Mary GrandPré. Arthur A. Levine Books, 1998.

Interest level: **Middle** • Lexile measure: **880L**
Fantasy

Unloved orphan Harry Potter can't remember the "accident" that killed his parents, but he discovers that they, and he, are quite remarkable in the world of magic when he receives the invitation to enroll at Hogwarts School of Witchcraft and Wizardry. In his first year there, he becomes a star of the Quidditch team and foils a plot to capture a stone containing the elixir of life. This English boarding school story stands out for its gripping plot and imaginative details. The characters, especially Harry's friends Ron Weasley and Hermione Granger and his protector Hagrid the giant, are memorable; the magic is delightful and sometimes frightening. In this fast-paced series opener, there's the death of a unicorn and the menace of the soul-stealer Voldemort. The sequels gets progressively darker; young readers may decide they want to leave volumes 4–7 (which include significant deaths) for later years.

The Night Fairy

By Laura Amy Schlitz. Illustrated by Angela Barrett. Candlewick Press, 2010.

Interest level: **Younger** • Lexile measure: **630L**
Fiction

This fairy story is set in the real backyard of an elementary-school librarian and story teller who created this tale to reflect her own childhood imaginings and the interests of her students. Flory, a night fairy, is already independent but less than three months old when a bat accidentally chews her wings. She takes refuge in a wren house, befriends a squirrel, and braves both a spider's web and a raccoon to save a trapped hummingbird. This is surprisingly realistic and totally enchanting. It has the appeal of Norton's *The Borrowers* and other stories of miniature people. Flory is determined and inventive; she has realistic fears and a child's emotional life. There's both suspense and a satisfying resolution. Short chapters make this very accessible. The art, chapter-heading miniatures, and full-page watercolors that show how tiny Flory is compared to the garden around her is delightful.

Charmed Life

By Diana Wynne Jones. Greenwillow Books, 1978.

Interest level: **Older** • Lexile measure: **720L**
Fantasy

Orphans Eric and Gwendolen Chant go to live in Chrestomanci Castle where Gwendolen defies the prohibition against magic, eventually revealing that she has been selfishly using her little brother's powers all along. The first published of many titles set in a series of magical worlds, this introduces the setting and magic rules. The current Chrestomanci, Christopher Chant, identifies Eric as the next in line to be the government official who keeps magic in check. A Chrestomanci-to-be begins with nine lives, but young Eric has already lost several. His recognition of his own potential and his sister's betrayal are the stuff of this inventive, engaging story. The author recommends beginning to read further titles in her Chrestomanci series with *The Lives of Christopher Chant* (1988) and *Conrad's Fate* (2005) before going on to *Witch Week* (1982) and *The Magicians of Caprona* (1980), which take place in the same worlds but involve the Chrestomanci only peripherally.

Quests and Adventures

OUNG PEOPLE HAVING ADVENTURES ON THEIR own has been a staple of children's literature for generations. These tales have perennial appeal. Sometimes the adventures are told episodically, as Homer recounts the adventures of Odysseus in the classical tale. Often, the narrative follows the archetypal pattern of the hero's journey. A protagonist whose life seems ordinary or unimportant answers a call to adventure and undertakes a heroic journey that will likely involve monsters and caves, a noble goal, some supernatural help, and some kind of reward, self-knowledge, or community benefit. The quest pattern makes for an exciting narrative and, once the setting and characters have been established, paves the way for many adventures. This section includes both classics and new titles. In some, the protagonists are talking animals. Three relate the adventures of grown-ups. Most have fantasy settings or elements of magic; other than suspenseful survival stories, it is hard to create an adventure starring children on their own in the setting of a realistic modern world. Look for quests and adventures in other sections of this bibliography as well; this story line appears in all kinds of stories and in books for all ages.

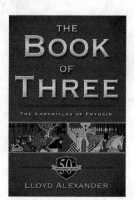

The Book of Three

By Lloyd Alexander. Henry Holt, 2014 (orig. 1964).

Interest level: **Middle** • Lexile measure: **770L**
Fantasy; Adventure

Assistant Pig Keeper Taran longs to be a hero, but when he gets caught up in the struggle against evil forces, he realizes that there is more to heroism than he had imagined. There are splendid characters here, including simile-spouting Princess Eilonwy; Hen Wen, the oracular pig; bard Fflewddur Flam; and hairy Gurgi, not to mention prince Gwydion himself. Alexander used a traditional quest pattern and elements of Welsh mythology to weave a splendid adventure that combines humor with thought-provoking questions about the nature of heroism. Sequels following Taran in search of his origins and destiny include *The Black Cauldron* (1965, a Newbery honor book), *The Castle of Llyr* (1966), *Taran Wanderer* (1967), and Newbery Medal–winning *The High King* (1968). These books get progressively darker; there are sad losses in the last adventure in particular. For its world building, story telling, language, and character development, this series may still be the best introduction to high fantasy available for young readers.

Loki's Wolves

*By Kelley Armstrong and Melissa Marr.
Illustrated by Vivienne To. Little, Brown, 2013.*

Interest level: **Middle** • Lexile measure: **690L**
Fantasy; Adventure

In South Dakota, descendants of Norse gods band together to stave off the end of the world. This first of a trilogy introduces thirteen-year-old Matt Thorsen, the sheriff's son, and the trouble-making cousins Fen and Laurie Brekke. After some sparring, the three set off to search for companions to challenge the monsters of the final battle. In chapters told from their different viewpoints, they encounter werewolves, trolls, Norns, and Valkyries. They also find the twins, Reyna and Ray; nice-guy Baldwin; and Odin's girlfriend, Astrid. Each carries some characteristic of a mythical ancestor; each may have skills to offer. But can they be trusted? Fast paced, action filled, and suspenseful, this is aimed at a slightly younger audience than Riordan's fantasies and would be a good introduction to the genre of myth-based adventure. In *Odin's Ravens* (2014), the friends descend to the underworld the Norse called Hel. *Thor's Serpents* will be published in 2015.

The Wonderful Flight to the Mushroom Planet

*By Eleanor Cameron. Illustrated by Robert Henneberger.
Little, Brown, 1954.*

Interest level: **Middle** • Lexile measure: **970L**
Fantasy; Adventure

In response to a newspaper advertisement, David Topman and Chuck Masterson build a spaceship and journey to a nearby planet, Basidium, ancestral home of the mysterious Tyco M. Bass, who provided their engine and fuel. Published in 1954, even before Sputnik, this traditional science fiction adventure is remarkably accurate in its space details (aside, of course, from the fictional planetoid) and full of the wonder at the idea of space exploration. The boys are between eight and eleven, both competent and naïve. Interestingly, in this old-fashioned story there are echoes of modern climate issues. Well-written science fiction for young readers is just as hard to find today as it was in the 1950s, and this satisfying read is still in print in paperback. Library collections may have sequels: *Stowaway to the Mushroom Planet* (1956), *Mr. Bass's Planetoid* (1958), *A Mystery for Mr. Bass* (1960), and *Time and Mr. Bass* (1967).

Gregor the Overlander
By Suzanne Collins. Scholastic, 2003.

Interest level: **Middle** • Lexile measure: **630L**
Fantasy; Adventure

Eleven-year-old Gregor follows his two-year-old sister Boots through the laundry-room grate in his New York apartment building and lands in an underland full of giant cockroaches, rats, and spiders waiting for him to fulfill an ancient prophecy. In this nicely worked-out quest adventure, Gregor does all he must but remains kind of surprised at himself. The creatures are easily imaginable (really, typecast villains). Gregor and Boots continue to visit this well-drawn underworld in four sequels: *Gregor and the Prophecy of Bane* (2004), *Gregor and the Curse of the Warmbloods* (2005), *Gregor and the Marks of Secret* (2006), and *Gregor and the Code of Claw* (2007). With allusions to geopolitics and Greek mythology, and graphic, gripping action, these plot-driven stories are not for the faint of heart, but they are more suitable for young readers than Collins's later, wildly popular Hunger Games series.

The Dark Is Rising

By Susan Cooper. Illustrated by Alan E. Cober.
Margaret K. McElderry Books, 1973.

Interest level: **Older** • Lexile measure: **920L**
Fantasy; Adventure

On his eleventh birthday, the winter solstice, Will Stanton learns he's one of the Old Ones, the Sign-Seeker. He must gather six magic signs in order to fight off the Dark, which threatens to freeze his world in an everlasting snowstorm. This grand fantasy, set in Buckinghamshire, England, is filled with ancient English and Welsh legends. Will, an authentic eleven-year-old, vacillates between childhood enjoyments and his newly acquired powers and responsibilities. Fear of the dark and the Dark pervades this Newbery honor book, a complete adventure though second in its series. It's probably the place older readers should start the series, which finishes up with *Greenwitch* (1974), Newbery Medal–winning *The Grey King* (1975), and *Silver on the Tree* (1977). Readers comfortable with the first two books will find nothing worse in the others, although the last has some philosophical musings, adding depth they may choose to ignore.

Over Sea, Under Stone

By Susan Cooper. Illustrated by Margery Gill.
Margaret K. McElderry Books, 2013 (orig. 1965).

Interest level: **Middle** • Lexile measure: **830L**
Fantasy; Adventure

On holiday in Cornwall, Barney, Simon, and Jane find a map leading them to a long-hidden treasure, a Dark Ages chalice, which they find and save from competing Dark forces, thanks to the help of Great-Uncle Merry. The adventure takes place in a menacing landscape with standing stones and rocky coastal shores. There are several dramatic escapes and even a kidnapping, plenty of action, and an Arthurian connection. Much of the action happens at night; toward the end, the boys crawl far into a cave. Barney, the youngest, is the hero here. Both family adventure and fantasy quest, this is less fantastical and lighter in mood than the others in Cooper's Dark Is Rising series. It was written first, in 1965, but is best read second, after *The Dark is Rising*, but before going on. Characters and settings mingle in subsequent stories.

Ophelia and the Marvelous Boy

By Karen Foxlee. Knopf, 2014.

Interest level: **Middle** • Lexile measure: **660L**
Fantasy

When the boy in the locked room on the museum's third floor asks Ophelia to help save the world, she knows she can't. She doesn't even believe in magic. Ophelia and her older sister, Alice, have traveled to a faraway frozen city where her father, a world expert on swords, prepares a museum exhibition. All three are still grieving the death of the girls' mother, a fantasy writer, only three months earlier. While her father works, Ophelia has time to explore, to hear the boy's story, and to look for the keys and the sword he asks her to find. Loosely based on Andersen's "The Snow Queen," this is set in a believable present day in which an asthmatic eleven-year-old would prefer the rigor of scientific thinking and her older sister might well be charmed by the promise of a beauty makeover. Inventive use of folktale elements distinguishes this quest adventure.

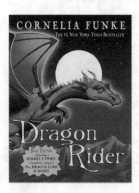

Dragon Rider

By Cornelia Funke. Illustrated by Cornelia Funke. Translated by Anthea Bell. Scholastic, 2004.

Interest level: **Middle** • Lexile measure: **710L**
Fantasy; Adventure

Silver dragon Firedrake and his brownie companion, Sorrel, seek the Rim of Heaven, a legendary dragon haven where he; his human rider, Ben; a stow-away homunculus, Twigleg; and other friends help him use brownie spit and dragon fire to rid the world of evil, gold-scaled Nettlebrand. This epic adventure makes use of legendary creatures in highly imaginative ways. This was Funke's first novel, hugely popular in Germany, but not published in this country until after the success of her more challenging titles, *The Thief Lord* (2001) and *Inkheart* (2003). Skillfully translated, this is humorous and suspenseful. Expertly paced story telling keeps readers going through the lengthy narrative; a who's who at the end helps recall the large cast of characters. There's also a map of their journey, from Scotland, across Europe, down and across the Arabian Peninsula, and up the River Indus to Tibet's mountains.

Odd and the Frost Giants

By Neil Gaiman. Illustrated by Brett Helquist. HarperCollins, 2009.

Interest level: **Older** • Lexile measure: **820L**
Fantasy; Adventure

Here, the versatile Gaiman uses Norse mythology to weave an elegant fantasy. Lamed in an effort to be a woodsman like his drowned Viking father, twelve-year-old Odd limps away from home and encounters a bear, a fox, and an eagle. These are the gods Loki, Thor, and Odin turned into animals by a Frost Giant. Odd travels with them to Asgard, where he outwits the giant, convincing him to leave and to take with him the endless winter he brought. In gratitude, the goddess Freya partially cures Odd's leg and he returns home, now grown so tall his stepfather doesn't even recognize him. This has folklore and trickster tale elements as well as a classic quest pattern, all woven together with quiet humor into what is really a novella—a taste of Norse mythology that should encourage readers to look for more.

Fortunately, the Milk

By Neil Gaiman. Illustrated by Skottie Young.
HarperCollins, 2013.

Interest level: **Middle** • Lexile measure: **680L**
Fantasy; Adventure

When the narrator's father goes out to get milk for their breakfast, he comes back with a series of preposterous stories to explain his delay. Space invaders, a time-traveling stegosaurus in a hot air balloon, piranhas, pirates, vampires, and volcanoes are all mixed up in a delightful sequence of narrow escapes and recursive stories. The boy and his older sister don't believe a word of this, interrupting occasionally to point out the absurdity. Numerous pen-and-ink cartoon illustrations, stylized images full of scribbles and angles, reinforce the humor and reveal the possible truth. A piece of eight stuck to the bottom of the milk bottle at the end will leave readers wondering. This is wacky and wonderful, appropriate for a much younger reader than Gaiman's darker *Coraline* (2002) and his Newbery Medal–winning *Graveyard Book* (2008).

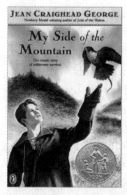

My Side of the Mountain

By Jean Craighead George. Illustrated by Jean
Craighead George. Dutton, 1999 (orig. 1959).

Interest level: **Older** • Lexile measure: **810L**
Adventure

Sam Gribley runs away to family land in the Catskills and survives for a year, living in a hollowed-out tree, making his own clothes and tools; fishing; trapping and gleaning; and training a falcon, Frightful, to hunt for him. This grand survival story ends with Sam's learning that he does appreciate people, too, including his large family. He begins his first-person account when snow first threatens to shut him inside his tree, but then goes back to the beginning in May and proceeds chronologically through the year. He includes diary entries. The author's illustrations include a small map, and drawings of fishhooks and traps and various helpful plants. The details of Sam's resourceful woodsmanship are just as interesting today as they were to readers of this Newbery honor book more than fifty years ago. *On the Far Side of the Mountain* (1990) and *Frightful's Mountain* (1999) continue the story.

The Escape of the Deadly Dinosaur
By Elizabeth Singer Hunt. Illustrated by Brian Williamson. Weinstein Books, 2007.

Interest level: **Younger** • Lexile measure: **760L**
Fantasy; Mystery

Jack Stalwart, nine-year-old secret agent for the Global Protection Force, travels through his magic map to the Natural History Museum in New York City to solve the mystery of the missing allosaurus toe. It is easy enough for the resourceful boy to solve the mystery, but then he has to deal with the full-sized dinosaur roaming the streets of New York, using a number of his high-tech tools. First in a series of fourteen mystery and adventure stories popular with good first- and second-grade readers, this volume, like the others, begins with a background for the series and for the particular adventure. This fast-paced series takes the intrepid adventurer from his home in England to countries around the world, from the Arctic to Australia, and finally to Egypt, where he finds and saves his older brother. It might have special appeal for readers who've enjoyed the Magic Treehouse books.

Redwall
By Brian Jacques. Illustrated by Gary Chalk. Philomel, 2007 (orig. 1986).

Interest level: **Middle** • Lexile measure: **800L**
Animal fantasy; Adventure

When peaceful Redwall Abbey is threatened by a band of rats led by Cluny the Scourge, the young mouse Matthias, who longs to be a warrior rather than a monk, seeks the legendary sword of an earlier defender, Martin the Warrior, in order to defeat the invaders. This first volume of a much-loved series (whose twenty-second and last title appeared after the author's death) introduces the pattern of adventures (often two story lines in alternating chapters), distinctive animal characters, delicious meals, pitched battles, and a writing style that consciously recalls Homeric epics—all characteristics of the series. Good and evil are clearly distinguished, strong female characters contribute to the fighting effort, and success is won through cooperation rather than authoritarian leadership. The lovingly realized medieval world has captivated young readers and hitherto non-readers for nearly thirty years.

Comet in Moominland

By Tove Jansson. Illustrated by Tove Jansson. Translated by Elizabeth Portch. Square Fish, 2010 (orig. 1951).

Interest level: **Middle**
Animal fantasy; Adventure

Moomintroll and his friends, Sniff and Snufkin, go on an expedition to discover the meaning of the mysterious tailed-star signs. Learning that a comet is threatening the earth, they set off to see the flaming comet for themselves. They have a variety of suspenseful adventures, rescue the Snork Maiden, and return with this new friend in time to hide safely in a cave with the Moomintroll family. This is the first full-length book in a hugely popular series starring the gentle, accepting imaginary creatures and their various friends and acquaintances. The Finnish author won the Hans Christian Andersen Award for the body of her work. This series (minus the first novella) has been reissued in attractive paperback editions with the original black-and-white illustrations by the author. This dreamlike kids-on-their-own adventure might have particular appeal for fans of *Winnie-the-Pooh*.

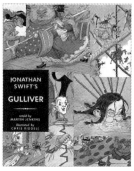

Jonathan Swift's Gulliver

Retold by Martin Jenkins. Illustrated by Chris Riddell. Candlewick Press, 2005.

Interest level: **Older**
Classics; Adventure

Here's a lively illustrated retelling of Lemuel Gulliver's four sea journeys at the turn of the eighteenth century. Each of these, Gulliver says, ended unexpectedly in unlikely parts of the world where he met tiny people, giants, distracted mathematicians, and honest, highly civilized horses whom he much preferred to human Yahoos. Jenkins's retelling retains some of the satirical flavor of the eighteenth-century original, written for adults, but removes much of the verbiage; it would be an ideal read for a twenty-first-century child. Swift's imagined worlds have become part of our heritage; Riddell's cartoons bring them to life. The fancily dressed Gulliver appears on the title page; an opening spread shows a map of his voyages. The text, set in columns, is often interrupted by sketches, and the illustrations are large, colorful, and detailed. There's much to appreciate in this adaptation, which retains all the original adventures.

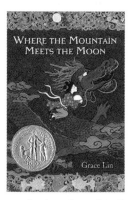

Where the Mountain Meets the Moon

By Grace Lin. Illustrated by Grace Lin. Little, Brown, 2009.

Interest level: **Middle** • Lexile measure: **810L**
Fantasy; Adventure

Inspired by tales she'd heard from her father and the advice of a goldfish she had set free, Minli journeys to find the Old Man of the Moon to learn how to change her family's fortune. She's joined on her way by a flightless green dragon who proves a faithful friend. Lin weaves elements of Chinese folklore together with her own inventions to create a remarkable quest adventure. Handsome book design adds to the appeal of this Newbery honor–winning fantasy. Papercuts serve as chapter headings as well as full-page color illustrations. The typography makes it easy to distinguish the framing story from the interspersed tales. Not only do Minli's parents miss her while she's gone, she misses them and comes to value what she had previously overlooked, a very satisfying ending to a memorable tale. A companion book, *Starry River of the Sky* (2012), stands alone but connects interestingly.

Silverwing

By Kenneth Oppel. Simon & Schuster, 1997.

Interest level: **Middle** • Lexile measure: **660L**
Animal fantasy; Adventure

Shade, a runty but quick-witted and curious first-year Silverwing bat, is separated from his flock on their migration south. In his efforts to be reunited with his mother and to learn the truth about the bands his father and his Brightwing friend Marina received from humans, he faces fearful challenges, including escaping from a pair of Central American vampire bats. This suspenseful survival story is full of intriguing natural history details about the habits and skills of North American bats. The story of Shade and his family continues in sequels, *Sunwing* (2000) and *Firewing* (2003), while a prequel, *Darkwing* (2007), focuses on bats' ancestors in the Paleocene era. In all these titles, animals attack and eat other animals—even their own species—sometimes gruesomely, but appropriately representing actual animal predation. Issues of war and peace making are important, too.

High Time for Heroes

By Mary Pope Osborne. Illustrated by Sal Murdocca. Random House, 2014.

Interest level: **Middle** • Lexile measure: **560L**
Historical fantasy; Adventure

Beginning with the twenty-ninth title in the Magic Tree House series, Merlin sponsors Jack and Annie on slightly longer missions to both mythical and real places. In this fifty-first, they journey to Thebes, Egypt, where they meet Florence Nightingale in 1850, long before she trained as a nurse. Magic mist allows them to become great rock climbers in order to rescue a baby baboon, but not for long enough to get them safely back down the cliff. Luckily, as always, their injuries have disappeared and no time has passed when they return to the treehouse. These later books are somewhat longer and more challenging, and the children seem older. But the stories are similarly fast paced and appealing, providing interesting if somewhat clichéd information about people and places in history. Since book 38 (and sporadically before that) the author has also written nonfiction companion books called *Magic Tree House Fact Trackers.*

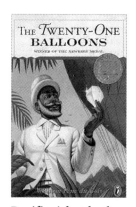

The Twenty-One Balloons

By William Pène du Bois. Illustrated by William Pène du Bois. Viking, 1947.

Interest level: **Older** • Lexile measure: **1070L**
Historical fantasy; Adventure

Retired school teacher Professor William Waterman Sherman, planning a year-long balloon voyage, lands unexpectedly on the island of Krakatoa just before it explodes in 1883. On that remote South Pacific island, the professor finds a restaurant-based community that's become unbelievably wealthy because of the local diamonds. Twenty families, having built an astonishing variety of homes, now spend their time experimenting with "modern" gadgetry such as steam engines and electricity. This nearly seventy-year-old Newbery Medal winner has echoes of *The Swiss Family Robinson* and *20,000 Leagues under the Sea.* It's a story of invention, adventure, treasure, and the benefits of working together. The fantasy setup is well done. Plentiful line drawings by the author may help twenty-first-century readers imagine this faraway world. For many, the best parts of this culturally ethnocentric classic are the descriptions of the interesting technology; others think this makes the story line drag.

Swallows and Amazons

By Arthur Ransome. Illustrated by Arthur Ransome "with help from Miss Nancy Blackett." Overlook Press, 2013 (orig. 1930).

Interest level: **Older** • Lexile measure: **800L**
Classics; Adventure

Children on their own, sailing, rowing, and camping on a lake, engaging in mock battles with other children who sail and with a presumed pirate, and finding buried treasure—what could be more exciting? This splendid English summer adventure is the first of a classic series. Roger, John, Susan, and Titty Walker, sailing Swallow, plan to join forces with Captain Nancy and Peggy Blackett, sailing Amazon, to fight with the Blacketts's uncle living on a houseboat nearby. The story is filled with camping and sailing details. There's a daring night sail, a burglary, and buried treasure. Roger is seven; the others are older, but still young enough to enjoy the elaborate game. All twelve titles were reissued in paperback by Godine in 2010, and Overlook Press has recently reissued this and its sequel, *Swallowdale* (1931), in hardcover bindings.

The Lightning Thief

By Rick Riordan. Hyperion, 2005.

Interest level: **Older** • Lexile measure: **740L**
Fantasy; Adventure

For twelve-year-old Percy Jackson, diagnosed with ADHD and dyslexia, everything changes when monsters begin to attack. He escapes to a summer camp where he learns he's a half-blood son of Poseidon and needed for a quest to the underworld to find and return Zeus's stolen thunderbolt. The fast-paced action draws readers in immediately. Percy's best friend and minder is a hoofed satyr named Grover; the companion on their journey is Annabeth, gray-eyed daughter of Athena. Elements of Greek mythology blend nicely with ordinary life and a quest pattern. Fun, funny, and hugely popular, this saga has spawned four increasingly violent sequels—*The Sea of Monsters* (2006), *The Titan's Curse* (2007), *The Battle of the Labyrinth* (2008), and *The Last Olympian* (2009)—as well as films and many imitations. Riordan followed this series with another, The Heroes of Olympus, which includes Percy and his friends but also material from later, Roman myths.

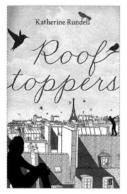

Rooftoppers

By Katherine Rundell. Illustrated by Terry Fan.
Simon & Schuster, 2013.

Interest level: **Middle** • Lexile measure: **490L**
Adventure

Orphaned children who live high above the Paris streets help Sophie search for her birth mother, lost twelve years earlier in a shipwreck from which Sophie floated away in a cello case. The baby was rescued and raised by Charles Maxim, now deemed an unsuitable guardian by child-care authorities. This story, set in today's London and Paris, is a modern adventure with a traditional feel. These children survive by their wits and their physical prowess; they leap from roof to roof and catch and eat birds and rats. Readers may stop breathing as Sophie walks a tightrope between two tall buildings and will delight in a serious fight between Sophie's friends and the railroad station gang. Appropriately for a children's book, Sophie does find her cello-playing mother, whom the child-care authorities would probably find no more suitable. By turns lyrical, whimsical, suspenseful, and glorious—this is a grand read.

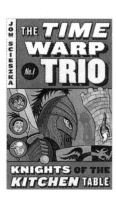

Knights of the Kitchen Table

By Jon Scieszka. Illustrated by Lane Smith. Viking, 1991.

Interest level: **Middle** • Lexile measure: **630L**
Historical fantasy

It was Fred who first opened The Book, Joe's birthday present from his magician uncle, and wished to see the pictured black knight. Joe, Fred, and Sam were instantly transported to the Middle Ages, where they vanquished the knight, met Merlin, and were knighted themselves by King Arthur. First of a lively series of humorous fantasies that take the three friends to the past and the future, this provides the pattern for the books that follow. Over the course of fifteen sequels (the last eight illustrated by Adam McCaulay) the Time Warp Trio meet notables such as King Tut and Dracula, as well as ancient Mayans, pirates, and Samurai warriors. Fast paced and predictable, this series is full of historical details, though it occasionally falls into stereotypes. Absurd situations, puns, bathroom humor, and an excess of explosions add up to stories that have had continuing appeal. Short and funny but also mind stretching.

Brave Irene

By William Steig. Illustrated by William Steig. Farrar, Straus, Giroux, 1986.

Interest level: **Younger** • Lexile measure: **AD630L**
Adventure; Fairy tales, original

When her dressmaker mother fell ill, Irene volunteered to take the finished ball gown to the duchess. Steig gives this young girl hurrying bravely through a blizzard to the castle an adventure just as heroic as boys have in folktales and fairy tales, illustrating it with colored line drawings in his characteristic style. The story opens and closes in Irene's cozy home. The scenes outside are overlaid with driving snow and quite dark as the journey becomes more difficult. The castle is appropriately fancy and well staffed, and the ball is just what a child might imagine. This has the look of a picture book, but the language is that of literature. When the "ill-tempered wind" opens the box, "The ball gown flounced out and went waltzing through the powdered air with tissue-paper attendants." A little bit scary and altogether satisfying whether read aloud or alone.

Chapter 10

Traditional Tales

···

MYTHS, LEGENDS, FOLKTALES, FAIRY TALES, AND fables are the stuff of tradition—stories that have their roots in antiquity. These ancient tales were often told to explain some phenomenon or event, or to teach some philosophical or moral lesson. They're the source of the traditional literary patterns and the allusions to myth or folklore that appear regularly in modern works for children and adults. In traditional tales, character development is minimal and the setting is merely a backdrop for the plot. Often these tales involve talking beasts, monsters, larger-than-life heroes and heroines, and magical powers. Many of the titles in this section are collections, not necessarily meant to be read from beginning to end. A few are original tales using traditional patterns. Children who come to these stories early will have a solid background for their further reading. Avid

Chapter 10

Traditional Tales

··

MYTHS, LEGENDS, FOLKTALES, FAIRY TALES, AND fables are the stuff of tradition—stories that have their roots in antiquity. These ancient tales were often told to explain some phenomenon or event, or to teach some philosophical or moral lesson. They're the source of the traditional literary patterns and the allusions to myth or folklore that appear regularly in modern works for children and adults. In traditional tales, character development is minimal and the setting is merely a backdrop for the plot. Often these tales involve talking beasts, monsters, larger-than-life heroes and heroines, and magical powers. Many of the titles in this section are collections, not necessarily meant to be read from beginning to end. A few are original tales using traditional patterns. Children who come to these stories early will have a solid background for their further reading. Avid readers will find familiar characters and plots. Titles in other sections of this bibliography may reflect traditional tales and folklore; in this section are the myths, legends, and wonder tales, themselves. Where a story or set of stories has been published in many editions and versions, I have tried to choose those that have particular appeal for young readers.

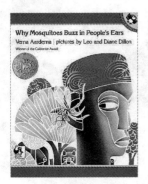

Why Mosquitoes Buzz in People's Ears: A West African Tale

Retold by Verna Aardema. Illustrated by Leo and Diane Dillon. Dial Books, 1975.

Interest level: **Younger** • Lexile measure: **770L**
Folklore

This retelling of a West African *pourquoi* tale explains the buzzing of mosquitoes as a long chain of events that included the death of an owlet and sad Mother Owl refusing to wake the sun. Engagingly shaped by an experienced story teller and illustrated with Caldecott Medal–winning images done with watercolor, pastels, ink, and cutout shapes, this has perennial appeal. Although the author was white, her interest in Africa and her realization that the vast number of folktales from various parts of southern and central Africa were largely unknown to American children, led her to retell a number of them. At the time, there was little emphasis on pinpointing the exact provenance of folktales, and publishers didn't feel the need to differentiate cultures or countries in that vast continent. Though the back matter would be different today, the story reads wonderfully, with an inviting repetitive refrain.

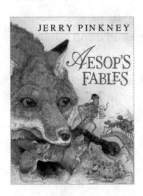

Aesop's Fables

Retold by Jerry Pinkney. Illustrated by Jerry Pinkney. Chronicle Books, 2000.

Interest level: **Younger** • Lexile measure: **760L**
Classics; Folklore

Pinkney retells and illustrates over sixty of Aesop's fables, some familiar and some lesser known. His language and sentence structure are formal, but not daunting, and his watercolor illustrations are delightful. Beginning with the endpapers, scenes from "The Tortoise and the Hare" in front and "Who Will Bell the Cat?" in back, they include tiny vignettes, full-page framed images, and some stretching across gutters. The center spread of "The Lion and the Mouse" will remind readers of Pinkney's more recent, Caldecott Medal–winning picture book. Many of his animals wear kerchiefs and some sport remarkable hats, but they're still realistic; his people come from all around the world. These 2,500-year-old tales have universal and lasting appeal; this oversized volume is a handsome collection. This, too, dates from a time when citing sources and explaining interpretations was less common in folklore published for children.

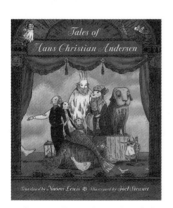

Tales of Hans Christian Andersen

By Hans Christian Andersen. Illustrated by Joel Stewart. Translated by Naomi Lewis. Candlewick Press, 2004.

Interest level: **Middle**
Classics; Fairy tales, original; Short stories

This is a beautiful presentation of thirteen of Andersen's most beloved wonder tales, enhanced with graceful introductions and appealing illustrations. The smooth translation by Lewis, a renowned Andersen authority, preserves the writer's humor and originality. The conversational tone suggests that readers are listening to a master story teller. Also humorous are the digitally created illustrations, including vignettes, tiny corner decorations indicating which tale is being told, and full-page scenes, some presented under a proscenium curtain that alludes to Andersen's fascination with the theater. This selection is particularly good, including familiar tales such as "The Princess and the Pea," "The Steadfast Tin Soldier," "The Little Mermaid," "The Ugly Duckling," "The Snow Queen," "The Little Match Girl," and "The Emperor's New Clothes." (The emperor is clearly naked, though drawn discreetly.) This oversized volume, a British import, is a perfect introduction to the nineteenth-century master for American children.

The Hero and the Minotaur: The Fantastic Adventures of Theseus

Retold by Robert Byrd. Illustrated by Robert Byrd. Dutton, 2005.

Interest level: **Middle** • Lexile measure: **AD1050L**
Mythology

Byrd combines several myths to construct his tale of the hero, Theseus, from the boy's childhood in exile to the young man's voyage to Athens to find his father; his journey to Crete, where he slew the Minotaur with the help of Daedalus and Ariadne; and the events of his return. Though this looks like a picture book, with text set directly on Byrd's careful art, it's a rich, challenging read, a worthy blending of many mythological strands. The story moves seamlessly along, including important, familiar details but softening and even omitting others that might be less appropriate for the age group. Stylized and intricate, the ink-and-watercolor wash illustrations include meticulous details of period costume, architecture, and design. The spread showing the attack of the fire-breathing Minotaur is particularly effective. There's a map on the end-papers. Larger-than-life characters and larger-than-life excitement make this an appropriate introduction to a classic story.

Robin Hood

Retold by David Calcutt. Illustrated by Grahame Baker-Smith. Barefoot Books, 2012.

Interest level: **Middle** • Lexile measure: **780L**
Classics; Folklore

Tricked into outlawry, Robin Hood gathers a band of followers who plunder and provoke the privileged and help the poor living in the environs of Sherwood Forest in medieval England. This well-crafted edition of these traditional tales includes verses from Robin Hood ballads and detailed, digitally manipulated paintings that almost have the look of anime. There are vignettes of woodland animals, portraits, and scenic double-page spreads. (Some illustrations have been truncated in the paperback edition and the back matter is missing, though the bibliography remains.) The familiar players are there—Little John, Maid Marian, Friar Tuck, and Alan-a-Dale—but this is a story of action, not character. Greed is punished and fighting prowess rewarded; the author doesn't dwell on the gory details. Smoothly told in episodic chapters, this is a grand version of a much-told tale.

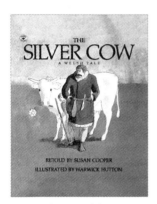

The Silver Cow: A Welsh Tale

Retold by Susan Cooper. Illustrated by Warwick Hutton. Atheneum, 1983.

Interest level: **Younger** • Lexile measure: **AD750L**
Folklore

Playing his harp as he watched his cows on the pasture surrounding a mountain lake, Huw Hughes, son of a miserly farmer, raises a magical white cow who produces more milk than any other and bears equally productive offspring until, in her old age, the greedy farmer decides to have her butchered. The farmer gets his comeuppance when the cow, her offspring, and the riches she'd brought disappear when the butcher raises his knife. This Welsh *pourquoi* tale, charmingly retold by Cooper, who had heard it as a child, explains how water lilies came to surround Llyn Barfog, "the bearded lake" high in the hills of Wales. Illustrated with watercolors, this is the first of a three-book series of British folktales by this author and illustrator reimagined for more modern children. Equally enjoyable are *The Selkie Girl* (1986) and *Tam Lin* (1991).

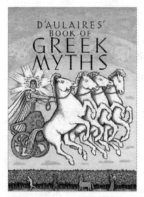

Ingri and Edgar Parin d'Aulaires' Book of Greek Myths

By Ingri and Edgar Parin d'Aulaire. Illustrated by Ingri and Edgar Parin d'Aulaire. Doubleday, 1962.

Interest level: **Middle** • Lexile measure: **1070L**
Classics; Mythology

This oversized album introduces the pantheon of twelve gods and goddesses and other major figures of Greek mythology: Zeus and his family, minor gods and goddesses, and Zeus's mortal descendants. The authors constructed this as a connected narrative, but readers can dip in and out. An index makes it easy to find the character you seek; the individual stories are short. The myths themselves have been toned down for young readers (using "marry" instead of "rape," for example). The illustrations are made up of pencil lines and shading, sometimes colored, but often black on brown. To modern eyes they may seem awkward, with unconventional perspectives, but they weren't meant to be realistic. The gods stand out appropriately. Many grown-ups remember this title fondly, often as a book they read and reread.

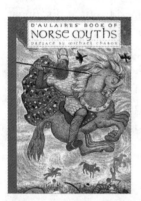

d'Aulaires' Book of Norse Myths

By Ingri and Edgar Parin d'Aulaire. Illustrated by Ingri and Edgar Parin d'Aulaire. New York Review of Books, 2005 (orig. 1967).

Interest level: **Older**
Mythology

This compendium of stories about the Aesir, the Norse gods, is mythology at its most gory. Beginning with the creation story and ending with Ragnarokk, the final battle, this husband-and-wife team introduce familiar characters such as Odin, Thor, Freya, and Loki and retell their tales. This is the stuff from which Wagner made his Ring Cycle and many writers have woven modern fantasies. The d'Aulaires's version is both vigorous and humorous. The illustrations—alternating black-and-white lithographs (some with spots of color or a pastel-colored background) with colored acetate prints—may seem pale to the modern viewer, but they're hard to forget. The book opens with a lineup of major characters and closes with a reader's companion that serves as an index and provides pronunciations and capsule biographies. The endpapers map the nine Norse worlds. This modern edition includes an appreciative introduction by Michael Chabon.

d'Aulaires' Book of Trolls

By Ingri and Edgar Parin d'Aulaire. Illustrated by Ingri and Edgar Parin d'Aulaire. New York Review of Books, 2006 (orig. 1972).

Interest level: **Middle** • Lexile measure: **AD1020L**
Folklore

Building on the success of their collection of Norse myths, the d'Aulaires produced a much shorter book for younger readers and listeners. Here they tell of the trolls who traditionally inhabited the Norwegian landscape, ugly subjects of countless folktales who were feared for their taste for human flesh and their ability to deceive. Rather than repeating specific tales, the authors describe what trolls are and what they do. We meet night trolls, forest trolls, mountain trolls, water trolls, trolls with one head or many, trolls with troll-cats and troll-roosters and fire-breathing horse steeds, as well as gnomes who mine gold underground and beautiful hulder maidens who will steal a boy's soul. This has more pictures than words, but the text is both challenging and satisfying. Again, they've illustrated these pages with a combination of black-and-white and colored prints in their recognizable, somewhat naïve style.

The People Could Fly: The Picture Book

By Virginia Hamilton. Illustrated by Leo and Diane Dillon. Knopf, 2004.

Interest level: **Older** • Lexile measure: **AD480L**
Folklore

A folksy retelling of an African folktale in which American slaves, miserable with their condition, fly away, one by one and then as a group, thanks to their heritage and the enchantment of an old man named Toby. This is a reissue of the title story in *The People Could Fly: American Black Folktales* (1985), with new illustrations by the much-honored Dillons. These include an homage to the late author, a lovely portrayal of the young Hamilton as a flying story teller on the last page. It is beautiful from start to finish. Black endpapers are embossed with shiny black feathers. The dialect recalls black English and reads aloud as if the story were being told orally, but there are no apostrophes or odd spellings to deter the young silent reader, and the paintings are splendid. The portrayal of slavery is appropriately harsh.

Just So Stories

By Rudyard Kipling. Illustrated by Barry Moser. Books of Wonder: Morrow, 1996 (orig. 1902).

Interest level: **Middle** • Lexile measure: **1190L**
Classics; Short stories

Here is a beautifully illustrated and attractively presented edition of Kipling's entertaining origin stories, which range around the world in their geography and natural history. A dozen *pourquoi* tales describe how the elephant got his trunk, the camel his hump, the rhino his wrinkles, and more, including how humans invented the alphabet. Each chapter is followed by a poem in which Kipling comments on the story. Written originally for the author's own children, these are full of engaging, rhythmic language, humor, and exaggeration. The child reader is addressed directly, often as "my Best Beloved." Some stories include dialect, which readers may find difficult, but for the most part these are quite accessible to the modern child. There are many editions of this classic still available, including some with Kipling's own illustrations and captions. Moser's watercolors look more modern.

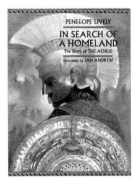

In Search of a Homeland: The Story of the Aeneid

By Penelope Lively. Illustrated by Ian Andrew. Delacorte Press, 2001.

Interest level: **Older**
Mythology

After the fall of Troy, Aeneas set out from the burning city with his elderly father and his young son, Iulus. Their goal was Italy, where the gods had prophesied he would be the founder of a new civilization that would become Rome. Virgil's Aeneid is a two-thousand-year-old Latin epic poem in the Homeric tradition. This retelling, published as a companion to Sutcliff's stories of the Trojan War and its aftermath, nearly matches up in terms of its epic adventure and endless warfare. The gods, now bearing their Roman names, take sides once again, so that the hero's journey is long and difficult. Andrew's colored pencil illustrations are scratchy and unfinished in appearance; some are additionally colorized. Although the people are similar to those in Lee's illustrations of the Sutcliff epics, these images don't have the same distant effect. The story will appeal to the same readers.

The Jesse Tree

By Geraldine McCaughrean. Illustrated by Bee Willey. Eerdmans, 2005.

Interest level: **Middle**
Bible stories

The framework for this retelling of twenty-four traditional Advent stories—from Adam and Eve in the Garden of Eden to the birth of Christ—is a small boy's visits to a carpenter carving a Jesse tree, a traditional means of depicting Jesus's family tree. These tales are smoothly told in a believably natural way; they're illustrated with slightly elongated figures that seem to fit. The realistic details of the boy's encounters with the craftsman connect these traditional narratives to a more modern world. The book itself is nicely designed, with heavy paper, ample leading, and digitally created illustrations on every spread. An image of the completed carving appears at the beginning and end. This offers an attractive and accessible way to introduce familiar Bible stories (mostly from the Old Testament) to children who haven't previously encountered them as well as an entertainment for the days of Advent for families following that tradition.

Hercules

Retold by Geraldine McCaughrean. Cricket, 2005.

Interest level: **Middle**
Mythology

Born of Zeus and a mortal woman and hated by Zeus's wife Hera, Hercules was noted for his strength from childhood. Thanks to Hera's meddling and maddened by drink, he killed his wife and children and was sentenced to ten years of bondage during which he performed seemingly impossible feats before being saved by Zeus and set among the constellations in the sky. Readers will sympathize with Hercules as much as they are revolted (as he is) by his murderous acts. McCaughrean's quartet of short novels describing heroes of Greek mythology also includes *Theseus* (2003), *Odysseus* (2004), and *Perseus* (2005). Slim volumes, with no illustrations beyond the covers, these smooth retellings keep readers' attention through exciting action, bloody battles, horrifying monsters, convincing human (and godly) relationships, and humor. They would be ideal preparation or follow-up for reading Rick Riordan's gripping tales.

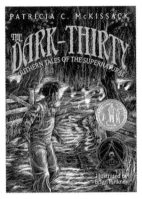

The Dark-Thirty: Southern Tales of the Supernatural

By Patricia C. McKissack. Illustrated by Brian Pinkney. Knopf, 1992.

Interest level: **Older** • Lexile measure: **730L**
Folklore, original; Short stories

Ten spooky tales, ghost stories, and a bit of horror suitable for telling at the half hour just before nightfall make up this Newbery honor–winning collection. These stories are original to the author but rooted in the African American experience and the story-telling tradition. Pinkney's black-and-white scratchboard illustrations add to the atmosphere. These are not for the very young; they include the attempt by a slaveholder to break apart a family and an actual lynching. But for readers ready for that history or already aware of it, they turn an unhappy past into tales to share and remember. A short introduction sets each story in context and, after the first two slave stories, the rest—including a haunted bus route, a child raised by a Sasquatch, and an evil-doing knickknack from an antique store—are scarily possible even today.

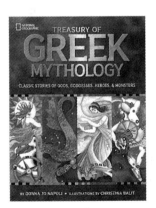

Treasury of Greek Mythology: Classic Stories of Gods, Goddesses, Heroes & Monsters

By Donna Jo Napoli. Illustrated by Christina Balit. National Geographic, 2011.

Interest level: **Middle** • Lexile measure: **860L**
Mythology

From the chaos that spawned Gaia to war and destruction caused by the beautiful Helen, this presents a coherent account of the most familiar Greek mythology lavishly illustrated with stylized portraits, borders, and vignettes. Carefully researched and beautifully written, this keeps your attention as a reader. The twenty-five stories are dramatic and certainly include Zeus's wandering eye, but they're not explicit; they're exactly as you'd want them told for younger readers. There are sidebars that connect stories to each other and, sometimes, to today's world; maps; a time line; a cast of characters (including equivalent Roman names and symbols); bibliography; suggested further research; and an extensive index. An opening family tree introduces the main characters visually, and the illustrations throughout include both stylized images and associated symbols. Much as I have loved the d'Aulaires's stories, I would choose this version for a family collection.

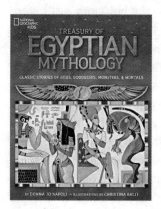

Treasury of Egyptian Mythology: Classic Stories of Gods, Goddesses, Monsters & Mortals

By Donna Jo Napoli. Illustrated by Christina Balit. National Geographic, 2013.

Interest level: **Middle** • Lexile measure: **860L**
Mythology

From Ra, the god of radiance, to Imhotep, human-turned-god of medicine and architecture, here's an introduction to the complex world of ancient Egyptian mythology. This lavishly illustrated oversized volume clearly lays out the main cast of characters: the great pesedjet of Ra and his nine children, grandchildren, and great-grandchildren, and more. Napoli explains the importance of the Nile in Egyptian culture and describes traditional funeral rites. There are maps, time lines, and even a culminating fast-facts list of deities. Each character is introduced with a colorful double-page image, memorable stories, and significant history. Each section has a slightly different design. There are distinctive borders and smaller illustrations throughout. Summarizing the mythology of a complex series of civilizations extending over three thousand years is difficult, and readers may come away with their heads swimming, but this is a grand place to begin. Napoli's *Treasury of Norse Mythology* will be published in 2015.

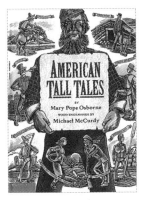

American Tall Tales

By Mary Pope Osborne. Illustrated by Michael McCurdy. Knopf, 1991.

Interest level: **Middle** • Lexile measure: **970L**
Folklore; Short stories

From Davy Crockett to Paul Bunyan, nine short stories describe larger-than-life men and women whose feats have inspired story tellers for generations. Each episode is lively and fresh, though grounded in earlier versions. There's an extensive bibliography. This oversized title opens with a map of the United States showing the part of the country identified with each character. Individual chapters are illustrated with colored woodcuts. Johnny Appleseed frees a trapped wolf; Stormalong wrestles a giant octopus; and, hammer in each hand, John Henry outdigs a steam drill. Some characters may be less familiar: Mose Humphreys fought fires in New York with a hand-carried pumper. Febold Feboldson set the prairies on fire to make rain. Women appear twice: Slue-Foot Sue marries Pecos Bill and, as a test of her own skills, rides his bronco, Widow Maker. The author also creates an adventure for Sally Ann Thunder Ann Whirlwind, Crockett's fictional wife.

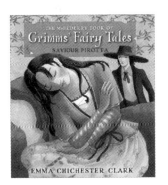

The McElderry Book of Grimms' Fairy Tales

Retold by Saviour Pirotta. Illustrated by Emma Chichester Clark. Margaret K. McElderry Books, 2006.

Interest level: **Younger**
Classics; Fairy tales; Short stories

For this fine collection for young readers, first published in England, Pirotta chose to retell ten tales from Wilhelm and Jacob Grimm, including those of Sleeping Beauty, Hansel and Gretel, Magic Bear, Rapunzel, Little Mouse and Lazy Cat, Snow White, six swans and the brave princess, Frog Prince, Rumpelstiltskin, and the twelve dancing princesses. These have been presented in a handsome, oversized volume with large font, generous leading, and sweet, gently old-fashioned illustrations. Many of the more gruesome details have been softened. These versions would be appropriate for children in early elementary-school grades but still retain important original particulars. Clark's whimsical paintings include one double-page spread per tale, numerous smaller images, and, on page corners, a flower identifying the story. The satisfying whole would be a perfect introduction to an enduring body of work.

Beowulf: A Hero's Tale Retold

By James Rumford. Illustrated by James Rumford. Houghton Mifflin, 2007.

Interest level: **Older** • Lexile measure: **740L**
Folklore

A splendid retelling of the earliest English hero saga, this is the story of Beowulf, hero of the Danes, Angles, and Saxons. As a youth, he slew the monster Grendel and Grendel's mother, and in his old age, he took on a fire-breathing dragon. Beowulf's story was told orally long before it was set down as an epic poem in Old English more than a thousand years ago. Rumford's version uses words from Anglo-Saxon almost exclusively, which gives his narrative power and an air of antiquity. At the same time he's shortened and simplified the tale for younger readers. Text and connected illustrations are set in boxes on spreads whose backgrounds provide foreshadowing of Beowulf's ultimate fate. The effect of these illustrations, done in pen and ink and finished in watercolors, is extraordinarily powerful, and yet, though the battles are gory, they are bloodless, unlike those in some other versions.

Cut from the Same Cloth: American Women of Myth, Legend, and Tall Tale

Collected and told by Robert D. San Souci. Illustrated by Brian Pinkney. Philomel, 1993.

Interest level: **Older** • Lexile measure: **1050L**
Folklore; Short stories

Fifteen short tales of heroines from various parts of the country and varying ethnicities make up this collection of myths, legends, and tall tales. Introduced with a map, the stories are organized by section of the country from east to west, including Alaska and Hawaii. Each is introduced with a handsome black-and-white scratchboard drawing. The protagonists include tricksters and larger-than-life strong women, warriors and sweet talkers, and even talking animals. They come from varied Native American tribal as well as colonial and African American traditions. Many include familiar themes or characters, but the focus is fresh. San Souci's retellings are based on extensive research; he provides a short introduction for each and includes a bibliography. This is not easy reading, and the dialect of some stories makes them even more difficult, but this is probably the broadest selection available for young readers. Jane Yolen introduces this set of wonder tales.

Black Ships Before Troy: The Story of The Iliad

By Rosemary Sutcliff. Illustrated by Alan Lee. Frances Lincoln Children's Books, 2005.

Interest level: **Older** • Lexile measure: **1300L**
Mythology

Sutcliff creates a glorious rendition of the traditional story of the Trojan War: from the golden apple thrown by the goddess of discord, to the theft of Helen, to the ten years of attack by the avenging Greeks. She includes the most memorable events, Achilles's sulk and the deaths of Patroclus and Hector, and goes on from where *The Iliad* leaves off to conclude with Achilles's death and the ploy of the Trojan horse. Her masterful story telling retains much of the flavor of the original, including striking metaphors and astonishing gore. There's heroism, death, dishonor, and grief. Readers will be left with a sense of both glory and futility. Not an easy read, this will particularly appeal to older voracious readers who are already aware of the machinations of Greek gods in human lives. Lee's Kate Greenaway Medal–winning watercolors are both monumental and distant, perfectly matching the story.

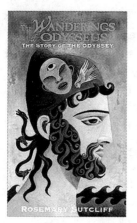

The Wanderings of Odysseus: The Story of The Odyssey

By Rosemary Sutcliff. Illustrated by Alan Lee. Frances Lincoln Children's Books, 2005.

Interest level: **Older**
Mythology

After the fall of Troy, Odysseus sets off for Ithaca with a fleet of twenty ships, but he incurs the wrath of Neptune for injuring a Cyclops. After a series of misadventures, he finally arrives home nine years later and, with his now grown son, frees his halls from the suitors of his faithful wife, Penelope. In this masterful retelling of a 2,700-year-old story, Sutcliff includes all major characters and episodes, concluding with a grand and gory battle. In Lee's misty watercolors, the monsters are monstrous and the women beautiful (and sometimes, like Greek statues, partially topless). The story is told in a surprisingly immediate way, full of visual details and suspense. The text is not easy, but it is presented in episodic chapters that make up a wonderful series of adventures for a young reader. This is a grand foundation for the many versions and allusions readers will encounter throughout their lives.

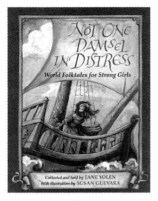

Not One Damsel in Distress: World Folktales for Strong Girls

Collected and told by Jane Yolen. Illustrated by Susan Guevara. Silver Whistle Books, 2000.

Interest level: **Older**
Folklore; Short stories

Thirteen traditional tales collected from around the world and retold in a lively fashion show that women were often heroes of the traditional sort, bearing and using whatever weapons were necessary to rescue the helpless, slay monsters, and achieve their goals. The arrangement of these stories is interesting—they often seem to contrast as much as possible in time, place, and experience so that the reader is impressed not only by each single tale, but also by their variety. This is a convincing demonstration that such tales have existed in every culture, and it's supported with an extensive bibliography. Readers like Yolen's own granddaughters, who respond in a final chapter, probably don't need convincing that girls can do brave things, but they will enjoy the examples from Atalanta the Huntress in Greece to Mollie Whuppie in England. A companion volume with male protagonists is *Mightier Than the Sword* (2003).

Chapter 11

Living Long Ago

· ·

STORIES AND TRUE ACCOUNTS FROM LONG AGO are often thought to be ideal material for young readers, increasing their understanding of history in appealing small doses. Sometimes the hook is time travel: a child from the present or recent past travels back to an earlier time, noticing things that were ordinary for people then but are extraordinary to us. (Imagine the smells of Shakespeare's England!) Other stories of the past come from the writer's memories or a relative's experience. They may be based on earlier accounts, even diaries. There are both fiction and nonfiction titles in this chapter. Many young readers don't care about that difference if the book is well written and the subject interests them. But they can still be helped to learn the distinction between characters, events, and details that have been imagined and those that can be documented.

Today, writers of both fiction and nonfiction usually base their historical writings on meticulous research. Readers may come to these books because they like history in general, or out of an interest in a particular time or place or even in a story's theme. This selection includes a variety of narrative forms and includes engaging family stories, adventures, and stories involving dogs and horses and baseball as well as more straight-forward history.

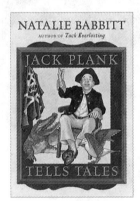

Jack Plank Tells Tales

By Natalie Babbitt. Illustrated by Natalie Babbitt. Michael Di Capua Books, 2007.

Interest level: **Middle** • Lexile measure: **860L**
Historical fiction; Short stories

Retired pirate Jack Plank entertains Miss Withers's boarders and guests in Saltwash, Jamaica, with stories from his seafaring past. This is a completely convincing eighteenth-century world of leisurely story telling and romantic piracy. The stories are not about plundering (which Jack didn't like). They're about ghosts and shipmates who turn into sea creatures, a crocodile who loves music, and a girl who was raised by seagulls. Original and imaginative but traditional in flavor, these are gently humorous and ideal for youngsters who are looking for not-too-scary stories about pirates. Also notable is the language, which is both immediate and kid friendly: "There's only one way to plunder: You have to yell and make faces and rattle your sword, and once you've got people scared, you take things away from them. That's what pirates do." Babbitt's illustrations grace each chapter heading and show major characters, too.

The Children of Green Knowe

By L. M. Boston. Illustrated by Peter Boston.
Harcourt, 2008 (orig. 1955).

Interest level: **Older** • Lexile measure: **880L**
Historical fantasy

When Tolly comes to visit his great-grandmother at Green Knowe, he discovers her ancient house filled with ghosts of children who lived there in the seventeenth century, at the time of the Great Plague, and whose lives are different from and yet similar to his own. This is the first in a series of books set at The Manor at Hemingford Grey, outside Cambridge, England, the author's home, now open to the public. They're a perfect gateway to historical times. An opening flood and a threatening topiary provide light suspense. Five sequels, also illustrated by the author's son, introduce other children, both modern and historical, who explore the out-of-doors, befriend animals, and confront forces of evil: *Treasure of Green Knowe* (1958) (called *Chimneys of Green Knowe* in the U.K.), *The River at Green Knowe* (1959), *A Stranger at Green Knowe* (1961), *An Enemy at Green Knowe* (1964), and *The Stones of Green Knowe* (1976).

King of Shadows

By Susan Cooper. Margaret K. McElderry Books, 1999.

Interest level: **Middle** • Lexile measure: **1010L**
Historical fantasy

As Nat Field rehearses with a troupe of boys recreating original Shakespeare performances in a replica of the Globe Theatre in London, he's suddenly transported back in time to the days when the Globe was new and Shakespeare himself directed and performed in the plays. Nat's been exchanged with another Nat Field, ill with bubonic plague, who was scheduled to play the part of Puck in *A Midsummer Night's Dream*. The time slip is handled smoothly, and the details of staging and performing the play, both in Shakespeare's time and today, are fascinating. Suspense comes not only from Nat's fear of being discovered, quickly replaced by fear of leaving Shakespeare, who helps him heal from the pain of losing his own father, but also from the possibility that Queen Elizabeth herself will see this play. Ideal for young readers who have heard or performed some Shakespeare themselves.

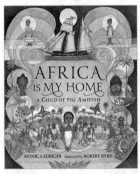

Africa Is My Home: A Child of the Amistad

By Monica Edinger. Illustrated by Robert Byrd. Candlewick Press, 2013.

Interest level: **Older** • Lexile measure: **890L**
Historical fiction

Sold to a slaver in Mendeland, West Africa, nine-year-old Magulu (Margru), gets caught up in a slave revolt on their ship, the *Amistad*. After years of legal battle, she's finally allowed to go home, returning to the United States only for teacher training at Oberlin College. In language that's usually formal, Margru tells her own story; it becomes poetry when she thinks of home. The narrative has been fleshed out with details from the author's extensive research and Byrd's detailed ink-and-watercolor illustrations throughout. Images and quotations from the time add authenticity. This fictional biography works well to introduce slave trade to middle-grade readers, personalizing the experience in a gentle and hopeful but not unrealistic way. A disturbing all-black spread is all readers need to imagine "seven weeks in a dark and airless hold." The contrasting pastels of the return voyage and her African home make the point.

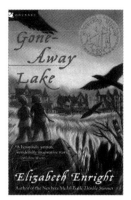

Gone-Away Lake

By Elizabeth Enright. Illustrated by Beth and Joe Krush. Harcourt, 2000 (orig. 1957).

Interest level: **Middle** • Lexile measure: **760L**
Adventure

Exploring the woods behind his family's new summer home, Julian, twelve, and his cousin Portia, ten,
discover the boggy remains of a lake and community of summer cottages with two elderly year-round
residents, Mrs. Cheever and her brother, Pindar Peyton, who encourage
them to set up a clubhouse in an empty cottage. Over the summer, they
explore the area, experiencing its wonders and what it was like to vacation
there in the 1890s. The freedom these mid-twentieth-century children had
adds another historical layer. The children and grown-ups alike are well-
developed characters: curious, capable, and interested in the natural world
around them. The language is rich and wonderful, the setting lovingly
depicted. The story is illustrated with occasional line drawings. Happily,
there's even a sequel to this still-appealing Newbery honor book: *Return to
Gone-Away* (1961), in which Portia's family summers in a once-stately
home.

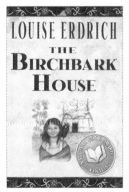

The Birchbark House

By Louise Erdrich. Illustrated by Louise Erdrich. Hyperion, 1999.

Interest level: **Middle** • Lexile measure: **970L**
Historical fiction

In her Ojibwe community on the shores of Lake
Superior in 1847, Omakayas pursues daily life in
a culture already changing under the influence of
voyageurs. The sole survivor of a smallpox epidemic
in her birth village, the seven-year-old was rescued and adopted as a toddler. She idolizes her older sister, resents her hyperactive next-younger
brother, and loves the baby. There are periods of plenty and famine,
joyful times and sad ones, especially when smallpox takes her beloved

baby brother. Learning of her adoption is a final step in this extraordinary year of growth. This is the first of a series by an acclaimed adult author that grew out of research into her own family history. Sequels following this family from their home island in Lake Superior westward to the Plains Country include *The Game of Silence* (2005), *The Porcupine Year* (2008), and *Chickadee* (2008), a grand survival story starring one of Omakayas's sons.

Locomotive

By Brian Floca. Illustrated by Brian Floca. Atheneum, 2013.

Interest level: **Younger** • Lexile measure: **840L**
Informational picture book

Following a family traveling from Nebraska to California on the newly completed transcontinental railroad, this outstanding Caldecott Medal winner illustrates in words and pictures the construction and train workers, the layout and mechanics of the engine, and the experience of the journey. There's a hefty text for good readers, set in short lines and stanzas on the illustrations, using interesting typographical effects. Floca picks out child-friendly details: the stove and toilet in the passenger cars; the food available at hash houses along the way. There's an illustration of the train traveling over a "rickety rickety rickety" narrow bridge and another of the explosion that would result if the fireman and the engineer didn't keep the water level just right. Some paintings spread across a page or two, most are vignettes, close-ups of passengers and trainmen and scenes from the journey. This tribute to transportation in the past also earned a Sibert honor.

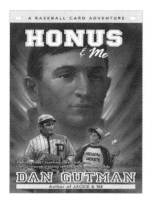

Honus and Me:
A Baseball Card Adventure

By Dan Gutman. Avon Books, 1997.

Interest level: **Middle** • Lexile measure: **690L**
Historical fantasy

Joe Stoshack uses baseball cards to travel in time. Here, he goes back to a World Series game in 1909 where Honus Wagner had a big day. This is the first of a long series of time-travel adventures that introduce an era and a player using photographs from the period. In each, Joe improves his own baseball skills and also faces a moral dilemma usually involving giving up large amounts of money that would make his life with his single mother easier. These carefully researched titles include endnotes distinguishing fact from fiction. Joe's ability is a dream come true for many readers. Heroes sports fans can meet in the sequels include Jackie Robinson, Babe Ruth, Shoeless Joe Jackson, Mickey Mantle, and players on the Milwaukee Chicks (part of the All-American Girls Professional Baseball League), Abner Doubleday, Satchel Paige, Jim Thorpe, Ray Chapman, Roberto Clemente, Ted Williams, and Willie Mays.

Shooting at the Stars:
The Christmas Truce of 1914

By John Hendrix. Illustrated by John Hendrix. Abrams, 2014.

Interest level: **Middle** • Lexile measure: **830L**
Informational picture book

In the early years of World War I, when eager young soldiers discovered that war was not the adventure they'd anticipated, there was an unexpected lull in the fighting when German and English soldiers emerged from their trenches and celebrated Christmas Day together in 1914. Using material from letters and interviews with participants, Hendrix imagines the Christmas truce, presenting it in the form of a letter from an English soldier to his mother. At first the letter is handwritten (printing, not script), but soon it alternates with regular type (and occasional hallooed messages from the Germans), set on pages of paintings that will help readers imagine the setting. Dark, drab, dreary in the cold wartime winter, even the colors seem to brighten after the soldiers get together. The accurate information is supplemented with an author's note, glossary, bibliography, and index. An excellent choice for young history buffs.

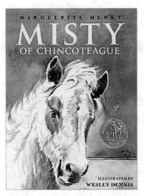

Misty of Chincoteague

By Marguerite Henry. Illustrated by Wesley Dennis. Rand McNally, 1970 (orig. 1947).

Interest level: **Middle** • Lexile measure: **750L**
Historical fiction

Living on a farm in Chincoteague, Virginia, where their grandparents raise and sell Assateague ponies, Paul and Maureen Beebe's dream of a pony they can keep comes true when Paul joins the annual roundup and they jointly buy Phantom and her young foal, which he names Misty. This Newbery honor book was based on a real family's Assateague ponies and the roundup and pony sale that still occur today. It's representative of the 1940s, but still a crackerjack story of children and the horse of their dreams. This is really Phantom's story. She continues to long for her home herd of wild ponies, and Paul eventually releases her, a sad decision but clearly the right one. *Stormy, Misty's Foal* (1963) continues Misty's story, and Henry followed these with many more horse stories still available, at least in paperback editions.

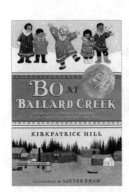

Bo at Ballard Creek

By Kirkpatrick Hill. Illustrated by LeUyen Pham. Henry Holt, 2013.

Interest level: **Middle** • Lexile measure: **840L**
Historical fiction

Living with two papas in an Alaskan gold mining camp in the early twentieth century might seem surprising, but for five-year-old Bo it's both ordinary and wonderful, made even better when she gets a brother. In the tradition of frontier stories, this is full of fascinating details about mining camp life, from a child's point of view. In an episodic narrative covering a year, readers, aided by Pham's occasional cheerful line drawings, are immersed in Bo's world. Bo has useful work to do and time to play, too. She has a best friend, Oscar, to share adventures and a wide range of acquaintances, from the camp and the nearby Eskimo village, who dotes on her. Bo greets life with enthusiasm; a reader can't help but be caught up by her story and hope for more. *Bo at Iditarod Creek* (2014) introduces some darker elements, but not inappropriately.

Our Only May Amelia

By Jennifer L. Holm. HarperCollins, 1999.

Interest level: **Older** • Lexile measure: **900L**
Historical fiction

The only daughter in a family of eight and the only girl child in the Nasel River settlement, a Finnish American logging and farming community in Washington State in 1899, May Amelia resents the expectation that she be a proper young lady. This independent twelve-year-old wants to do everything her brothers do. This gets her into trouble, over and over. When her longed-for baby sister finally arrives, she doesn't live long. In a painful climax, the hateful grandmother who has come to live with them accuses the blameless child of being responsible for the infant's sudden death. This Newbery honor book features a fresh, convincing first-person voice and lots of details about the time and place. May Amelia's story continues into 1900 in *The Trouble with May Amelia* (2011), which is filled with events that graphically demonstrate the difficulties of pioneer life.

The Evolution of Calpurnia Tate

By Jacqueline Kelly. Henry Holt, 2009.

Interest level: **Older** • Lexile measure: **830L**
Historical fiction

In the summer of 1899, another only daughter, eleven-year-old Calpurnia Tate, screws up her courage to talk to her fearsome grandfather. She discovers a man who encourages her interest in the natural world around her. Together they discover a new species of sedge near their home in rural Texas. The plant will bear their name. More importantly, she discovers what she really wants to do with her life in a world where the only science thought appropriate for a wealthy young woman is the science of housewifery. Chapter headings come from *On the Origin of Species*, and this is truly about evolution, both of an intelligent young woman and in the natural world. Callie V is a very likeable character in an interesting time and place, pure pleasure for the reader who enjoys spunky girls who aren't resigned to their fate. *The Curious World of Calpurnia Tate* (2015) continues her story.

Dash

By Kirby Larson. Scholastic, 2014.

Interest level: **Middle** • Lexile measure: **570L**
Historical fiction

Everything changed for fifth grader Mitsi Kashino in 1942, with the United States at war with Japan. Her best friends turned away from her, her family was sent to a Japanese internment camp, and she had to leave her beloved dog, Dash, behind. The kernel of this story is true—there was an actual Japanese American girl who loved, left, and was eventually reunited with her dog—but Larson makes this much more than that by personalizing Mitsi's experience in ways that will engage middle-grade readers: losing friendships, worrying about her brother's new activities, finding a new friend in a new place. There are rich historical details, but the author distances the worst experiences. While Mitsi and her family are uncomfortable, they are, at least, together. The letters Mitsi receives from her dog, left with a neighbor, have a surprising source, and their eventual reunion is very satisfying.

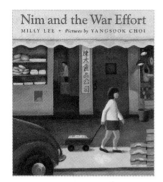

Nim and the War Effort

By Milly Lee. Illustrated by Yangsook Choi. Farrar, Straus, Giroux, 1997.

Interest level: **Younger** • Lexile measure: **AD510L**
Historical fiction; Picture book

During World War II, when the children at Nim's school collected newspapers for the war effort, she outsmarts her biggest rival in the contest, sneaky, bigoted Garland Stephenson. This is a warm, gently humorous story that requires some understanding of the time—the racism during the war against Japan that made Chinese American families like Nim's suspect, the ways that war affected people's lives at home, and the residential segregation that made Nim's trip outside of San Francisco's Chinatown a particularly brave effort. Using her own childhood memories, the author clearly reveals the family's culture. Nim has calligraphy and Chinese language lessons, eats rice for breakfast, and watches her grandfather light incense at the family's ancestral altar. He worries that she's shamed the family. Though a picture book, with large paintings full of the brown tones of the past, the text is extensive and more appropriate for the elementary-school reader.

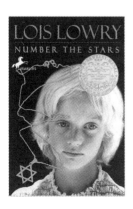

Number the Stars

By Lois Lowry. Houghton Mifflin, 2014 (orig. 1989).

Interest level: **Older** • Lexile measure: **670L**
Historical fiction

Pretending that her best friend Ellen is her sister is just the first of the ways ten-year-old Annemarie Johansen, like other patriotic Danes, helps her neighbors escape to Sweden when the Germans occupying Denmark decide to relocate the Jews of that country in 1943. This Newbery Medal winner is often the first book children read about World War II and their first encounter with Nazi policies. It's moving and gently suspenseful, an appropriate introduction. The focus is the Danish resistance, not the Jewish experience; the novel ends with the end of the war in Denmark, not the Rosen family's return. In an afterword, Lowry relates truths behind her fiction. Readers ready for grimmer details might move on to Yolen's *The Devil's Arithmetic* (1988), in which a modern Jewish girl travels back in time to a Polish village and a concentration camp.

Sarah, Plain and Tall

By Patricia MacLachlan. Harper & Row, 1985.

Interest level: **Middle** • Lexile measure: **560L**
Historical fiction

Anna and her little brother, Caleb, love Sarah, the mail-order bride from Maine who has come to live on their prairie farm and be their new mother. Telling details reveal the life of prairie pioneers: the loneliness (the home of the nearest neighbor is too far to walk); the harsh reality of a hailstorm; the joy of sliding down a mountain of hay. Every word of this short, Newbery Medal–winning text is as carefully chosen as for a poem. The children's occasional sadness is palpable: Anna, when she remembers the mother who died when Caleb was born, and both children when Sarah hitches up a wagon to go to town by herself and they fear she's planning to leave. The family grows in sequels *Skylark* (1994), *Caleb's Story* (2001), *More Perfect than the Moon* (2004), and *Grandfather's Dance* (2006), which demonstrate the healing power of writing and the cycle of life.

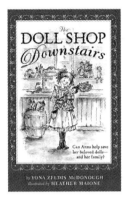

The Doll Shop Downstairs

By Yona Zeldis McDonough. Illustrated by
Heather Maione. Viking, 2009.

Interest level: **Middle**
Historical fiction

In Manhattan's Lower East Side in early twentieth
century, Anna-in-the-middle helps in the family's
doll repair shop and suggests that they make their
own dolls after war with Germany makes it impossible to get porcelain repair parts. This warm family story, reminiscent of
All-of-a-Kind Family, annotated later in this chapter, was inspired by the
actual beginnings of the Madame Alexander doll enterprise. There are
descriptions of doll play, family chores, and Jewish holiday celebrations as
well as the normal sibling back-and-forth relationships. Since their family
is too poor for them to have fancy dolls of their own, Sophie, seven; Anna,
nine; and Trudie, eleven, adopt dolls waiting for repair, and worry about
their owners reclaiming them. There's even a glossary defining unfamiliar
terms. Sweet gray-scale drawings add to the period feel. A sequel, *The Cats
in the Doll Shop* (2011), adds a cousin from Russia to the family.

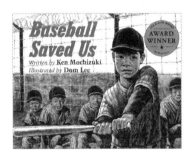

Baseball Saved Us

By Ken Mochizuki. Illustrated by Dom Lee.
Lee & Low, 1993.

Interest level: **Younger** • Lexile measure:
AD550L • **Historical fiction; Picture book**

In 1942, when the narrator's Japanese
American family is moved to an internment camp in the desert, his father helps construct a baseball field, organizing teams for both grown-ups and children. Watching and playing, the
boy develops skills that help him fit in at home when they are allowed to
return. A short author's note, wisely placed at the beginning, provides all
the background needed to set up this narrative, which begins in the camp
"in the middle of nowhere . . . behind a barbed wire fence." While racism
underlies the entire experience, the focus is the small, skinny boy. The text

includes details about the camp experience: endless lines, family disruptions, ever-present guards. Lee's paintings make the setting more real; this is not a comfortable place. When the war is over, the narrator still gets called "Jap" and "Shorty" but, in true sports story tradition, he triumphs. A powerful picture book for reading children.

Blizzard!: The Storm That Changed America

By Jim Murphy. Scholastic, 2000.

Interest level: **Older** • Lexile measure: **1080L**
Nonfiction

Eyewitness accounts and newspaper reports enliven this dramatic story of the blizzard of 1888, which stopped trains in their tracks and shut down the East Coast, especially New York City, for nearly a week, prompting drastic changes in the way weather is forecast in this country. Related drawings and photographs from the time enhance the text. In a complicated but page-turning narrative, Murphy weaves together the stories of many individuals, not all of whom survived. From a former senator who insists on walking home in the storm to a divinity student trapped on a train to children who spent a night in a snow cave, these stories are gripping and memorable. Though storm forecasting and snow removal have improved significantly in the last 125 years, blizzards are still a formidable threat. This is narrative nonfiction at its best.

Ship of Dolls

By Shirley Parenteau. Candlewick Press, 2014.

Interest level: **Middle** • Lexile measure: **670L**
Historical fiction

For readers still cherishing their own dolls, this little piece of history may be especially welcome. Set in Portland, Oregon, in 1926, the background of this moving story of a child's adjustment to a new family arrangement is a real event: an exchange of dolls between Japan and the United States, conceived as a message of peace. Forced to live with her grandparents while her "flapper" mother performs, what eleven-year-old Lexie Lewis most wants is a chance to get to San Francisco to be with her mother again. The school's Japanese doll letter-writing contest might be her ticket, but her classmate, privileged mean girl Louise Wilkins, is also determined to win. Small lies play a big part in this heartwarming story of friendship, dolls, and family love. The third-person narrative reflects Lexie's point of view, justifying the impulses that get her into trouble.

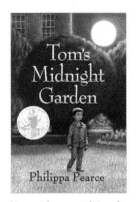

Tom's Midnight Garden

By Philippa Pearce. Illustrated by Susan Einzig. Oxford University Press, 2008 (orig. 1958).

Interest level: **Middle** • Lexile measure: **860L**
Fantasy

Sent off to stay with an apartment-dwelling aunt and uncle to avoid the measles, Tom finds a magical garden, accessible only in the middle of the night, and a playmate in Hatty, the little girl who lives there. This classic time-travel fantasy won a Carnegie Medal as the most distinguished children's book published in Great Britain; it still resonates today. It's a story of loneliness, children's play, and life long ago in late-Victorian Britain. There's even a grand ice-skating expedition down river during an unusually hard winter freeze in 1895. Tom wrestles with theories of how time works, given that his garden visits take place in different seasons and different stages of Hatty's childhood, but he finally realizes that his visits coincide with the dream memories of the elderly woman living upstairs in the grand house, now broken up into apartments, that was her childhood home.

Esperanza Rising

By Pam Muñoz Ryan. Scholastic, 2000.

Interest level: **Older** • Lexile measure: **750L**
Historical fiction

Called "my queen" by her friend Miguel, the housekeeper's son, Esperanza was a privileged child until bandits killed her father, the owner of a prosperous Mexican farm, the night before her thirteenth birthday. She and her mother were forced to emigrate with Miguel's family and start over as farm workers themselves in central California. This moving riches-to-rags story, set in the Depression years of the early 1930s, is partially based on the real-life experiences of the author's grandmother, who worked on a company farm in the San Joaquin Valley. Ryan weaves in historical and political background, the threat of strikes and the "voluntary repatriation" of hundreds of thousands of Mexicans and Mexican Americans. But the heart of the story is Esperanza's maturation as she learns to care for babies, do housework, and, later, paid work on the farm. A little-told story from U.S. history that deserves its many awards.

All-of-a-Kind Family

By Sydney Taylor. Illustrated by Helen John. Delacorte Press, 2005 (orig. 1951).

Interest level: **Middle** • Lexile measure: **750L**
Historical fiction

Early in the twentieth century, in New York's Lower East Side tenements, five sisters who share a single room demonstrate the joys of growing up in a large, loving, and close-knit family. This much-loved title remains a favorite for its detailed descriptions of the family's life and Jewish practices. Each chapter is a stand-alone story; each reader will find a particular favorite among the five girls. Ella, at twelve, is the oldest in this book; Gertie, four, is the youngest. Their little brother, Charlie, is born in the last chapter. The original illustrations, line drawings, add to the period atmosphere. Four sequels carry the family through World War I and beyond. To follow the family growing up, the books should be read out of publishing order. Follow this title with *All-of-a-Kind Family Downtown* (1962) and then *More All-of-a-Kind Family* (1954), *All-of-a-Kind Family Uptown* (1958), and *Ella of All-of-a-Kind Family* (1978).

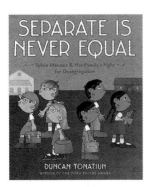

Separate Is Never Equal: Sylvia Mendez and Her Family's Fight for Desegregation

By Duncan Tonatiuh. Illustrated by Duncan Tonatiuh. Abrams, 2014.

Interest level: **Younger** • Lexile measure: **AD870L**
Informational picture book

School desegregation efforts began long before the *Brown v. Board of Education* decision in 1954 and involved many ethnic groups. In 1944, when third grader Sylvia Mendez and her siblings tried to attend their neighborhood school in Westminster, California, they were turned away, sent to the inferior "Mexican school." Her parents' three-year court battle integrated schools in Orange County and paved the way for a law integrating all California schools in 1947. The author-illustrator tells this story from Sylvia's point of view, beginning with the discomfort of her first day in the newly integrated school and then looking backward to her parents' legal battle. Folk-art-inspired illustrations, usually extending across the spreads, support the story, but there is a solid text for elementary-school readers. In conclusion, there's an author's note, plus photos of the Mendez family and the schools, glossary, bibliography, and index.

Little House in the Big Woods

By Laura Ingalls Wilder. Illustrated by Garth Williams. HarperCollins, 1953 (orig. 1932).

Interest level: **Middle** • Lexile measure: **930L**
Historical fiction

Chronicle of a year five-year-old Laura Ingalls's family spent in a cabin in the forest outside Pepin, Wisconsin in the 1870s. As pioneers, they grew or hunted everything they ate and made nearly everything they used. This first of eight titles in the series appeals especially to early readers because of Laura's age. Cheese and maple syrup making; Christmas festivities; a rollicking square dance; the visit of a bear; and descriptions of their cozy home, furnishings, and Laura's new doll are just some of the memorable details. Sadly, even in this revised edition, these books, reflect outmoded attitudes about Native Americans, African Americans, and women's roles. Parents can help their children place these attitudes in their historical context, discussing how times have changed and making sure their children read stories of U.S. history written from other points of view. Erdrich's Birchbark House series, annotated earlier, makes for an interesting parallel.

Real Places and People

MANY, MANY YOUNG READERS WANT TO READ about real things, real places, and real people. They want to know if something really happened, if a place really exists, if a person really did all the things he or she is said to have done. Like all of us, they have favorite subjects. Readers will read anything they can find on their current passions, skipping or skimming over parts that don't seem accessible or interesting. This selection includes only a tiny fraction of the true stories available for children. It introduces some authors and some series they might enjoy. It also includes some books that were never meant to be read straight through but are suitable for browsing.

Today, even nonfiction published for young teens is generously illustrated, with a look that adults might associate with picture books but a level of text and information far beyond the ken of a six-year-old. One publisher has even reissued a number of titles originally published in a larger, picture-book format. The new editions, the size and shape of chapter books, are intended for school-age readers. "Being older and being more accomplished readers, these kids want their books to reflect the maturity and mastery they feel," explained Mary Lee Donovan, editorial director at Candlewick Press. Some of these are annotated or mentioned below. Books that fall loosely into the "informational picture book" category can be good choices for younger readers. You can find far larger selections of informational picture books in my earlier annotated bibliographies, *Picturing the World* (2013) and *Bugs, Bogs, Bats, and Books* (2014).

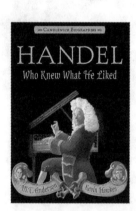

Handel, Who Knew What He Liked

By M. T. Anderson. Illustrated by Kevin Hawkes. Candlewick Press, 2013 (orig. 2001).

Interest level: **Middle**
Biography

From his early childhood, Handel was determined to be a musician, to play, compose, and perform what he liked. He studied secretly, against his father's will. He fought a duel with a friend over who would accompany the friend's opera. He studied in Italy, fell in love with Italian opera, and brought that style of music to England. When the fad for his operas faded, he turned to writing opera-like music for Biblical passages. His Messiah is still beloved and regularly performed. Anderson's lively biography strikes a humorous tone from the very beginning. It's full of amusing anecdotes but respects Handel's stature. This eighteenth-century musician is still ranked among the greats today. Hawkes's stately paintings befit the times, but they're funny, too. This reformatted edition of a picture book biography is a treat for any reader.

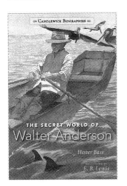

The Secret World of Walter Anderson

By Hester Bass. Illustrated by E. B. Lewis.
Candlewick Press, 2014 (orig. 2009).

Interest level: **Middle** • Lexile measure: **850L**
Biography

Here's another reformatted picture book biography. "The most famous American artist you've never heard of" lived in a cottage on the Mississippi coastline but spent most of his life painting the natural world on deserted Horn Island, twelve miles offshore. The text focuses on Walter Anderson's work in the 1950s and 1960s, describing his reclusive habits and some creatures he encountered. Watercolor illustrations show both his beloved island and the astonishingly painted locked room in his cottage. A lengthy author's note, more for adults, goes further into Anderson's troubled life and includes reproductions of some of his work. Other biographies reissued in the new format include *Vision of Beauty: The Story of Sarah Breedlove Walker* (Lasky, 2012); *Skit-Scat Raggedy Cat: Ella Fitzgerald* (Orgill, 2013); *Footwork: The Story of Fred and Adele Astaire* (Orgill, 2013); *John Muir: America's First Environmentalist* (Lasky, 2014); and *Lady Liberty: a Biography,* (Rappaport, 2014). Biographies of Henry Aaron and Ted Williams are scheduled for 2015.

America Is under Attack: September 11, 2001: The Day the Towers Fell

By Don Brown. Illustrated by Don Brown.
Roaring Brook Press, 2011.

Interest level: **Older** • Lexile measure: **840L**
Nonfiction

On September 11, 2001, four airplanes were taken over by followers of Osama bin Laden. Three planes attacked the twin towers of the World Trade Center in New York and the Pentagon outside Washington, D.C. Another crashed before hitting an unknown third target. Nearly three thousand people were killed. Brown begins with a brief explanation and tells just a few stories, enough to give the flavor of the event without fully expressing the horror, an appropriate introduction for young readers. This is the fourth in Brown's Actual Times series, introductory history that's a step up from informational picture books. The text is set on a background of pen-and-watercolor illustrations, and there's a bibliography. Other titles in the series include *Let It Begin Here* (The American Revolution, 2008), *All Stations! Distress* (The Titanic, 2008), *Gold! Gold from the American River!* (The California Gold Rush, 2011), and *He Has Shot the President* (Lincoln's assassination, 2014).

Crazy Horse's Vision

By Joseph Bruchac. Illustrated by S. D. Nelson. Lee & Low, 2000.

Interest level: **Younger** • Lexile measure: **420L**
Informational picture book; Biography

A young Lakota boy, called Curly for his hair, rides a wild horse, kills his first buffalo, and, prompted by a battle in which white soldiers unjustly attack his camp, goes on an early vision quest. He grows up to be the Lakota leader called, in English, Crazy Horse. Acrylic paintings, done in the traditional ledger book style by an enrolled tribal member, enhance this fictionalized account of the childhood of one of the leaders at the Battle of Little Bighorn. The endpapers depict another melee with armed soldiers and Sioux warriors, but in the illustrations these battles are bloodless. For readers who can deal with violence, this is an excellent depiction of native traditions. Lengthy afterwords add to the story of Crazy Horse's life and explain the artist's choices. Bruchac also told the story of Sitting Bull in *A Boy Called Slow* (1994).

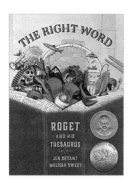

The Right Word: Roget and His Thesaurus

By Jen Bryant. Illustrated by Melissa Sweet.
Eerdmans, 2014.

Interest level: **Middle** • Lexile measure: **590L**
Informational picture book; Biography

A boy who loved to make lists grows up to write a famous book of words. For a word-loving child, this Sibert Medal winner is both a fascinating biography and an introduction to the idea of a thesaurus. Bryant introduces Peter Mark Roget as a lonely, shy child, born in 1779. He moved often and took refuge in books and in "scribbling" lists of words (Latin and English) and things. He began classifying ideas as Linnaeus had classified plants and animals. He wrote his first thesaurus for himself. An enlargement was published in 1852 after he'd made a reputation as a learned man. Sweet's Caldecott honor–winning art is amazing. These inventive collages include hand-lettered word lists (Roget's own) and watercolor sketches of Roget's life, sometimes in comic-like panels. There are bits and pieces of old books, images from the time, and words everywhere, a joy for any eager reader.

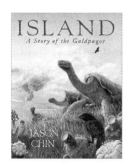

Island: A Story of the Galápagos

By Jason Chin. Illustrated by Jason Chin.
Roaring Brook Press, 2012.

Interest level: **Middle** • Lexile measure: **900L**
Informational picture book

Words and dramatic watercolor paintings work together in this imagined, but scientifically based account of the formation, population, evolution through natural selection of the plants and animals, and eventual end of an island. An afterword explains that the epilogue, describing the arrival of humans after six million years, shows Darwin's explorations in the Galápagos chain off the coast of Ecuador. In double-page spreads and small boxes, the illustrations demonstrate change. At first the island itself grows. All kinds of animals arrive. Finally, the species themselves become modified: beaks grow, shells are reshaped, and wings shrink. Front endpapers identify thirty-six Galápagos species, each with a small sketch. In the back, a map labels the different islands; an inset shows their location in the Western Hemisphere. This is both a simple explanation and a vivid demonstration of evolution as a series of gradual changes over a long period of time.

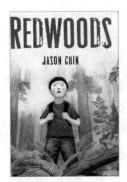

Redwoods

By Jason Chin. Illustrated by Jason Chin.
Roaring Brook Press, 2009.

Interest level: **Middle** • Lexile measure: **NC1100L**
Informational picture book

In this interesting combination of fantasy and science fact, an Asian American boy reading a book about redwoods on the subway imagines it so vividly it comes to life around him. After he finishes his reading—and his fantasy treetop tour—he leaves the book on a park bench, where a little girl picks it up and begins to have the same experience. The author weaves in many facts about these giant trees, ending with an afterword about redwoods in danger. The prose is straightforward exposition, not especially engaging; it is the imagery that carries the narrative arc while adding information. The invention and imagination in these detailed watercolors set this book apart. Details of the boy's real life interrupt but don't stop the vision he sees in his mind as he reads; he's a true reader. Don't miss the flying squirrel! A similar title is Chin's *Coral Reefs* (2011).

The Scraps Book: Notes from a Colorful Life

By Lois Ehlert. Illustrated by Lois Ehlert.
Beach Lane, 2014.

Interest level: **Middle** • Lexile measure: **640L**
Biography

Using bits from previously illustrated books as well as new material and scraps from her own memories, Ehlert demonstrates how she became the kind of artist she is. She begins at the beginning, in a childhood filled with opportunities and supplies for making things. A few well-chosen photos show young Lois and her parents, the house she lived in, and even the worn surface of the folding art table she used. She describes where she gets ideas and the kinds of materials she uses. She's messy! Many early able readers have already heard many books read aloud. They may well be familiar with *Chicka Chicka Boom Boom* and other titles. (A spread showing book covers serves as a reminder.) This colorful, relatively easy-to-read biography may send them back to old favorites or forward to read about other children's authors and illustrators while encouraging them to try some art themselves.

Who Was Ben Franklin?

By Dennis Brindell Fradin. Illustrated by John O'Brien. Grosset & Dunlap, 2002.

Interest level: **Middle**
Biography

Ben Franklin was a man of many talents, an excellent subject for this first of a lengthy series of biographies for young readers that are surprisingly good reads. Fradin's engaging narrative is full of information and anecdotes that reveal something about Franklin's personality. The author sensibly begins with an overview explaining this Founding Father's importance and grabs attention with an exciting vignette. After that, he surveys Franklin's childhood, his printing career, his inventions, diplomatic efforts, and participation in the beginnings of our country. Lively black-and-white illustrations interrupt and surround the text, often detailing and explaining things described. This wildly popular series, written by a variety of authors, now profiles people as disparate as Steve Jobs, J. K. Rowling, Louis Armstrong, King Tut, and Bruce Lee. The one hundredth title will appear in 2015. Cover caricatures and a small trim size add to the appeal. A new spinoff is the What Was? series.

The Boston Tea Party

By Russell Freedman. Illustrated by Peter Malone. Holiday House, 2012.

Interest level: **Middle** • Lexile measure: **NC1130L**
Nonfiction

Determined not to pay the hated new tea tax, colonists disguised as Mohawk Indians boarded three British ships in Boston Harbor on December 16, 1773, and threw both chests and tea into the harbor, an opening salvo in the American Revolution. Well known for his stellar nonfiction for older readers, Freedman presents this entry in his long-running Library of American History series in a particularly accessible way. The story of this pivotal event is focused and clearly told, with enough background so that even readers with little prior knowledge of American history can understand what happened and why. The text is set on watercolor paintings that are as accurate and carefully fact-checked as the text. There's appropriate back matter, too, a bibliography, time line, source notes, and index. An exemplary introduction to a writer who has perfected the art of distilling history for young readers so that it's accurate, engaging, and meaningful.

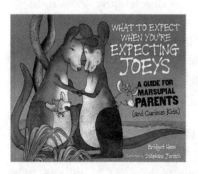

What to Expect When You're Expecting Joeys: A Guide for Marsupial Parents (and Curious Kids)

By Bridget Heos. Illustrated by Stéphane Jorisch. Millbrook Press, 2012.

Interest level: **Middle** • Lexile measure: **660L**
Informational picture book

This tongue-in-cheek introduction to the animal group that includes opossums, kangaroos, koalas, and even Tasmanian devils is framed as questions and answers for expectant parents. The process is unique among mammals, with teeny, tiny "pinkies" spending time in their mother's pouch (or a belly fold), where they nurse and develop further before emerging; the author goes on to describe childhood as well. Painted pen-and-ink sketches of fond marsupial parents and their offspring add to the humor. There's just enough information about where these animals live and what they eat to make readers want to learn more. A glossary and suggestions for further reading and websites add value to this offbeat approach to learning about the natural world that targets exactly the stage young readers most want to know about. They may also enjoy *What to Expect When You're Expecting Larvae* (2011) and *What to Expect When You're Expecting Hatchlings* (2012).

Minn of the Mississippi

By Holling Clancy Holling. Illustrated by Holling Clancy Holling. Houghton Mifflin, 2008 (orig. 1951).

Interest level: **Middle** • Lexile measure: **910L**
Informational Picture Book

Over a period of forty years, Minn, a three-legged snapping turtle, makes her way down the Mississippi River in this leisurely narrative nonfiction picture book. Holling decorates his lengthy text with full-page paintings and carefully labeled marginal drawings. Published in 1951, this Newbery honor book is much loved for its sweeping story and depth of detail about the geography, geology, flora, fauna, and history of the area. Depictions of Native and African Americans are dated but respectful of their contributions to American history and culture. Dialect reflects the speech differences of different parts of the country even at the time of writing. Minn's journey is sometimes calm, sometimes perilous, and always interesting. Similarly, *Paddle to the Sea* (1941) explores the Great Lakes; *Seabird* (1948) sails the seas; *Tree in the Trail* (1942) watches history along the Santa Fe Trail; and a hermit crab called *Pagoo* (1957) wanders the ocean's edges.

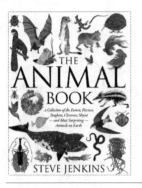

The Animal Book: A Collection of the Fastest, Fiercest, Toughest, Cleverest, Shyest—and Most Surprising—Animals on Earth

By Steve Jenkins. Illustrated by Steve Jenkins. Houghton Mifflin, 2013.

Interest level: **Younger** • Lexile measure: **IG1030L**
Nonfiction

This encyclopedic album is the culmination of twenty years of experience in finding amazing facts and creating realistic cut-and-torn paper illustrations of the animal world. Jenkins has chosen more than three hundred creatures, large and small, exotic and familiar, prehistoric and present-day, for this demonstration of astounding diversity. After a section of definitions, he organizes his examples into chapters on animal families, senses, predators, defenses, extremes, and the story of life. More animal facts appear in the final section, which serves both as index and quick reference. Most spreads have an explanatory paragraph and then a number of examples, each with an animal image and a sentence or two of details set on white background. Each chapter ends with a chart. Jenkins fills out this appealing celebration with a description of his bookmaking process, which is also on his website. For researchers and browsers alike, a treasure.

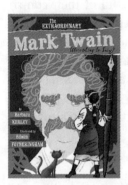

The Extraordinary Mark Twain (According to Susy)

By Barbara Kerley. Illustrated by Edwin Fotheringham. Scholastic, 2010.

Interest level: **Middle** • Lexile measure: **AD1090L**
Informational picture book; Biography

Determined to set the record straight about her famous father, thirteen-year-old Susy Clemens writes her own biography describing his appearance; his character; his good and bad habits; his childhood in Hannibal, Missouri; and good times at her aunt's New York farm. Through Susy's eyes the reader is introduced to a loving father, a man who enjoyed cats and was often distracted from his work, and a philosopher as well as someone who told funny stories. Much of this comes from Susy's original journal. Quotations, misspellings and all, have been printed in script and tipped into the oversized pages. Fotheringham's stylized illustrations add amusing details. Equally engaging biographies by this author-illustrator combination include *What to Do About Alice?: How Alice Roosevelt Broke the Rules, Charmed the World, and Drove Her Father Teddy Crazy!* (2008), *Those Rebels, John and Tom* (2012), and *A Home for Mr. Emerson* (2014).

A Voice of Her Own: The Story of Phillis Wheatley, Slave Poet

By Kathryn Lasky. Illustrated by Paul Lee.
Candlewick Press, 2012 (orig. 2003).

Interest level: **Middle** • Lexile measure: **940L**
Biography

At a slave market in Boston in 1761, a couple named Wheatley bought a seven-year-old girl they named Phillis, for the ship that brought her from Africa. Impressed with her quick mind, they gave her an education unusual for any woman of the time. She began writing poetry that so impressed her owners and others that it was collected and published in England, the first book ever written by a black American woman. In this fictionalized biography Lasky concentrates on Wheatley's younger years, imagining Wheatley's thoughts and feelings, including the overriding image of her mother making an offering to the sun. There are a few short lines from her poems. Lee's acrylic paintings will help young readers envision the historical setting. This reformatted picture book includes the bibliography the first edition lacked. Lasky has written a similar biography of *Eratosthenes, The Librarian Who Measured the Earth* (1994).

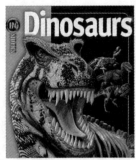

Dinosaurs

By John Long. Simon & Schuster, 2007.

Interest level: **Middle**
Nonfiction

This first volume in the eye-catching Insiders series provides an overview of the field and a more focused look at eleven species. Each spread combines an introductory paragraph with more detailed information in captions explaining parts of the striking computer-generated illustrations. The first half of the book introduces general dinosaur anatomy and behavior, dinosaur evolution, and the work of paleontologists. The change over time of imagined reconstructions of iguanodons demonstrates how scientists continue to reinterpret fossil findings. The In Focus section describes particular species, setting them in time and illustrating most in scenes with vegetation appropriate to the era. Each is compared to the size of a ten-year-old boy. With an embossed cover, striking illustrations, intriguing information, and appropriate comparisons, this series has terrific child appeal. A dozen other titles cover subjects ranging from the human body to knights and castles to the universe and space exploration.

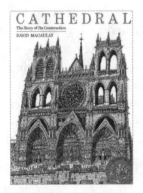

Cathedral: The Story of Its Construction

By David Macaulay. Illustrated by David Macaulay. Houghton Mifflin, 2013 (orig. 1973).

Interest level: **Older** • Lexile measure: **1120L**
Nonfiction

Macaulay chronicles the construction of a Gothic cathedral in an imagined town in the thirteenth century, "the longest, widest, highest, and most beautiful cathedral in all of France." In this, his first book, he uses a fictional narrative to describe the building process, but, as all his later titles, it's his intricately detailed pen-and-ink drawings (newly done with color for this edition) that provide the explanation. He shows the important workers; their equipment, tools, and techniques; and the structure in progress. In the background of spreads showing the rising cathedral is the changing townscape: small houses with thatched roofs and smoke coming out of windows being replaced by larger timbered houses with real chimneys and shingled roofs. This Caldecott honor book was followed by others accurately explaining the design, construction, engineering, and even destruction of major edifices, including *Pyramid* (1975), *Castle* (1977), *Unbuilding* (1980), *Mill* (1983), and *Mosque* (2003).

The New Way Things Work

By David Macaulay and Neil Ardley. Illustrated by David Macaulay. Houghton Mifflin, 1998 (orig. 1988).

Interest level: **Middle** • Lexile measure: **1180L**
Nonfiction

For the curious, mechanically inclined child, this hefty compendium of explanations of the workings of familiar machines and devices and the scientific principles behind them will provide years of reading and rereading. Five chapters present the mechanics of movement, harnessing the elements, working with waves, electricity and automation, and the new digital domain. A final section describes the invention of specific machines. All this is loosely held together by humorous stories about wooly mammoths and features Macaulay's colorful, detailed, and carefully labeled illustrations along with technical writer Ardley's clear explanations. This revision of a popular title adds a whole new chapter on computers and digital systems. Though some details have changed (floppy disks have disappeared, for example), the principles they describe are still valid, and digital systems work the same way. Everyone in the family will enjoy this browser's book.

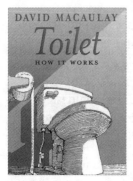

Toilet: How It Works

By David Macaulay and Sheila Keenan. Illustrated by David Macaulay. David Macaulay Studio, 2013.

Interest level: **Younger** • Lexile measure: **AD740L**
Nonfiction; Early reader

This engaging early reader describes the system in our bodies that produces waste products, the toilets in our bathrooms, and the systems that remove and purify waste from our homes. Simple but accurate explanations are presented in a not-too-difficult text. The illustrations will help still-struggling readers and the appeal is universal. The authors describe both home septic and public waste water collection and treatment systems. Illustrations add humor. In one, the long line for a public bathroom includes a dog, a family with a dead fish, and a pregnant woman dubiously eyeing the plumber with a plunger behind her. In another, a big-city apartment wall is cut away to show a tower of kitchen sinks and next-door bathrooms, some in use. End matter offerings include words to know, an index, and suggestions for further research. This winning new series also includes *Castle* (2012), *Jet Plane* (2012), and *Eye* (2013).

Louisa: The Life of Louisa May Alcott

By Yona Zeldis McDonough. Illustrated by Bethanne Andersen. Henry Holt, 2009.

Interest level: **Middle** • Lexile measure: **890L**
Informational picture book; Biography

This straightforward, strikingly illustrated presentation of the nineteenth-century life of the author of *Little Women* describes some events that influenced her and demonstrates parallels and differences from people and events in that famous novel. This has the look of a picture book, with text set in boxes on double-page illustrations, but it's just right for the reader who has fallen in love with the March family and wants to know more about the author. Stylized gouache and pastel illustrations are full of birds and flowers as well as images of Louisa and the family she loved. Appended is a selection of quotations from the author about herself, her life, and her opinions; two poems written in childhood; added facts and dates; and a recipe for New England Apple Slump. McDonough's *Little Author in the Big Woods: A Biography of Laura Ingalls Wilder* (2014) is similar.

Darwin

By Alice B. McGinty. Illustrated by Mary Azarian. Houghton Mifflin, 2009.

Interest level: **Middle** • Lexile measure: **1060L**
Informational picture book; Biography

Looking at this beautifully illustrated biography of the noted naturalist, one might almost imagine opening one of Darwin's own leather-bound journals. Inside, a clear conversational narrative describes his life from childhood, through his famous *Beagle* voyage, to his years of work on his theory of natural selection, and eventual success. This is accompanied by detailed woodcut illustrations, hand-tinted with watercolors, as well as quotations from the naturalist's own writings, presented in script on scraps of yellowed paper. From the fossil on the title page to the Galapagos finch on the closing copyright page, illustrative vignettes sprinkled around the text add to the story. The author emphasizes Darwin's passion for collecting and experimentation. She addresses, but doesn't dwell on, his hesitations to publish his controversial ideas, so at odds with church teachings. Of the many Darwin titles published to mark his anniversary, this is particularly attractive.

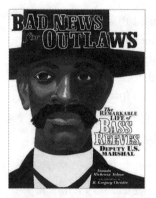

Bad News for Outlaws: The Remarkable Life of Bass Reeves, Deputy U.S. Marshal

By Vaunda Micheaux Nelson. Illustrated by R. Gregory Christie. Carolrhoda Books, 2009.

Interest level: **Middle** • Lexile measure: **860L**
Informational picture book; Biography

Born into slavery, Bass Reeves, a head taller than most men, crack shot, and "honest as the day is long," served for thirty-two years as U.S. marshal in the Oklahoma Indian Territory, until Oklahoma became a state in 1907. Nelson tells his story chronologically in double-page spreads, each with only a paragraph or two of text with picturesque language. "Bass was as right as rain from the boot heels up." Examples of Reeves's tricks and disguises provide humor. At one point he pets a skunk! The narrative is set in boxes on sepia-toned pages or with a background of Christie's oil paintings. The exemplary end matter includes a glossary of western words, a time line, suggestions for further reading, ancillary material, and a selected bibliography. This solid information presented in an entertaining matter introduces an important and relatively unfamiliar figure in frontier and African American history.

Josephine: The Dazzling Life of Josephine Baker

By Patricia Hruby Powell. Illustrated by Christian Robinson. Chronicle Books, 2014.

Interest level: **Younger** • Lexile measure: **790L**
Informational picture book; Biography

In the 1920s, when Josephine Baker set out to conquer the world with her dancing, the United States wasn't ready for an African American dancer but Paris was. She became a star who shone in France not only for her dancing, but also for her contributions as a spy in World War II and her rainbow family of twelve children. The text is a free verse poem, set in acts that chronicle her life from its beginnings (1906–1917) to the difficult but triumphant end (1947–1975). Stylized illustrations, acrylic paintings, are jazzy and wonderful, suggesting her flexible body, her high energy, and, sometimes, the anger underneath. Who can resist Josephine on the streets of Paris with her leopard with its diamond collar? Or Josephine as a stunt pilot looping a heart in the sky? Like its subject, this lengthy picture book biography is a triumph.

Octopuses! Strange and Wonderful

By Laurence Pringle. Illustrated by Meryl Henderson. Boyds Mills Press, 2015.

Interest level: **Younger** • Lexile measure: **930L**
Nonfiction

This most recent title in a long-running series introduces the most intelligent invertebrate of all—the octopus. These short-lived, ocean-dwelling cephalopods are shape-changing masters of camouflage, capable of hiding in plain sight or in tiny spaces or in the inky blackness of a cloud they've generated to avoid predators. This is the twelfth title in Pringle's Strange and Wonderful series, books that introduce curious creatures with a smoothly written narrative and lifelike, accurate watercolor illustrations that support and enhance the text. From *Alligators and Crocodiles* (2009), through *Cicadas* (2010), to *Whales* (2012), and to *Scorpions* (2013), the author has chosen creatures with particular appeal for young readers and provided enough information for enthusiasts as well as helpful back matter, including suggestions for further research. For readers who prefer a straight narrative to exposition or collections of facts, these are ideal invitations to explore the natural world.

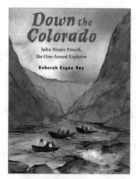

Down the Colorado: John Wesley Powell, the One-Armed Explorer

By Deborah Kogan Ray. Illustrated by Deborah Kogan Ray. Farrar, Straus, Giroux, 2007.

Interest level: **Middle** • Lexile measure: **NC1070L**
Informational picture book; Biography

In spite of losing an arm in the Civil War, John Wesley Powell continued his lifetime passion to explore the natural world, most notably leading an expedition down the Colorado River, which was the first ever recorded to pass through the Grand Canyon. This picture book biography stands out for its relatively lengthy and well-crafted story. After briefly covering his childhood and Civil War service, the author concentrates on the Colorado expedition, emphasizing its danger and difficulty. Suspense is heightened by the use of double-page spreads where the reader sees small boats and churning rapids and, worse, Powell clinging to the rock face high above the river. Ray's dramatic paintings make liberal use of shades of brown and red; their colors blend into the yellowed paper of the text pages. Organized chronologically and topically, the text is quite suitable for middle-grade readers, who will appreciate the map and time line.

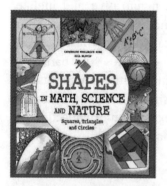

Shapes in Math, Science and Nature: Squares, Triangles and Circles

By Catherine Sheldrick Ross. Illustrated by Bill Slavin. Kids Can Press, 2014.

Interest level: **Middle** • Lexile measure: **970L**
Nonfiction

Shapes in nature, shapes in the world, shapes in math and crafts and games—this compilation of three earlier titles about squares, triangles, and circles invites kids to play with geometry as they think about it. It's attractively designed, an oversized book full of surprising facts and interesting ideas as well as hands-on activities. While the school connections are obvious, this would also interest a child intrigued by facts in general and math in the world. Cheerful pen-and-ink drawings with watercolor wash add energy and interest and occasionally spill out of the page borders, suggesting further possibilities. The many craft and construction suggestions could provide hours of fun. Can you make a cubic bubble? What can you build with reconstituted dried peas and toothpicks? Are chocolate chip cookies better as balls or disks?

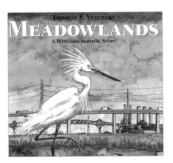

Meadowlands: A Wetlands Survival Story

By Thomas F. Yezerski. Illustrated by Thomas F. Yezerski. Farrar, Straus, Giroux, 2011.

Interest level: **Middle** • Lexile measure: **AD1020L**
Informational picture book

A surprising number of plants and animals survive and even thrive in urban environments. This charming history of a once-trashed wetlands near New York City documents the destruction and resurrection of a natural area known as the Meadowlands. A relatively challenging text describes human use from as long ago as the time of the Lenni Lenape, the mid-twentieth-century toxic wasteland, and subsequent development. Ecosystem restoration happened largely naturally in the remaining protected area of wetlands. The author-illustrator's watercolors show the story, bordered by tiny related images. Clearly identified, these intriguing details will keep readers' attention. They show not only plants and animals to be found in this natural world, but also the works of humans, from bits of trash in the dump to the vehicles that pass by daily. Readers will not need to live in the area to be heartened by the story.

Chapter 13

Humor

H UMOR MAY BE THE MOST DIFFICULT THING TO
write. It can also be the most difficult category
for a parent or other advisor to find just the
right book to recommend. What one person
finds funny, another thinks is dumb, or just
doesn't get. Dav Pilkey's Captain Underpants (a
series that didn't make it into this selection) appeals mightily to
second-grade boys but not to most adults. Boys and girls in the
early elementary grades enjoy bathroom humor, pratfalls, wacky
characters, melodramatic exaggerations, and knock-knock jokes.
Eventually they come to appreciate satire and language play
(though some may have enjoyed those all along). There is humor
in many of the titles annotated throughout this book; the ones in
this section are particularly good suggestions—I hope!—for the
child who is looking for a funny book.

Mr. Popper's Penguins

By Richard and Florence Atwater. Illustrated by Robert Lawson. Little, Brown, 2011 (orig. 1938).

Interest level: **Middle** • Lexile measure: **910L**
Fiction

When his polar-exploring hero Admiral Drake sends Mr. Popper a penguin, the Minnesota house painter is thrilled. He names the bird Captain Cook, keeps it in his refrigerator, acquires a mate he calls Greta, and then puts the pair and their ten children in his basement before training them to march and dance and taking them on tour across the country. The details of this seventy-five-year-old Newbery honor book are dated, of course, but the humor is not. Mr. and Mrs. Popper will do anything to make their penguins comfortable: drill holes in the refrigerator door, turn off the heat in the winter, and install a freezing plant and swimming pool for them in the basement. Traveling with a troupe of penguins is not easy, and the authors get plenty of mileage out of the animals' antics. Lawson's illustrations add to the hilarity.

Flat Stanley

By Jeff Brown. Illustrated by Tomi Ungerer. Harper & Row, 1964.

Interest level: **Younger**
Fantasy; Adventure

Flattened by a bulletin board that fell in his bedroom, Stanley finds many advantages in his new shape. He gets mailed to California and captures art thieves. This is the first of a long series of titles describing Stanley's adventures: five more Lambchop family stories written by the original author, and twelve, so far, in the Flat Stanley's Worldwide Adventures series written by Sara Pennypacker and, more recently, Josh Greenhut. Ungerer was the original illustrator; his color-washed drawings added sophistication. Since 2009 all titles have been illustrated or reillustrated by Macky Pamintuan. He has also provided the art for spinoff I Can Read titles and a picture book version. These look more like animated cartoons and will be the ones familiar to the many thousands of elementary-school students who have participated in Flat Stanley projects over the years. But the Ungerer illustrations are classy and worth the effort to find.

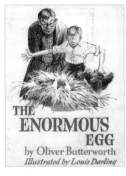

The Enormous Egg

By Oliver Butterworth. Illustrated by Louis Darling. Little, Brown, 1956.

Interest level: **Older** • Lexile measure: **900L**
Fantasy

Nate Twitchell tells about the dinosaur that hatched from an egg from one of his family's hens: how he raised the animal as a pet in Freedom, New Hampshire, and then went with him to Washington, D.C., to the Smithsonian Museum and the National Zoo. The story has been so popular that there is now a statue of the triceratops he called Uncle Beazley in Washington's National Zoo. Nathan is twelve but seems young. The cultural setting is dated—especially in its gender roles—but the underlying story of a boy and his unusual pet is just as appealing as it was sixty years ago. It's clear about the triceratops's needs; just satisfying its enormous appetite becomes a major issue. It's also funny and just suspenseful enough to make a very satisfying read.

How to Train Your Dragon

By Cressida Cowell. Little, Brown, 2004.

Interest level: **Middle** • Lexile measure: **990L**
Fantasy

Scrawny son of the tribal chief, Hiccup Horrendous Haddock III has little hope of passing the Dragon Initiation Program, and even less when the dragon he captures is toothless. But his cleverness saves the day when two ancient Sea Dragons come ashore on the Island of Berk. This send-up of traditional hero tales has ample portions of bathroom humor, caricatured bad guys, and amoral dragons who like old jokes. Hiccup's nickname is Useless, but, of course, his ability to speak dragon—a language proscribed by his father, Stoick the Vast—turns out to be immensely useful. Scribbles and scrawls characterize the drawings. This purports to be a training manual replacing an earlier volume, which suggested that dragons could be trained only by yelling at them. Underneath the kid-pleasing slapstick is a well-constructed story of a boy and his dragon guaranteed to make readers laugh. First of a long series.

The BFG

By Roald Dahl. Illustrated by Quentin Blake. Farrar, Straus, Giroux, 1982.

Interest level: **Middle** • Lexile measure: **720L**
Fantasy

Orphaned Sophie spies a big, friendly giant in the middle of the night. Caught on his nightly dream-delivering rounds, he takes her to his home. But other giants are not so friendly; they snatch children in their sleep. Sophie and the BFG concoct a plan to capture and imprison his nine human-eating neighbors. Blake's illustrations show a grandfatherly gentleman with enormous ears and a sweet smile, a most lovable giant, especially in contrast to his neighbors Bloodbottler, Fleshlumpeater, Childchewer, and others. The BFG mixes up his words constantly, makes up new meanings, and creates glorious puns. "I cannot be helping it if I sometimes is saying things a little squiggly," he explains. "There never was any schools to teach me talking." The language play is the best thing about this delightfully preposterous story that involves the Queen of England before it resolves.

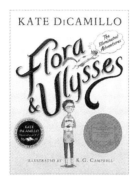

Flora & Ulysses: The Illuminated Adventures

By Kate DiCamillo. Illustrated by K. G. Campbell. Candlewick Press, 2013.

Interest level: **Middle** • Lexile measure: **520L**
Fantasy

After being nearly swallowed by a vacuum cleaner, a squirrel develops superhero powers and undying affection for Flora, the cynical ten-year-old who saved his life with CPR. Together, squirrel and girl try to avoid her mother's efforts to terminate him and direct her daughter toward more "normal" preoccupations. Ulysses writes messages on her mother's typewriter. He vanquishes an attack cat and escapes a kidnapping. The two meet William Spiver, a lonely boy with an immense vocabulary temporarily staying with his Great-Aunt Tootie in the house next door, and the widowed Dr. Meescham, also lonely, who lives next door to Flora's father. One implausible event after another is related in a combination of serious narrative and graphic panels that add up to genuine humor and a surprisingly realistic and poignant story of loss and recovery.

By the Great Horn Spoon!

By Sid Fleischman. Illustrated by Eric Von Schmidt. Little, Brown, 1992 (orig. 1963).

Interest level: **Older** • Lexile measure: **730L**
Historical fiction; Adventure

In 1849, twelve-year-old Jack Flagg and his Aunt Arabella's capable butler, Praiseworthy, sail from Boston to California hoping to find enough gold to save the Flagg family home. With humor and heaps of local color, Fleischman weaves a tall tale about gold prospectors that includes a scoundrel named Cut-Eye Higgins, a race at sea, grizzly bears, a bushel of neckties, a patently unfair fight, and a surprise happy ending. This is the first of a loosely connected series of tales about California history, including *Bandit's Moon* (1998), in which a girl joins a band of outlaws, and *The Giant*

Rat of Sumatra: or, Pirates Galore (2005), in which the Boston boy takes up ranching. Humor, exaggeration, and barely believable escapades characterize all of Fleischman's work, but the good guys (and gals) are also ethical and compassionate.

The Whipping Boy

By Sid Fleischman. Illustrated by Peter Sís.
Greenwillow Books, 1986.

Interest level: **Middle** • Lexile measure: **570L**
Adventure

When Prince Brat misbehaves, as he often does, a street brat named Jemmy is called in for a whipping. When the prince runs away, he insists that Jemmy come too, and when both are captured by famous highwaymen, Jemmy stands in for the prince in a different way and engineers their escape. First they flee through a deep dark forest and meet a bear; then they ride in a hot potato man's cart; finally, there's a suspenseful chase through sewers. Cutwater and Hold-Your-Nose-Billy are as dastardly as you might hope for without actually being violent, and there's also a dancing bear. Set in an unspecified medieval time and place, this rollicking adventure is funny from start to satisfying finish. Sís's intricate pen-and-ink illustrations are an added attraction. This won a Newbery Medal nearly thirty years ago, but its humor is timeless.

Rotten Ralph Helps Out

By Jack Gantos. Illustrated by Nicole Rubel.
Farrar, Straus, Giroux, 2012 (orig. 2001).

Interest level: **Younger** • Lexile measure: **430L**
Early reader

When Sarah tries to create a school project about Egypt, her badly behaved cat, Rotten Ralph, is not helpful. Short chapters with helpful illustrations describe a disastrous trip to the library and grand messes with water and sand as well as an inventive solution. There's plenty of humor and some solid information about ancient Egyptian culture, enough to spark curiosity. This is the first in a five-book series of beginning readers starring a duo first introduced to young readers and listeners in a popular picture book string published between 1976 and 2009. The text of the early reader format is often less difficult to read than the picture book text, but the size and shape of this format may be more appealing to young people looking for "real books."

Great-Grandpa's in the Litter Box

By Dan Greenburg. Illustrated by Jack E. Davis. Grosset & Dunlap, 1996.

Interest level: **Younger** • Lexile measure: **570L**
Fantasy

Zack, a ten-year-old magnet for the paranormal, goes to a shelter to get a kitten and comes home with an aging tomcat who claims to be his reincarnated great-grandfather. Grandpa turns up his nose at cat food, preferring herring with sour cream. He smokes cigars, likes his schnapps, and provides the family money in a happy ending. This series, probably aimed at reluctant readers, has also been popular with early eager readers who enjoy the preposterous situations, the general wackiness, and the fact that there are thirty titles. Short sentences, bathroom humor, and snappy dialog add to the appeal. Stylized black-and-white illustrations reinforce the oddball effect. Later books in the series deal with parallel universes, curses, mind reading, out-of-body experiences, time travel, and more.

Bunnicula: A Rabbit-Tale of Mystery

By Deborah and James Howe. Illustrated by Alan Daniel. Atheneum, 1979.

Interest level: **Middle** • Lexile measure: **700L**
Animal fantasy; Mystery

Chester, the family cat, notices that the Monroe's new pet, a baby rabbit found at a showing of *Dracula*, keeps odd hours and sucks the juices out of its food. He puts two and two together: it's a vampire rabbit. None of Chester's efforts to warn the family work so he sets himself to keeping the rabbit from eating. This is an anniversary edition of a title much loved for its clever premise, humor, engaging narrator (the bumbling dog Harold), and interesting vocabulary. The book's popularity has inspired sequels (written by James Howe after his wife's death): *Howliday Inn* (1982), *The Celery Stalks at Midnight* (1983), *Nighty-Nightmare* (1987), *Return to Howliday Inn* (1993), *Bunnicula Strikes Again!* (1999), and *Bunnicula Meets Edgar Allan Crow* (2006) —as well as an animated TV special and even an early reader series.

Earwig and the Witch

By Diana Wynne Jones. Illustrated by Paul O. Zelinsky. Greenwillow Books, 2012.

Interest level: **Middle** • Lexile measure: **760L**
Fantasy

With the help of the witch's black cat, Thomas, Earwig manages to make her new home with Bella Yaga and her sidekick, the Mandrake, as comfortable as was her old home in the orphanage where everyone did exactly as she wished. A solid straightforward plot, engaging characters, and humorous magic mark a posthumously published chapter book that should prepare young readers for years of reading the author's work. There is nothing too scary—the cat and Earwig's friend Custard are frightened but Earwig is not. This "unlovable" character gets to be just what any kid would like to be—ruler of all—but she has to work at it. Zelinsky's delightful line drawings add to the humor of this last story, another fine fantasy by a writer popular with both children and adults.

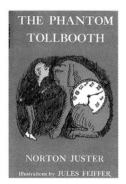

The Phantom Tollbooth

By Norton Juster. Illustrated by Jules Feiffer. Random House, 1961.

Interest level: **Middle** • Lexile measure: **1000L**
Fantasy; Adventure

Bored by everything in life, Milo finds a package in his room that turns out to contain a Phantom Tollbooth, the entrance into amazing adventures in the Kingdom of Wisdom. Accompanied by Tock, a watchdog, and Humbug, a bug, he journeys through Dictionopolis and Digitopolis. The trio rescue the princesses Rhyme and Reason from the Castle in the Air and reunite the kingdom. Milo meets the Whether Man, Faintly Macabre (the not-so-wicked Which), King Azaz the Unabridged, the Mathemagician, the Terrible Trivium, and more. This beloved fantasy, though clearly preaching an appreciation for daily life and schoolwork, is as appealing today as it was fifty years ago, thanks to the humor of both the sophisticated wordplay and the cartoons. Every child has been bored at one time or another, but many have found this tollbooth an entrance to endless entertainment.

Gooney Bird Greene

By Lois Lowry. Illustrated by Middy Thomas. Houghton Mifflin, 2002.

Interest level: **Younger** • Lexile measure: **590L**
Early reader

The new kid at Watertower Elementary School tells the most amazing stories, and they're absolutely true. Gooney Bird Greene, who likes to be right in the center of things, is the center of this laugh-out-loud school story as she tells her classmates how she got her name, how she came from China, how she got her diamond earrings, and how her cat was consumed by a cow. The interesting things that seem to happen to her result from the interesting ways she uses language. The author artfully weaves a number of useful hints about story telling around Gooney Bird's stories. This clever second grader even gets her classmates to tell tales of their own. Five sequels continue Gooney Bird's second-grade year: *Gooney Bird and the Room Mother* (2005), *Gooney Bird the Fabulous* (2007), *Gooney Bird Is So Absurd* (2009), *Gooney Bird on the Map* (2011), and *Gooney Bird and All Her Charms* (2014).

The Birthday Ball

By Lois Lowry. Illustrated by Jules Feiffer. Houghton Mifflin, 2010.

Interest level: **Middle** • Lexile measure: **870L**
Fairy tales, original

At her sixteenth birthday bash, bored Princess Patricia Priscilla will have to choose among three deplorably disgusting suitors, Prince Percival of Pustula, Duke Desmond of Dyspepsia, and the conjoined Counts of Coagulatia. But before she has to make her choice, she enjoys herself for a few days, sneaking out into the village disguised as a peasant, enrolling in school, and doing so well she charms the handsome schoolmaster. The romantic outcome is predictable, but the exaggeration and wordplay along the way will please any reader. Lowry's language delights. The egalitarian princess can't help addressing her cat in rhymes: "No need . . . to be surreptitious, Delicious." The Conjoint Counts, one (two?) of her suitors, delight in bathroom jokes. Triplet serving girls sing about the supper. This delightful spoof on traditional tales is illustrated with Feiffer's humorous caricatures.

The Pushcart War

By Jean Merrill. Illustrated by Ronni Solbert.
New York Review of Books, 2014 (orig. 1964).

Interest level: **Older** • Lexile measure: **1020L**
Historical fantasy

After traffic became nightmarish in New York City because of the volume of trucks and a Mammoth Moving truck driver who ran down the pushcart of a flower peddler in a fit of road rage, street vendors fought back with pea shooters and peace marches. Writing as if she were a historian, and setting her tale in what was then the future, Merrill looks back from 1986 to events twelve years earlier. This children's classic has worn well. It's fun, funny, and relevant today. At one point Old Anna, the apple peddler, says pushcarts aren't the menace, "It is plastic bags!" Children play a significant part in the battle. This fifty-year-old story about politics, the use of power, justice and injustice, and civil disobedience is a thought-provoking read for an able third- or fourth-grade student.

Doctor Proctor's Fart Powder

By Jo Nesbø. Illustrated by Mike Lowery. Aladdin, 2010.

Interest level: **Middle** • Lexile measure: **830L**
Fantasy

In Oslo, Norway, Lisa and her new neighbor, Nilly, befriend an eccentric inventor whose fart powder makes enormous but scent-free blasts and offers the possibility of sending people into space without space ships. But down the street live bullies Trym and Truls whose greedy father convinces the police that Nilly and Dr. Proctor should be jailed and has his sons steal the invention. The fast-paced plot includes an escape through Oslo's sewers, a hungry anaconda, an Independence Day celebration, and plenty of explosions. This child-pleasing title, sure to appeal to fans of Roald Dahl and Dav Pilkey, is the first of a series by Norway's most famous crime writer. Sequels published in this country include *Bubble in the Bathtub* (2011), *Who Cut the Cheese?* (2012), and *The Magical Fruit* (2013).

The Best Christmas Pageant Ever

By Barbara Robinson. Illustrated by Judith Gwyn Brown. Harper & Row, 1972.

Interest level: **Older** • Lexile measure: **930L**
Fiction

When "the worst kids in the history of the world" decide to take part in the annual Christmas pageant, their contributions are memorable. The six Herdman siblings, an uneducated, unsupervised family of delinquents, discover the Christmas story. Unlike the narrator and his friends who've acted their parts unquestioningly for years, these ruffians want to know more. How could people let a pregnant woman sleep in a stable? Why didn't Mary get to name her own baby? What kind of "cheap king" gives oil as a present? The children's questions are thought provoking, and their antics still amuse. This is funny any time of year. First published as a magazine story and later as a book, this has been the basis for plays, a TV movie, and a picture book that no longer conveys the more serious theme. Sequels include *The Best School Year Ever* (1994) and *The Best Halloween Ever* (2004).

Sideways Stories from Wayside School

By Louis Sachar. Illustrated by Adam McCauley. HarperCollins, 1998 (orig. 1978).

Interest level: **Middle** • Lexile measure: **460L**
Fiction; Short stories

Loosely connected but self-contained chapters describe the students and teachers in the classroom on the thirtieth story of Wayside School (built sideways so that it's tall instead of long). These venerable stories will not seem dated to today's readers. They'll be too busy laughing at the teacher who turned into an apple, the student who counted her mosquito bites, and the three inaptly nicknamed Erics, not to mention the dead rat. The wordplay is delightful, and there's also plenty of slapstick and recurring tropes like the horrendous food of the lunch lady, Miss Mush. This has spawned a TV series and four sequels, two with math and logic puzzles: *Wayside School Is Falling Down* (1989), *Wayside School Gets a Little Stranger* (1995), *Sideways Arithmetic from Wayside School* (1989), and *More Sideways Arithmetic from Wayside School* (1994). The first edition was illustrated by Dennis Hockerman.

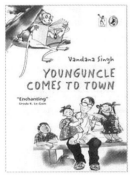

Younguncle Comes to Town
By Vandana Singh. Illustrated by B. M. Kamath. Viking, 2006.

Interest level: **Younger** • Lexile measure: **920L**
Fiction

When Younguncle comes to visit his family in northern India, adventures follow. He solves the railroad station's pickpocket problem; he saves his sister from an unwise marriage; gets the monkeys to help him retrieve the milkman's stolen cow; and restores peace to an animal sanctuary. No one can remember the real name of this Mary Poppins-like character, but Younguncle is much loved by his nieces and nephews. The author, a U.S. resident, grew up in India hearing her family's stories of rural life. She has recreated that world for modern readers in both countries. These lively stories are full of local color and include unfamiliar foods, arranged marriages, clear class divisions, wild drivers, and animals in the road. The unfamiliar setting and sophisticated vocabulary will make this challenging for young independent readers, but they'll be rewarded with laugh-out-loud humor and satisfying endings involving comeuppances for the rich and haughty.

Lulu and the Brontosaurus

By Judith Viorst. Illustrated by Lane Smith.
Atheneum, 2010.

Interest level: **Younger** • Lexile measure: **910L**
Fantasy

For her birthday, spoiled Lulu didn't get the bronto-saurus she wanted, so she stomped off to the woods to find one. Not surprisingly, the gigantic dinosaur would rather have Lulu for a pet. Curiously, dino-saurs don't respond to tantrums. They like good manners. And Lulu gets homesick. This tongue-in-cheek story is charmingly presented in a small book with gray-scale drawings done with pencil on textured paper and playful changes of font. The book design will be familiar to young readers who have encountered Leach's designing brilliance in picture books illustrated by Smith, her husband. They're a perfect match for this metafictional text with its exaggerated setup and obvious moral. The reader is given a choice of three different endings, too. Don't be surprised to hear Lulu's song over and over. It's catching. "I'm gonna, gonna get / A bronto-bronto-bronto / Brontosaurus for a pet."

Chapter 14

Compelling Characters

OME CHARACTERS FROM CHILDREN'S LITERA-
ture have taken on lives of their own. Everyone
knows their names. Harry Potter (annotated in
chapter 8) is one example; Peter Rabbit (chapter 7) is another. Many books in this section
also have characters everyone knows. We met
them in our own childhood reading and listening, in movies and
television shows, and in constant references in popular culture.
Paddington Bear, Mary Poppins, Winnie-the-Pooh, Anne of Green
Gables, Pippi Longstocking, and Heidi are world-famous names
from stories that were first published in countries other than the
United States, sometimes in languages other than English. Other
characters in stories that are listed in this chapter are less well
known, but they are so compelling that once readers meet them

they will never forget them. For children who like meeting new and interesting personalities in their reading, these titles will fill the bill.

Little Women

By Louisa May Alcott. Illustrated by Stacy Carson Hubbard. Sterling, 2012 (orig. 1868–1869).

Interest level: **Older** • Lexile measure: **1300L**
Classics

The four March sisters grow up in a world where girls are expected to look forward to being wives and mothers, an era when social position is very important. Tempting as it is to introduce youngsters to Meg, Jo, Beth, and Amy as soon as possible, this much-loved family story is better for experienced readers. Filled with the minutiae of Victorian daily life, including unfamiliar clothes and customs, the action is frequently interrupted by homilies that were customary at the time but are uncommon in today's children's books. And, it's truly sad. Published first as two stories, most editions now combine them. Be sure your copy has all forty-seven chapters; don't settle for an abridged edition with dumbed-down language. Old-fashioned as it is, the book still resonates today. Sequels include *Little Men,* about the school Jo and her husband run, and *Jo's Boys,* about the adult lives of those schoolboys.

A Bear Called Paddington

By Michael Bond. Illustrated by Peggy Fortnum. Houghton Mifflin, 2008, (orig. 1958).

Interest level: **Younger** • Lexile measure: **750L**
Animal fantasy

When Mr. and Mrs. Brown discover a bear in Paddington Station, they find him so endearing that they bring him home to join their family. He proves to be polite, well meaning, good company, and an able shopper. He tends to make messes and to take things literally, grounds for much of the humor. There are now thirteen novels in the main series, each organized into stand-alone chapter adventures. There are also picture books, board books, several TV series, apps, and a forthcoming movie. The original title and most of the subsequent ones have been slightly revised and reset to appear more readable. In this anniversary edition, the line illustrations have been colorized. One of the most familiar characters in all of children's literature, this lovable bear has been commemorated in bronze and sits on the concourse of the Paddington Station of the London Underground today.

The Secret Garden

By Frances Hodgson Burnett. Illustrated by Inga Moore. Candlewick Press, 2008 (orig. 1911).

Interest level: **Middle**
Classics

Sour and spoiled at ten, orphaned Mary Lennox leaves India and comes to live at Misselthwaite Manor in Yorkshire, where, thanks to the friendship of country boy Dickon, she flowers with the flowering of a secret garden. She also discovers her ailing cousin, Colin, and helps him heal, too. This beloved classic has had many iterations. This is a particularly nice edition, oversized and with a highly readable typeface. There are plentiful ink-and-watercolor images of the hundred-room house, gardens, and children, and vignettes of the flowers and animals, all set on thick, creamy paper. With full-page pictures and plenty of vignettes, this is immensely inviting. Don't get an abridged edition; make sure you get the original text with all its glorious description and its crotchety characters. Readers may struggle with the dialect, but it's worth it. This is another story no one forgets.

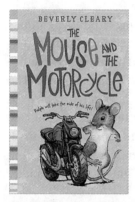

The Mouse and the Motorcycle

By Beverly Cleary. Illustrated by Jacqueline Rogers. HarperCollins, 2014 (orig. 1965).

Interest level: **Younger** • Lexile measure: **860L**
Animal fantasy

When a young hotel guest lines up his model cars and a motorcycle on a bedside table, adventurous Ralph S. Mouse, who loves motorcycles, doesn't think twice. A little bit reckless and quite courageous, he takes off. Before his adventures are over he's befriended a human boy, discovered peanut butter, ventured outside, and performed a heroic deed. Though the story may seem a bit dated, Ralph's enthusiasm will ring true to anyone who has made a toy go by saying "Pb-pb-b-b-b." The pace is fast and details are surprisingly realistic and familiar. Sequels include *Runaway Ralph* (1970), in which the fearless mouse escapes to a summer camp but is imprisoned in a cage, and *Ralph S. Mouse* (1982), in which he goes to school and comes home with a fast car. Originally illustrated by Louis Darling and Paul Zelinsky, these were reillustrated in 2006 by Tracy Dockray, and again in 2014.

Bud, Not Buddy

By Christopher Paul Curtis. Delacorte Press, 1999.

Interest level: **Older** • Lexile measure: **950L**
Historical fiction

When his latest foster home placement doesn't work out, ten-year-old Bud Caldwell hits the road to look for the man he thinks might be his father, Herman E. Calloway, performing with a band in Grand Rapids, Michigan, in 1936. This satisfying Newbery Medal winner stars a determined kid with a suitcase full of memories and a burning need to find family. Along the way he meets a variety of memorable characters. His world is the hardscrabble world of the depression era: with Hoovervilles full of men and families with little to eat and no place to go, hostility toward labor organizers, and pervasive prejudice that led to laws against African Americans owning real property or even spending the night in some towns. Bud is fortunate to land with the band family of Herman E. Calloway and the Dusky Devastators of the Depression and to discover the joys of jazz music.

Matilda

By Roald Dahl. Illustrated by Quentin Blake. Viking, 1988.

Interest level: **Middle** • Lexile measure: **840L**
Fantasy

Ignored by her parents and nourished by a friendly librarian, Matilda is already reading and calculating like a much older student when she enters school, where she will need all of her big brainpower to outwit the bullying headmistress, Miss Trunchbull, and restore her teacher Miss Honey's inheritance. The humor of this perennial favorite lies in the small child's ability to outwit powerful grown-ups, first by clever (probably dangerous) tricks and then with a surprising new ability: telekinesis. Matilda's bingo-playing mother and dishonest father as well as the beastly school administrator (eventually revealed as Miss Honey's wicked aunt) are over-the-top awful. Their exaggerated loathsomeness adds to the pleasure readers will take in their downfall, as Matilda does. But Matilda's loving teacher and sensible librarian come off well, and readers will rejoice that Matilda can grow up in their care. Blake's caricatures add to the joy.

Amber Brown Is Not a Crayon

By Paula Danziger. Illustrated by Tony Ross. G. P. Putnam's Sons, 1994.

Interest level: **Younger** • Lexile measure: **720L**
Fiction

Third-grader Amber Brown faces the impending move of her best friend, Justin Daniels, with whom she's shared Oreo cookies since their preschool days.

Justin's father has a new job in Alabama. Justin won't talk about his move. They fight and stop speaking. These natural ways of coping with impending loss can be very painful. Amber describes the days leading up to Justin's move in a first-person, present-tense narrative that's surprisingly upbeat in spite of the pain. Losing a best friend is no fun, but the realistic, fast-paced narrative also shows the ways these two have supported each other. Occasional cartoon-style illustrations are just a bit messy, like this appealing character. This is the first in a series that takes Amber through fourth grade, concentrating mostly on issues surrounding her parents' divorce and mother's remarriage. Danziger completed nine books; Bruce Coville and Elizabeth Levy have added two more titles so far.

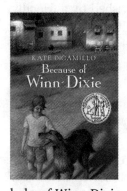

Because of Winn-Dixie

By Kate DiCamillo. Candlewick Press, 2000.

Interest level: **Middle** • Lexile measure: **610L**
Fiction

A stray dog named for the grocery store where India Opal Buloni found her wins the hearts of everyone in the small Florida town where Opal's father has come to preach at the Open Arms Baptist Church. With the help of Winn-Dixie, the ten-year-old find friends in the library, the neighborhood, and the church community, including five-year-old Sweetie Pie Thomas; pinch-faced (and grieving) Amanda Wilson; Miss Franny Block, the librarian; the Dewberry brothers; and Gloria Dump, old and blind, but not a witch. The smiling dog also helps her father come out of his shell and talk about her long-gone mother. Opal tells her tale in a believable Southern voice. With a diverse cast of well-developed, intriguing characters, a convincing setting, and an underlying lesson—that, like Miss Franny's candy, lives contain both sadness and sweet—this Newbery honor book is a special treat.

Harriet the Spy

By Louise Fitzhugh. Illustrated by Louise Fitzhugh. Delacorte Press, 2014 (orig. 1964).

Interest level: **Middle** • Lexile measure: **760L**
Fiction

When her nurse, Ole Golly, leaves, and her class-mates discover and read the notebook in which she has been recording critical truths about them, Harriet M. Welch's sixth-grade year seems to be a disaster, but she recovers by learning about retraction and apologies. Now fifty years old, this story still resonates, showing the ins and outs of class-room friendships, the ability of kids to hurt each other, and the workings of a quirky and imaginative mind. Harriet's family is traditional, but her best friend, Sport, lives with his father; Beth Ellen with her grandmother; and Rachel with only her mother. These relatively privileged New York City children see their play as work; they take it seriously. To modern eyes they seem young, making this particularly suitable for a younger reader. Sequels include *The Long Secret* (1965) and *Sport* (1975). Skip efforts by other authors to resurrect the inimitable Harriet.

Julie of the Wolves

By Jean Craighead George. Illustrated by John Schoenherr. Harper & Row, 1972.

Interest level: **Older** • Lexile measure: **860L**
Fiction

Running away from an arranged marriage, thir-teen-year-old Miyax (Julie) finds herself lost on the Arctic tundra, her survival dependent upon Inuit skills her father had taught her and her ability to communicate with a pack of wolves. Beautifully written by an author who knew and loved that part of the world, this is full of vivid description and animal lore. For most young readers, details of Julie's short-lived marriage and even her final sad statement "the hour of the wolf and the Eskimo is over" disappear in the suspense of the gripping story, the details of learning to communicate with the wolves, and the tools and techniques she uses. More sophisticated readers will appreciate the descriptive language and strong sense of place. Two sequels, *Julie* (1994) and *Julie's Wolf Pack* (1997), have less staying power than this Newbery Medal winner.

Meet Danitra Brown

By Nikki Grimes. Illustrated by Floyd Cooper. Lothrop, Lee & Shepard, 1994.

Interest level: **Younger** • Lexile measure: **NP**
Poetry

A series of poems introduces Zuri Jackson's friend, Danitra Brown, secret sharer, bike rider, story teller, "the most splendiferous girl in town." More character sketch than story, this collection of thirteen poems is beautifully brought to life by Cooper's radiant oil-wash paintings whose shades of brown show the two lively girls and their city surroundings, neighbors, apartments, and activities inside and out. Danitra has "Coke-bottle" glasses and a mind of her own. She wears only purple and plans to win a Nobel Prize for her writing. This title and its sequels look like picture books, but the content is more appropriate for elementary-school readers. In *Danitra Brown Leaves Town* (2005), the poems cover the summer Danitra goes to visit relatives and include more about Zuri. *Danitra Brown Class Clown* (2005), illustrated by E. B. Lewis, extends their friendship through the next school year.

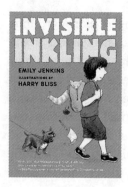

Invisible Inkling

By Emily Jenkins. Illustrated by Harry Bliss. Balzer + Bray, 2011.

Interest level: **Middle** • Lexile measure: **570L**
Fantasy

Since his best friend has moved away, Hank faces fourth grade on his own until he rescues an invisible creature who becomes his new companion. Inkling is a bandapat—a furry, endangered animal from the wilds of Peru, or maybe Ukraine. He's come to Hank's Brooklyn neighborhood because he loves squash. Hank's parents own an ice-cream shop called the Big Round Pumpkin. There's no squash there, but Inkling's mistake is understandable. He stays around eating pizza and helping Hank deal with a bully at school. Hank describes his life so convincingly that readers will easily believe in his imaginary friend. He has a real friend too, Sasha Chin, the girl downstairs, who supports him in his struggles. This funny school and friendship story includes plentiful dialog and engaging gray-scale illustrations. Hank is still in fourth grade in *Dangerous Pumpkins* (2012) and *The Whoopie Pie War* (2013).

Ella Enchanted
By Gail Carson Levine. HarperCollins, 1997.

Interest level: **Middle** • Lexile measure: **670L**
Fantasy

Ella finds it almost impossible to live with the fairy gift she received at her christening, the charm of obedience, which requires her to follow any order, even the horrendous ones given by her odious classmate, Hattie. Worse, Hattie eventually becomes one of her two stepsisters. Ella's playful nature wins her the love of Prince Char, but how can she marry him with such a curse? She'd endanger the kingdom. This reworking of the Cinderella story is funny and clever, fully worked out both in the details of the enchantment and in the more complex trajectory of the fairy tale. This won its first-time author a Newbery honor in 1998 and still reads very enjoyably. Levine has gone on to write numerous other fractured fairy tales including a series of six Princess Tales that are shorter than *Ella*, but similarly charming.

Pippi Longstocking

By Astrid Lindgren. Illustrated by Lauren Child. Translated by Tiina Nunnally. Viking, 2007 (orig. 1950).

Interest level: **Middle** • Lexile measure: **870L**
Fiction

Only nine years old, Pippi Longstocking is nevertheless astonishingly strong and determinedly independent. She leads her better-behaved neighbors, Tommy and Annika, into amazing adventures. This new occupant of Villa Villekulla is a red-headed orphan who claims to have spent her entire previous life at sea with her ship captain father. Unfortunately, he was blown into the ocean. He's left her plenty of money so she can do what she likes, and she certainly does. Her horse lives on her porch; she lifts it down when she's ready to ride. On the day she goes to school, she does nothing but ask rude questions. When burglars visit, she exhausts them with dancing, and when she goes to the circus, she performs. Her exaggerated misbehavior hasn't lost any of its appeal over sixty years. This fresh translation uses more modern language.

Julia Gillian (and the Art of Knowing)

By Alison McGhee. Illustrated by Drazen Kozjan. Scholastic, 2008.

Interest level: **Middle** • Lexile measure: **810L**
Fiction

Nine-year-old Julia Gillian prides herself on her Art of Knowing: her ability to communicate with her dog Bigfoot, and the certainty that the book she doesn't want to read will have an unhappy ending. This first of a trilogy introduces Julia, her school-teaching parents, her large, loving dog, her Minneapolis neighborhood, and her babysitter and friend, Enzo. Her summer has included some frustrations: her parents are busy, the newspaper headlines are depressing, she can't make the claw machine in the nearby hardware store disgorge the meerkat she wants. When she does finish the book about the boy and his dog, it has the unhappy ending she feared. Readers should be prepared for a similar, and well-handled, death in the third of the series. In *Julia Gillian (and the Quest for Joy)* (2009) she's in fifth grade, in *Julia Gillian (and the Dream of a Dog)* (2010) in sixth.

Winnie-the-Pooh

By A. A. Milne. Illustrated by Ernest H. Shepard. Dutton, 1988 (orig. 1926).

Interest level: **Younger** • Lexile measure: **790L**
Classics

Christopher Robin's stuffed animals, Winnie-the-Pooh, Piglet, Eeyore, Owl, Kanga and her baby Roo, and Rabbit (with all his friends and relations) have adventures in the Hundred Acre Wood. These characters are distinctive and memorable: Pooh, who thinks mostly about eating; Owl, who talks about things you're not interested in with words you don't understand; Piglet, who would like to be bigger and better; Eeyore, who always sees the worst of things, and Kanga, the consummate mother. This title was soon followed by *The House at Pooh Corner,* in which bouncy Tigger joins the crew and Christopher Robin, now going to school, pulls away. Both books are decorated with Shepard's black-and-white line drawings, to which gentle color has been added in some editions. This favorite read-aloud book is likely to become a repeated read-alone for children who love to read.

Anne of Green Gables

By L. M. Montgomery. Aladdin, 2014 (orig. 1908).

Interest level: **Middle** • Lexile measure: **990L**
Classics

Red-haired Anne Shirley, brought by mistake from an orphanage to the Prince Edward Island farm of siblings Matthew and Marilla Cuthbert, who needed a boy, wins their hearts with her positive, imaginative approach to the world. This beloved story follows Anne from the age of eleven, when she arrived, through her years in the local school, her year at Queen's Academy, where she gets her teaching license (at sixteen), and Matthew's death. It has spawned sequels that carry her well into her forties, plays, movies, and TV series. The flowery prose is full of description of the landscape, which the author must have loved as much as Anne does. There are various versions available; this is the most recent hardcover publication. Sequels about Anne herself include: *Anne of Avonlea* (1909), *Anne of the Island* (1915), *Anne of Windy Poplars* (1936), *Anne's House of Dreams* (1917), and *Anne of Ingleside* (1939).

Clementine: Friend of the Week

By Sara Pennypacker. Illustrated by Marla Frazee.
Hyperion, 2006.

Interest level: **Younger** • Lexile measure: **790L**
Fiction

Third-grader Clementine doesn't understand why her teacher is always saying, "Pay attention!" This lively, distractible child pays attention to everything. But, perhaps it was because she was a little bit angry at her sometime best friend, Margaret, that she "helped" her cut her hair off. And, because a clementine is a fruit, she thinks it only fair to give her little brother vegetable names such as "Spinach" and "Rutabaga." Clementine's first-person voice is spot-on, and Frazee's illustrations fit perfectly. Much of this is laugh-out-loud funny. They live in the basement apartment of the building her father manages; her artist mother works at home. Her parents' love for their lively, impulsive, original child shines through and readers love her, too. Six equally funny sequels complete this irresistible series, following Clementine to the end of third grade and the birth of the family's new baby.

Cartwheeling in Thunderstorms

By Katherine Rundell. Simon & Schuster, 2014.

Interest level: **Middle** • Lexile measure: **720L**
Fiction

Growing up untamed on a Zimbabwean farm, Wilhelmina (Will) loves life and the world around her. But when her father's death leaves her orphaned and the farm owner's new wife sends her to boarding school in England, it will take all her courage to survive. Independent, determined, skilled in all things farm-related but unschooled, Will is wild and wonderful, an unforgettable character you can't help loving—even the monkeys do. Just as memorable is the Zimbabwean farm setting the author lovingly details. This old-fashioned story has a plot right out of the nineteenth century, but it's also a grand and relatively modern survival story. Not only does Will run wild on the farm; she runs away in London, escaping the cruelty of her classmates. But some adults and young people appreciate her honesty and bravery. Thankfully, Will emerges untamed, with her character intact.

Maniac Magee: A Novel

By Jerry Spinelli. Little, Brown, 1990.

Interest level: **Middle** • Lexile measure: **820L**
Fantasy

Larger-than-life Jeffrey "Maniac" Magee, orphaned by a train accident, runs from an unhappy foster home to find a new one, first with Amanda Beale and her family, then with Grayson, an aging minor league baseball player. When Grayson dies, he tries living with the buffalo in the zoo, the bigoted and fearful MacNabs, and the Pickwells who take everybody in, before he returns to the Beales again. Along the way, in homes of blacks and whites, the race-blind eleven-year-old tries to contribute to racial harmony; he's not always successful. However the book ends happily and optimistically when his running companion, Mars Bar, rescues one of the MacNab twins from the railroad trestle that Maniac, who can do almost anything, can't face. This Newbery Medal–winning fantasy is set in the realistic world of a small, racially polarized Pennsylvania town on the Schuylkill River.

Heidi

By Johanna Spyri. Illustrated by Cecil Leslie.
Translated by Eileen Hall 1956. Puffin, 2009
(orig. 1880).

Interest level: **Older** • Lexile measure: **960L**
Classics

Five-year-old Heidi is brought to live with her grandfather, the reclusive Alm-Uncle, in his remote Alpine cottage. Her delight in that mountain world is so contagious that generations of children have fallen in love with her and with the Alps, at least as Spyri, who grew up there, described it. Alas, Heidi's aunt takes her away from this happy home to be the companion for Clara, an invalid in Frankfurt. Heidi is so desperately unhappy that she is sent back. Clara comes to visit and is miraculously cured. The extensive discussion of God's will and ways may surprise modern readers, but they'll be charmed by Heidi's natural exuberance and by the beauty of the setting. Many readers prefer the out-of-print Helen Dole translation illustrated by Leonard Weisgard, but there are two recent editions of this translation: this paperback, with an introduction by Eva Ibbotson, and a hardcover (2014) in the Puffin in Bloom series.

Mary Poppins

By P. L. Travers. Illustrated by Mary Shepard.
Harcourt, 2006 (orig. 1934; rev. 1981).

Interest level: **Middle** • Lexile measure: **830L**
Classics

The Banks family's new nanny arrives on the east wind and slides up the banister into the hearts of

Jane, Michael, and the baby twins. She takes the older children on expeditions, including a tea party in the air and a midnight trip to the zoo. The original story was revised in 1984, when Travers wrote a new "Bad Tuesday" chapter, describing their trip around the world. Unlike the movie character, the original Mary Poppins is a grumpy older woman. Her magic is left unexplained. Set in an idealized Edwardian England, the story is dated, but, as revised, not objectionable, and the sheer good fun of the episodic adventures remains. This can be found packaged together with Travers's five sequels: *Mary Poppins Comes Back* (1935), *Mary Poppins Opens the Door* (1943), *Mary Poppins in the Park* (1952), *Mary Poppins in Cherry Tree Lane* (1982), and *Mary Poppins and the House Next Door* (1988).

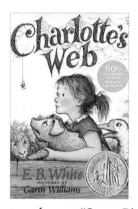

Charlotte's Web

By E. B. White. Illustrated by Garth Williams. HarperCollins, 2012 (orig. 1952).

Interest level: **Middle** • Lexile measure: **680L**
Animal fantasy

The runt of the litter, the young pig Wilbur, was saved first by Fern Arable's love and later by the remarkable friendship of the spider Charlotte, who described him over the course of their summer together as "Some Pig," "Terrific," "Radiant," and "Humble" in her web. This classic animal fantasy can also be read as a story about death as a natural part of life. Death threatens first in the opening, when Fern's father plans to kill Wilbur, and is faced bravely by Charlotte at the end of the book. (The ending is hopeful for readers, because generations of Charlotte's offspring remain in Wilbur's life.) Both the farm setting and the foods (for the pig, the rat, and the people) are lovingly described in language that deserves to be read both aloud and alone, over and over. This anniversary edition has a forward by Kate DiCamillo.

The Blossoming Universe of Violet Diamond

By Brenda Woods. Nancy Paulsen, 2014.

Interest level: **Middle** • Lexile measure: **670L**
Fiction

The summer eleven-year-old Violet expects to be deadly dull turns out to be just the opposite when she finally meets the black grandmother she never knew. Starting with the appealing honey-colored face on the cover, this coming-of-age book directly addresses racial issues and how it feels to be a biracial child. Violet's African American father died before she was born; his mother's anger kept her estranged. Curious, Violet Googles her grandmother and discovers she's a well-known artist with an upcoming show in Seattle. When Violet and her mother go, the first encounter is disastrous, but the grandmother relents. The determined preteen goes to visit her in Los Angeles, meeting other members of the Diamond family, experiencing an all-black world for the first time, and coming to feel that she has filled in parts of the puzzle of her own identity. Moving and affirming.

Chapter 15

Complicated Plots

....

THIS LAST SECTION HIGHLIGHTS BOOKS WITH multiple plot strands; mysteries that encourage readers to observe and make connections along with the protagonist; and fantasies and adventures with an extra layer of meaning that will keep readers thinking long after the action is over. Sometimes the narrative structure is complicated, with alternating narrators or stories within stories. These are appropriate titles for children with more reading experience, boys and girls who read without conscious effort, and who not only visualize the action, characters, and setting, but have room in their minds to think about what has happened in a story and what it means. These titles range from relatively easy reads, like the Cam Jansen series, to the multilayered constructions of Elaine

Konigsburg and Ellen Raskin. Many of them are well suited for repeated rereadings, and some have considerable appeal for adults as well.

Cam Jansen: The Mystery of the Stolen Diamonds

By David A. Adler. Illustrated by Susanna Natti. Puffin, 2004 (orig. 1980).

Interest level: **Middle** • Lexile measure: **420L**
Mystery

Cam Jansen's photographic memory helps her identify the real thieves in a jewelry store robbery. This is the first of a long series of short mysteries starring the fifth grader and her friend, Eric. These challenge young readers to discover the clues Cam notices. Cam may be too successful to be realistic, but judging by her many adult fans, young mystery readers have gobbled these stories up and never forgotten them. This adventure could be scary: Cam ends up in an abandoned house with Eric's baby brother and three jewel thieves. Luckily, sensible Eric has gone for the police; all ends well. Cam and Eric often go off on their own in early titles; later, they're less likely to put themselves into dangerous situations. In 1998, Adler added an early reader spin-off, the Young Cam Jansen series, with less complex stories. Stick to the originals.

The Strange Case of Origami Yoda

By Tom Angleberger. Illustrated by Tom Angleberger. Amulet Books, 2010.

Interest level: **Middle** • Lexile measure: **760L**
Fiction

Trying to figure out how to navigate the sixth-grade social world, Tommy has his friends contribute chapters about their experiences with their clueless classmate Dwight's origami Yoda finger puppet who seems to be able to reveal truths and the future. The hand-done-and-illustrated design contributes to the convincingly sixth-grade approach. This entertaining school story has been so successful that it has been followed by five sequels following most of the same characters through the seventh grade and their school's experiment with standardized test prep programs: *Darth Paper Strikes Back* (2011), *The Secret of the Fortune Wookiee* (2012), *The Surprise Attack of Jabba the Puppett* (2013), *Princess Labelmaker to the Rescue!* (2014), and *Emperor Pickletine Rides the Bus* (2014). The boy-girl relationships are age appropriate, and the series has been popular with early able readers in younger grades who connect with the public school setting and enjoy the lively humor.

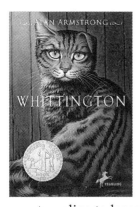

Whittington

By Alan Armstrong. Illustrated by S. D. Schindler. Random House, 2005.

Interest level: **Middle** • Lexile measure: **760L**
Historical fantasy; Animal fantasy

A barn cat, descended from one that supposedly made Dick Whittington's fortune in England, tells the story of that fourteenth-century merchant to an audience of rescued animals and two children, one struggling to learn to read. This is a charming combination of historical fiction and modern-day story, with a few talking animals for good measure. The framing narrative is set in the barn, where Bernie, a gas station owner, keeps a pair of horses, a duck, a rooster, bantam hens, and other animals no one else wants. The twenty-first-century Whittington, the feline story teller, finds a home there, too. The fact that Bernie's grandchildren, frequent visitors, can understand and speak with the animals just as Whittington communicated with his cat in the Middle Ages is taken for granted. The history, the natural history, and Ben's dyslexic efforts are all depicted accurately and entertainingly in this Newbery honor book.

Chasing Vermeer

By Blue Balliett. Illustrated by Brett Helquist.
Scholastic, 2004.

Interest level: **Middle** • Lexile measure: **770L**
Mystery

Outsiders Petra Andalee and Calder Pillay discover a shared interest in coincidence and patterns and become involved in a mystery involving a stolen Vermeer painting and questionable art attribution as part of their sixth-grade studies. With pentimento clues in all the illustrations, letters to decode, a missing friend, suspicious strangers, and plenty of red herrings, this ingenious puzzle is sure to appeal to fans of *From the Mixed-up Files of Mrs. Basil E. Frankweiler* annotated below. The characters are unique and believable, the setting on the University of Chicago campus unmistakable, and the action apparently random but coming together to form a satisfying pattern. Along the way, readers learn quite a lot about Vermeer's art, and the culminating chase is quite suspenseful. More recent editions have interesting afterwords. Two sequels explore other forms of art: *The Wright 3* (2006) and *The Calder Game* (2008). *Pieces and Players* will appear in 2015.

Alice's Adventures in Wonderland

By Lewis Carroll. Illustrated by Helen Oxenbury.
Candlewick Press, 1999 (orig. 1865).

Interest level: **Middle** • Lexile measure: **950L**
Classics

Alice follows a rabbit down a hole and into a dream world where nothing, not even her size, is certain. She meets remarkable, memorable characters and attends both a mad tea party and a trial in which the characters turn into a pack of cards. Adults may remember this story with Tenniel's original illustrations, or with Disney's. Oxenbury's Alice is much younger, somewhere between five and eight, with long, unruly blond curls and, often, a smile. This edition has been thoughtfully designed to present a classic text to a younger reader. With a larger font and increased leading it looks, and is, more readable. This won England's Kate Greenaway Medal for its illustrations; the prize is deserved. The image of Alice holding the baby who has just become a pig captures the delightful bizarreness of Carroll's classic fantasy. An equally delightful companion is *Alice Through the Looking Glass* (2009).

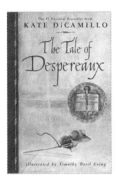

The Tale of Despereaux: Being the Story of a Mouse, a Princess, Some Soup, and a Spool of Thread

By Kate DiCamillo. Illustrated by Timothy Basil Ering. Candlewick Press, 2003.

Interest level: **Middle** • Lexile measure: **670L**
Animal fantasy; Adventure

Because of his father's perfidy and for the sake of his love for the Princess Pea, a tiny but unusually talented mouse faces the dungeon's depths and dangerous rats. At the same time, the rat Roscuro, in love with the light, plans to kidnap the princess to keep her light in the dungeon. He enlists the kitchen maid, Miggery Sow, who dreams of being a princess herself. These stories intertwine in a delightfully old-fashioned quest adventure told with a grand, exaggerated vocabulary and many asides to the reader. The old-fashioned air extends to the book's design, with deckle-edged pages, and the gray-scale illustrations labeled with a line from the story. Funny and fun, with just enough suspense to keep a reader on edge, this won its author her first Newbery Medal.

Under the Egg

By Laura Marx Fitzgerald. Dial Books, 2014.

Interest level: **Middle** • Lexile measure: **790L**
Mystery

Theodora's dying grandfather's last words, "Look under the egg," lead Theo and new friend Bodhi into the puzzle of identifying a painting, possibly a Raphael and possibly stolen, that has been long concealed in his studio, and then finding its proper owner. This mystery, in the tradition of *From the Mixed-up Files of Mrs. Basil E. Frankweiler* and *Chasing Vermeer* (both annotated in this section), is up to date enough to include computer research by the unschooled tech whiz, Bodhi. Thirteen-year-old Theo is very knowledgeable about art history but also practical and competent; she has been running the household for her reclusive mother. There are helpful librarians in the public library and the Center for Jewish History, visits to the Met and to a Holocaust survivor in a retirement community, and the sights and smells of New York City streets. The mystery is solved a bit too conveniently at the end, but the whole is a grand read.

Escape from Mr. Lemoncello's Library

By Chris Grabenstein. Random House, 2013.

Interest level: **Older** • Lexile measure: **720L**
Mystery

Eccentric gamemaker Luigi Lemoncello builds a new library for his town and challenges gamer Kyle Keeley and eleven classmates to a lock-in preview. "Find your way out of the library using only what's in the library" are his instructions. The seventh graders use book clues and references, an electronic learning center, and even a holographic image of Mr. Lemoncello's childhood librarian. The diverse characters are not particularly well developed; the mystery is what matters here. The author uses the hints and tricks and escape hatches of board and video games to enhance his intricate and suspenseful story. Teamwork, patience, and perseverance are rewarded. This homage to Willy Wonka and children's literature in general is a solid, tightly plotted read, full of puzzles to think about, puns to groan at, and references to children's book titles.

A Tangle of Knots
By *Lisa Graff. Philomel, 2013.*

Interest level: **Middle** • Lexile measure: **840L**
Fantasy

Eleven-year-old Cady, whose baking talent is demon-
strated by the included cake recipes, finally finds a
real home in a story as convoluted as the knots tied
by the mysterious man in the gray suit. There are
many story lines, following a disparate set of characters: a man whose lost
suitcase has led to a lifetime of buying suitcases and their contents; an
orphan who can bake just the right cake for anyone; another likeable girl
with no talent and her worthless brother; a famous author whose stroke
renders her speechless; a woman who matches up orphans with adoptive
parents; and a gray-suited man who prophesies cryptically at turning
points. As the story progresses, secrets are revealed and connections made
right up to the magical happy ending. Set in Poughkeepsie, New York, this
truly tangled tale is another treat.

Alvin's Secret Code
By *Clifford B. Hicks. Illustrated by Bill Sokol.
Henry Holt, 1963.*

Interest level: **Middle**
Mystery

The discovery of a scrap of paper with an apparently
meaningless message leads Alvin Fernald and his
friend Shoie Larson into the amazing world of codes
and cryptography and the discovery of buried treasure. This is the second
of ten books about Alvin and his "Magnificent Brain" (the first being *The
Marvelous Inventions of Alvin Fernald,* 1960). These titles are dated in many
ways, but this one still has the best introduction to secret codes there is in
children's fiction. Alvin and Shoie find codes everywhere. They enjoy
decoding the numbers in shoes and on store price tags, they learn something about the history of cryptography, and help solve a historical mystery. There are clear explanations along the way, given by their new friend,

Mr. Link, a spy in World War II. A lengthy appendix includes definitions and examples, practice messages, and instructions for making simple coding tools.

Eight Days of Luke

By Diana Wynne Jones. Greenwillow Books, 1988 (orig. 1975).

Interest level: **Middle**
Fantasy

A boarding school break becomes more interesting when David's imaginary curse conjures up Luke and a host of other characters from Norse mythology and he has to right a long-ago wrong. With a foster family that would make the Dursleys seem pleasant, orphaned David is much in need of a magical friend, but perhaps not one who loves to light fires and make mischief. In order to save his friend from returning to a horrendous prison, David must journey into a fantasy world full of pinball machine players and another where three witches share a single eye. This adventure long predates Harry Potter's, but it will appeal to the same audience. It's an excellent suggestion for a follow-up. The mythological characters are introduced properly in the back matter, and the chatter about cricket can be safely ignored.

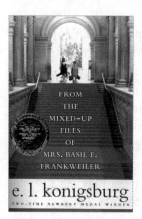

From the Mixed-up Files of Mrs. Basil E. Frankweiler

By E. L. Konigsburg. Illustrated by E. L. Konigsburg. Atheneum, 2002 (orig. 1967).

Interest level: **Older** • Lexile measure: **700L**
Fiction

Claudia and Jamie Kincaid run away from their suburban home to the Metropolitan Museum of Art, where they hide for a week and learn a secret about a new museum acquisition that might be a statue by Michelangelo. This Newbery Medal winner is an all-time favorite. Eleven-year-old Claudia, a good planner, initiates this adventure. She wants to come home different. She picks her nine-year-old brother to join her because he's good with money. They explore the museum, evade detection, and, in their efforts to solve the mystery of the marble angel, visit the formidable Mrs. Frankweiler herself, who turns out to be the narrator. Satisfyingly, they do come home different, inside. Along the way, runaways and readers both learn much about the museum. A perfect book for an able reader.

The View from Saturday
By E. L. Konigsburg. Atheneum, 1996.

Interest level: **Older** • Lexile measure: **870L**
Fiction

Epiphany Middle School sixth graders had never won academic bowl competitions until Mrs. Olinski, returned to teaching after a crippling accident, put together the Souls, an oddly related group who worked well together, practiced diligently, and triumphed at the New York State finals. When asked, their teacher could hardly explain why she chose Noah, who had been best man at the Florida wedding of Ethan's grandfather and Nadia's grandmother, and new student Julian Singh who had invited the three to tea, to form her winning team. Courage and compassion are important themes in this complex book, told in chapters that alternately focus on team members' experiences and on Mrs. Olinski's. There are endless connections, and it's all expertly woven together with challenging language and thought-provoking ideas. Quiz bowl questions and answers are included, too, in this still-popular Newbery Medal winner.

Mrs. Frisby and the Rats of NIMH

By Robert C. O'Brien. Illustrated by Zena Bernstein. Atheneum, 1971.

Interest level: **Middle** • Lexile measure: **790L**
Animal fantasy

When her son Timothy falls sick and Mrs. Frisby, a mouse, seeks help, she's directed to a colony of very special rats who are happy to be of assistance, while planning a larger move of their own. This Newbery Medal–winning classic stands up very well for modern readers in spite of the fact that the protagonist is an adult and the story opens leisurely. The premise of a National Institute of Mental Health experiment on rats and mice is a believable one, and the narrative is so full of convincing details that it is easy to accept the reading, the mechanical abilities, and even the moral qualms of the rat band. The author left room for a sequel; his daughter, Jane Conly, produced two that are reasonable adventures though not as compelling as the original story: *Racso and the Rats of NIMH* (1986) and *R-T, Margaret, and the Rats of NIMH* (1990).

The Westing Game

By Ellen Raskin. Dutton, 2003 (orig. 1978).

Interest level: **Older** • Lexile measure: **750L**
Mystery

Sixteen potential heirs of Samuel W. Westing are asked to solve the mystery of his death. One of them must be the murderer. They are paired up curiously, given some apparently random words as clues, $20,000, and the promise that the solver will be his sole heir. This puzzle mystery won both the Newbery Medal and the Boston Globe-Horn Book Award. Raskin's complicated plot weaves together unique characters. While the focus shifts from one to another, readers most often follow angry Turtle Wexler, unhappy younger sister of the beautiful Angela; Judge J. J. Ford, first African American elected to a judgeship in Illinois; and teenager Christos Theodorakis, whose unidentified illness has progressed to a point where he's confined to a wheelchair and speaks with difficulty. There's plenty of humor. The plot takes countless twists. Solving the puzzle doesn't answer the true question, and readers learn what happens to these characters in the future.

The Invention of Hugo Cabret: A Novel in Words and Pictures

By Brian Selznick. Illustrated by Brian Selznick. Scholastic, 2007.

Interest level: **Middle** • Lexile measure: **820L**
Historical fiction

Hugo Cabret, orphaned and abandoned, lives within the walls of a Paris train station in 1931. He works to keep the clocks running and to repair an automaton he thinks might have a message from his father, but which turns out to have a surprising connection to Georges, the toymaker whose shop is across the way, and to the history of early movies. Caught stealing a part for his project, Hugo goes to work for Georges and meets his granddaughter, Isabelle. Together, the children solve the mystery of the automaton and of Georges's background. This hefty, Caldecott Medal-winning tale is told in both words and pictures. These black-and-white pencil drawings can almost make you believe you are looking at a screen in a darkened room. The adventure, related in the text and both supported and embellished by the images, is suspenseful and the reading experience unforgettable.

The Bad Beginning

By Lemony Snicket. Illustrated by Brett Helquist. HarperCollins, 1999.

Interest level: **Middle** • Lexile measure: **1010L**
Fiction

The three orphaned Baudelaire youngsters, Violet, fourteen; Klaus, twelve; and Sunny, a toddler just beginning to talk, are placed by Mr. Poe, the executor of their parents' estate, with their most local relative, the evil Count Olaf, who hatches a plan to make Violet marry him in order to get their money. This first in the wildly popular Series of Unfortunate Events is a broad spoof on Victorian children's books, though readers won't know that. It's certainly not for the fainthearted or empathetic child, but the humor of the endless misfortunes and the use (and explanation) of interesting vocabulary contribute to the series' appeal. Snicket (Daniel Handler) narrates the books, often addressing the reader directly. The absurdities and endless mystery may keep readers going through the thirteen books in the series plus a series of prequels and some spin-offs.

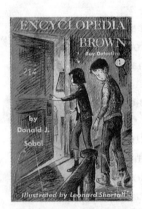

Encyclopedia Brown, Boy Detective

By Donald J. Sobol. Illustrated by Leonard Shortall. Thomas Nelson, 1963.

Interest level: **Middle** • Lexile measure: **560L**
Mystery; Short stories

Ten short examples of splendid detective work of the son of the Idaville police chief, ten-year-old Leroy Brown, whose logical thinking and wide-ranging knowledge have earned him the nickname "Encyclopedia." This first of a series of twenty-nine similar collections of solve-it-yourself mysteries sets the pattern while introducing the boy detective; his partner, Sally Kimball; and his perennial enemy, Bugs Meany. Explanations for Encyclopedia's clever solutions are given at the end of the book; sometimes they depend on outside knowledge, but often they can be deduced through extra-careful reading. This first title was published in 1963, two were numbered fifteen, and number twenty-eight came out in 2012, the year the author died. Throughout the series, the fifth-grade boy detective has not aged and continues to charge only twenty-five cents a day for his services. This series has stood up well, continuing to appeal to readers who enjoy a mental challenge.

Three Times Lucky

By Sheila Turnage. Dial Books, 2012.

Interest level: **Older** • Lexile measure: **560L**
Mystery

In Tupelo Landing, North Carolina, foundling and rising sixth grader Mo LoBeau tells how she and her friend Dale solve a mystery even more serious than the identity of her Upstream Mother. Who murdered their neighbor, Mr. Jesse, and kidnapped Colonel and Miss Lana, the couple who've raised her and run the cafe that feeds most of their small town? The out-of-town detectives who've turned up to investigate the murder don't seem to be solving anything. This satisfying mystery, a Newbery honor book, has plenty of humor, false trails, and local color. The spunky heroine who tells the story washed up in Tupelo in one hurricane and finds out what she's really searching for in another. In *The Ghosts of Tupelo Landing* (2014), Mo and Dale lay the ghost of The Old Tupelo Inn to rest by solving the ghost's murder and allowing her friends to say goodbye.

The Case of the Stolen Sixpence

By Holly Webb. Illustrated by Marion Lindsay. Houghton Mifflin, 2014.

Interest level: **Middle** • Lexile measure: **770L**
Mystery

Aspiring to be a detective like her hero, the Sherlock Holmes-like Gilbert Carrington, Maisie Hitchins solves the mystery of her new puppy's origins and, more importantly, finds the real thief in the butcher shop where her friend George worked until he was sacked for thievery. A dogged, determined girl stars in this series of mysteries for elementary-school readers. Maisie's grandmother runs a boarding house in Victorian London. In this first episode, observant Maisie finds a puppy whose owner had tried to drown him. Thanks to the help of tenant Professor Tobin, she convinces her grandmother to let her keep him. Another tenant, actress Miss Lotte Lane, helps her disguise herself to make her investigations. There are enough interesting characters to provide fodder for many further episodes. Though this is the first to be published in this country, six have appeared in England, where they're very popular.

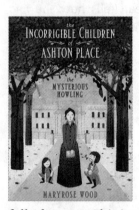

The Mysterious Howling

By Maryrose Wood. Illustrated by Jon Klassen. Balzer + Bray, 2010.

Interest level: **Middle** • Lexile measure: **1000L**
Fantasy

Proud graduate of the Swanburne Academy for Poor Bright Females, fifteen-year-old Miss Penelope Lumley takes a position as governess for three foundlings in a grand English country home full of secrets. This is a tongue-in-cheek version of the traditional Victorian governess story, full of humor, sensible sayings of Agatha Swanburne, and hints about the mysterious origins of Alexander, Beowulf, and Cassiopeia, found running wild in the forest of Ashton Place, and of their governess. These children howl like wolves from time to time. Is someone purposely setting them off? Readers may well want to have all the titles in this planned six-book series at hand before beginning because the endings of *The Hidden Gallery* (2011), *The Unseen Guest* (2012), and *An Interrupted Tale* (2013) are cliff hangers. *The Unmapped Sea* will come out in 2015. So far, complications and clues mount up, but there are plenty of revelations, too.

Finding Books for the Eager Reader

FINDING BOOKS FOR THE EARLY, EAGER READER can be a great joy for parents, caregivers, teachers, and librarians, but it can also be stressful. The titles mentioned in this bibliography represent one person's suggestions, not a definitive or prescriptive list. Some entries are books read by young, eager readers I have known as a teacher, librarian, parent, and grandparent. Some are newer books I think these children would enjoy. And many were suggested by other teachers, librarians, booksellers, and parents who reminded me of wonderful titles, old and new.

Parents I talked to were big fans of school and public librarians who had been helpful in their search for books for their voracious readers. "That's what you've got librarians for, because they can lead you to things you wouldn't normally read," one said. But as well as compliments, I heard sad tales, too: about a librarian (not a children's literature specialist) who recommended a disturbing but wildly popular dystopia, *The Hunger Games,* for a second grader; and a teacher who assigned a series she remembered fondly, Nancy Drew, for her able readers' enrichment. There are so many other possibilities available these days that it shouldn't be necessary to rely on current bestsellers or our own childhood favorites.

What is important is to know the child: to think about his or her emotional maturity, life experience, and reading experience. A beginning reader can be put off by a book that looks too long, whose type is too small, and whose words are unfamiliar. Teachers and librarians often suggest the "rule of thumb" test to help young readers choose suitable books. Read the first page, putting up a finger every time you encounter a word you don't know. If you get to your thumb, you've found five words. Put the book back on the shelf to take out later.

Background knowledge and experience make a huge difference in reading comprehension and reading enjoyment. There is a paradox here: we call on experience to comprehend and enrich our reading, but we read to get experience. Reading a book can help unfamiliar subjects and situations become familiar, but that happens only after children have found some connections.

Some children are frightened by stories of ghosts and witches, or by stories where people get hurt or die, whether fairy tales and fantasy or realistic novels. Others have no problem with scary stories or violence but may not be ready (or their parents may not be ready) for edgy subjects.

A website that can be helpful in checking a suggested book for difficult or painful situations and for potentially inappropriate content is Common Sense Media's Best Books for Kids (www.commonsensemedia.org/book-lists). This independent nonprofit offers (among other things) book reviews by trained and identified reviewers along with reader comments. It evaluates both quality and age appropriateness and provides summaries and other information in sections titled "Parents Need to Know," "Families Can Talk About," and "Content Grid." These entries include user reviews from parents and kids and offer suggestions for alternative titles. About one-third of the titles in this bibliography have been evaluated there.

Parents, caregivers, teachers, and librarians who are not children's literature specialists can look for suggestions in a variety of other places. Many public libraries have created lists of good books for early, eager readers under titles such as "Chapter Books for Early Readers" or "Gentle Fiction for High-Level Readers." Many libraries own more general annotated bibliographies of good books for children, which can be mined for titles that might be suitable for early able readers. Anita Silvey has made a career of suggesting good reading for young people. Anyone advising young readers will certainly want to consult her *100 Best Books for Children: A Parent's Guide to Making the Right Choices for Your Young Reader, Toddler to Preteen* (2005), *Children's Book-a-Day Almanac* (2012), and her website, http://childrensbookalmanac.com. Earlier bibliographies include *The New York Times Parent's Guide to the Best Books for Children: 3rd Edition* (2000), by children's book review editor Eden Ross Lipson, and Kathleen Odean's *Great Books for Girls* (2002) and *Great Books for Boys* (1998). Author Jon Scieszka has good suggestions for titles that have special appeal for boys on his website (www.guysread.com/books), but he includes few annotations. And, finally, Roger Sutton and Martha V. Parravano, the editors of *The Horn Book Magazine*, have collected a fine set of suggestions and advice from colleagues, reviewers, and contributors in *A Family of Readers* (2010).

There are extensive booklists on the American Library Association website, www.ala.org/alsc/booklists. Here you can find lists of Newbery award winners and honor books, longer lists of Notable Books for Children, suggestions for building a home library and for summer reading, lists of graphic novels (a category that also includes graphic nonfiction), books with particular appeal for tweens, and many more developed by the Quicklist Consulting Committee and others. And don't forget that many picture books have challenging text. The Cooperative Children's Book Center at the University of Wisconsin gives the Charlotte Zolotow Award every year for outstanding writing in a picture book. A list that links to annotations of their winners and honor books can be found at http://ccbc.education.wisc.edu. The Society of Children's Book Writers and Illustrators also gives an award for picture book text, as well as awards in other categories. Reading Rockets (www.readingrockets .org/books/awardwinners) is a good place to look for links to children's book awards in general.

Many book review magazines and websites also provide "read-alike" suggestions along with reviews of a specific title. This is especially good for a child who has exhausted a series and wants more like it. The *Kirkus* (www.kirkus.com) site is open to the public. Other databases such as Novelist K-12 and Children's Literature Comprehensive Database may be available through your public library.

Eager young readers with access to the Internet will find that today's authors typically have websites with (usually) up-to-date lists of their titles and links to additional information readers may like to have about the authors, characters, and books they love. A striking example is J. K. Rowling's Pottermore (www.pottermore.com), with its games and videos and additional writings and reader contributions. Most sites are far less professional, but still have appeal for fans. Many of these sites also offer a link for children to write the author with questions and comments.

Some parents have joined or organized book clubs where their reading children can talk about titles with other reading children. Many, many schools and libraries have such groups, and they can enrich a child's reading experience. Any good book discussion reveals how much our own reading experience depends on what we've brought to the book, and such discussions can enrich our understanding of the text. Able readers who have a chance to share their reading experiences with other like-minded readers are especially fortunate. And, like many adults, many children look first to their peers for reading suggestions.

Guiding early, able readers is often more a matter of keeping up than offering direction. Adults who have this privilege will be most successful if they take joy in the process without fretting about each and every jolt along the way. Children have remarkable sense and resilience. They will take from their reading what they need and leave the rest. Enjoy the ride!

Subject Index

A
ability, 219
acting, 61–62
actors and actresses, 147–148
adoption, 56, 59–60, 61–62, 102, 152–153
adventure, 29–30, 52–53, 70, 80,
    81–83, 88–89, 96, 100–101, 106, 109,
    111–114, 118, 120, 124, 125–126,
    130–131, 149, 184–185, 187, 188,
    191, 222. See also quest adventure
Aeneas (Legendary character), 135
Africa, 72–73, 209
Africa, West, 18–19
African Americans, 13, 20–21, 37–38, 68,
    69, 77–78, 134, 137, 173, 178–179,
    200–201, 204, 212, 222–223
African folklore, 34–35
agricultural laborers, 160
Alaska, 203–204
Alaska history (1867–1959), 152–153
Alcott, Louisa May (1832–1888), 176–177
Alps, Swiss (Switzerland), 210
American Library Association (ALA), 229
American poetry, 34–35, 37–38, 39–40, 41
Amistad (Schooner), 148
Ancient Egypt, 188–189
animal fantasy, 79–80, 83

animals. *See also specific animals*
    domestic, 215
    generally, 42–43, 114, 128, 134–135, 172
    mythical, 116–117
    talking, 21–22, 27–28, 79–80, 86,
        119–120, 128–129, 198–199
apartment houses, 26, 208
apprentices, 105
architecture, gothic, 174–175
art, 216, 217–218
art museums, 165, 220–221
artists, 59–60, 165, 168–169
Assateague Island, Virginia, 152
Association for Library Services to Children
    (ALSC), 8
athletes, 209
author websites, 230
authors, 172–173, 176–177
authorship, 75
automobiles, 96–97, 100–101

B
babysitters, 77
background knowledge and experience as
    factor in reading comprehension and
    reading enjoyment, 228–230

231

Baker, Josephine (1906–1975),
  178–179
baking, 219
ballet, 61–62
ballooning, 123
balls (parties), 226
baseball, 151, 157–158
baseball cards, 151
bats, 84, 122
beaches, 28
bears, 198–199, 207
behavior, 98, 196
biography, 86, 165, 172–173, 177, 180
birthdays, 192, 196
blizzards, 126, 158
boarding schools, 108–109, 209
boardinghouses, 225–226
boggarts, 97, 99
book clubs, 230
booklists, 229–230
books and reading, 66–67, 74, 168, 170, 218
Botswana, 72–73
brigands and robbers, 188
Brooklyn (New York, N. Y.), 204–205
brothers, 20, 56
brothers and sisters, 21–22, 24–25, 26–27,
  29–30, 50, 51, 52–53, 58, 59–60, 62,
  88–89, 99, 101, 103, 106, 110, 114,
  153, 223–224
bullies, 76, 193, 204–205

C
California, 160, 187–188
Canada, 97
carpentry, 135–136
castles, 102–103
cathedrals, 174–175
cats, 80–81, 86–87, 91, 102, 188–189,
  190–191, 215
characteristics of "underground readers," 2
characters in literature, 197–198.
  See also specific characters
Charlotte Huck Award, 12
Charlotte Zolotow Award, 229–230
Cherokee Indians, 61
chickens, 21
Children's Literature Comprehensive
  Database, 230
Chincoteague ponies, 152
Chinese Americans, 27, 57, 66–67, 71–72,
  155

Chinese folklore, 121–122
Chinese New Year, 56–57
Christmas, 194
Cinderella (legendary character), 44–45
city and town life, 38, 204
civil rights movements, 161
Clemens, Susy (1872–1896), 172–173
clubs, 68, 80–81
Colorado River (Colo.-Mexico), 180
comets, 120
Common Sense Media's Best Books for Kids,
  228–229
complicated plots, 213–214
composers, 164
concentration camps in the United States,
  157–158
Concord, Massachusetts, 71–72
conduct of life, 192
contests, 56–57, 74, 98, 155, 218, 221,
  222–223
Cooperative Children's Book Center
  (University of Wisconsin), 229
Corfu Island (Greece), 52
Cornwall, Great Britain, 115–116
cousins, 28
cowboys, 23
cows, 59
Crazy Horse (approximately
  1842–1877), 166
crickets, 91
criteria for good books, 7–16
cryptography, 219–220

D
dancers, 178–179
Darwin, Charles (1809–1882), 177
death, 75–76, 211
Denmark, 155–156
detective and mystery stories, 31, 62,
  72–73, 102, 214, 216, 217–218,
  219–221, 222–223, 224, 225–226
diaries, 71, 77–78
Dickinson, Emily (1830–1886), 91–92
dinosaurs, 29–30, 119, 174, 185, 196
disability, 59–60, 199, 221, 222–223
divorce, 48
dogs, 28, 32, 53–54, 67, 90–91, 103,
  154–155, 202, 206–207
dolls, 87, 157, 158–159
domestic animals, 215
Dominican Americans, 48

donkeys, 52
dragons, 82–84, 116–117, 121–122,
    185–186
ducks, 29

E
early reader as subject, 30
eccentrics, 30, 165, 193, 195, 210–211,
    214–215
editorial changes, books reissued with,
    13–14
Egypt, Ancient, 188–189
Egyptian mythology, 138
Ehlert, Lois (1934–), 168–169
elephants, 108
emigration and immigration, 60
emotions, 73
empathy, 69–70
engaging gifted readers, 1–6
England, 59–60, 108–109, 115, 159, 209,
    210–211
England, history, 147
    English folklore, 130–131, 140
    English poetry, 34, 40, 41
enthusiasm for reading, 1–6
escapes, 222
Eskimos, 152–153, 203–204
Europe, 96–97
Excellence in Poetry award, 12
explorers, 180

F
fables, 128–129
fairies, 34, 99, 102, 109
fairy tale characters, 44, 105, 205
fairy tales, 104, 121–122, 129,
    139–140, 217
families, 18–19, 20–21, 24–25, 39–40,
    47, 48, 50–51, 52–57, 58–59, 59–60,
    61, 66, 72, 75, 76, 87, 88, 100–101,
    149–150, 152–153, 154, 156, 157,
    158–159, 160–161, 162, 187, 198,
    201, 206–207, 208, 219
fantasy, 79–80, 83–84, 88, 95–96,
    102–103, 187, 210–211, 216–217
fantasy, animal, 79–80, 83
farm life, 85, 211
fathers, 118, 152–153
fear, 71–72, 206–207
feral children, 226

ferrets as pets, 55
finding books, 227–230
finger puppets, 214–215
Finnish Americans, 153
fire departments, 23–24
fireworks, 108
first day of school, 30–31, 73
flatulence, 193
floods, 59
Florida, 55-56, 202
folklore. *See also* mythology
    Africa, 34-35
    China, 121–122
    England, 130–131, 140
    Germany, 139–140
    Norway, 133
    United States, 134, 139, 141
    Wales, 131
    West Africa, 128
folktales, 127–128
forests and forestry, 89
found objects (art), 34–35
foundlings, 102, 225
foxes, 90
Franklin, Benjamin (1706–1790), 86, 169
freedmen, 178
friendship, 19–21, 22, 27–28, 57, 58, 65,
    66–67, 68, 69, 70, 71–72,
    74–76, 87, 89, 91, 109, 124, 155–156,
    159, 193, 199, 201–202, 203, 204,
    208, 211, 217–218, 221
frogs, 27–28
frontier and pioneer life, 152–153, 156,
    162, 178

G
Galapagos Islands, 167–168
games, 218
gardens, 159, 199
Geisel Award, 8–9
geometry in nature, 180–181
George, Saint (d. 303), 83–84
German folklore, 139–140
ghosts, 137, 147
giant sequoia, 168
giants, 117, 132–133, 186
gifted readers, encouraging, 1–6
girls, 41–42, 187
Globe Theatre (Southwark, London,
    England), 147–148
gods, 113, 117, 132–133, 137–138

gold miners, 152–153
gothic architecture, 174–175
governesses, 226
grandfathers, 52, 60, 61, 154, 155, 210
grandmothers, 58, 98–99
Great Britain
    Cornwall, 115–116
    generally, 167
    Victorian era (1837–1901), 105
    Yorkshire, 199
Great Depression, 160, 200–201
great-grandfathers, 189
Greece, 52
Greek mythology, 124–125, 132,
    137–138, 141–142

H
Hackensack Meadowlands (N.J.), 181
haiku, 38
hamsters, 105–106
Handel, George Frideric (1685–1759), 164
Hawaii, 76
Hercules (Roman mythology), 136
heroes, 112, 116, 117, 130, 135, 136,
    137–138, 139, 140, 209
heroines, 126, 141, 143
Himalaya Mountains, 103–104
Hispanic Americans, 161
historical writings, 145–146
history of the United States. See United
    States history
Holocaust, Jewish (1939–1945), 217–218
homeless persons, 125
homework, 188–189
horror tales, 137
horses, 23, 152
human-animal relationships, 88–89
humans and bats, 122
humor, 43, 183
humorous stories, 22, 23–24, 30, 50, 56,
    59–60, 67, 71, 80, 90–91,
    96–99, 103–104, 118, 184, 185–189,
    190–192, 193, 194–195, 196, 201,
    206, 208, 223–224

I
ice cream parlors, 204–205
identity, 219, 225
illustrators, 168–169
imaginary creatures, 103

imaginary places, 216–217
imaginary playmates, 24–25, 204–205
imagination, 22, 24–25, 49, 75–76
immigrants, 74–75, 157
immigration and emigration, 60
India, 195
Indian territory, 178
Indians of North America. See Indigenous
    peoples of the Americas
Indigenous peoples of the Americas, 61,
    149–150, 166
individuality, 27, 49
internment camps, 154–155
interpersonal relations, 209
invalids, 210
inventors, 169, 193
islands, 92, 152

J
Japanese Americans, 154–155,
    157–158
jealousy, 22
Jesse trees, 135–136
Jesus Christ, 135–136
Jewish life, 157, 160–161

K
Kansas (19th century), 156
kidnapping, 104
kindergarten, 30–31
King Arthur, 100
kings, queens, rulers, etc., 102–103, 116
knights and knighthood, 101,
    125–126
Korean Americans, 75
Krakatoa (Indonesia) eruption of 1883, 123

L
Lakota Indians, 166
Latinos, 48
letters, 74–75
lexicographers, 167
Lexile Framework for Reading, 5
libraries, 218
listening, 82
little people, 88
locomotives, 150
London, England, 104, 105, 198–199, 209
London, England (19th century), 225–226

loss (psychology), 77
lost and found possessions, 29
love, 82
loyalty, 90–91

M
machinery, 175
magic, 29–30, 95–96, 97, 100–102,
    103, 105–106, 108–110, 116, 131,
    190–191
magicians, 122–123
marsupials, 170–171
mathematics, 36–37
mature themes in books, 14–16
medical care, 25
Méliès, Georges (1861–1938), 223
melodrama, 223–224
Mendez, Sylvia (1936–), 161
Mexican Americans, 160
mice, 81, 85–86, 88–89, 91–92, 93–94,
    119–120, 200, 217, 222
middle ages, 125–126, 130–131, 174–175
Minneapolis, Minnesota, 206–207
minotaur (Greek mythology), 130
mischief, 97
missing persons, 114, 125
Mississippi, 165
Mississippi River, 171
mistaken identity, 188
moneymaking projects, 49
monsters, 105, 113
Moomins (characters), 120
motorcycles, 200
mountain life, 210
moving, household, 55–56, 60, 69, 105–106,
    201–202
multiracial families, 28, 56, 96–97,
    212
murder, 225
museums, 116, 185
music, 85–86, 93
mystery and detective stories, 31, 62, 72–
    73, 102, 214, 216, 217–218, 219–221,
    222–223, 224,
    225–226
mythical animals, 116–117
mythology. *See also* folklore
    Egyptian, 138
    Greek, 124–125, 132, 137–138,
        141–142
    Norse, 113, 117, 132–133, 220

    Roman, 135
    Welsh, 112
myths, 127–128

N
nannies, 55, 210–211
Narnia (imaginary place), 107–108
narrative structure, 9–10
National Book Award for Young People's
    Literature, 10–11
National Council of Teachers of English, 12
natural history, 21–22, 167–168
naturalists, 118–119, 154, 177
nature, 36, 38
nature conservation, 181
neighborhoods, 206–207, 217–218
neighbors, 19, 23–24, 26, 56, 57, 69–70
Netherlands, history, 51
New England, 185
New York, New York, 26, 52–53, 80–81,
    90–91, 119, 157, 158, 193, 217–218,
    220–221
Newbery award, 10–11
Nightingale, Florence (1820–1910), 122–
    123
nonfiction books, 11–12
Norse mythology, 113, 117, 132–133, 220
North Carolina, 225
Norway, 103, 193
Norwegian folklore, 133
Notable Books for Children, 229
Novelist K–12, 230
novels in verse, 35, 77
nursery schools, 26–27
nurses, 122–123

O
ocean travel, 88–89
octopuses, 179
Odysseus (Greek mythology),
    142
Ogala Indians, 166
Ojibwa Indians, 149–150
Oklahoma, 178
Oman, 60
Orbis Pictus Award, 12
origami, 214–215
orphans, 62, 103, 105, 116–117, 125, 186,
    190–191, 199, 201, 206, 207–208,
    209, 210, 219, 220, 223–224, 226

outer space, 18
outlaws and robbers, 130–131, 178, 188, 214
owls, 81

P
parallel universes, 104
Paris, France, 90–91, 125
peddlers, 193
penguins, 184
Pensacola, Florida, 55–56
people with disabilities. *See* disability
pets, 29, 35, 67, 184, 196
picture books, 7–9
pigs, 23–24, 85, 211
pioneer and frontier life, 152–153, 156, 162, 178
pirates, 146
play, 147
pleasure, reading for, 3–4
plots, complicated, 213–214
poetry
    American, 34–35, 37–38, 39–40, 41
    English, 34, 40, 41
    generally, 12, 33, 35–36, 37, 39, 41–45, 63, 84, 91–92
    20th century, 41
    world, 39–40, 42
poets, 59, 173
politicians, 185
ponies, 24
Poughkeepsie, New York, 219
Powell, John Wesley (1834–1902), 180
prejudices, 75, 157–158, 209
Prince Edward Island, 207–208
princesses, 102–103, 139–140, 192, 205
printers, 169
prisoners, 116
prodigies, 201
Puerto Rico, 21–22
puppets, 34–35
puzzles, 222–223

Q
queens, kings, rulers, etc., 102–103, 116
quest adventure, 108, 111–112, 114–117, 119–120, 121–122, 124–125, 217, 220

R
rabbits, 82, 90, 190
raccoons, 80
railroad stations, 223
railroads, 150
rats, 222
reading comprehension and reading enjoyment, background knowledge and experience as factor in, 228–230
Reading Rockers, 230
real places and people, 163–164
recluses, 217–218
Redwoods, 168
Reeves, Bass (1838–1910), 178
reincarnation, 189
responsibility, 55
restaurants, 225
robbers and outlaws, 130–131, 178, 188, 214
Robin Hood (legendary character), 130–131
robots, 223
Roget, Peter Mark (1779–1869), 167
roller skating, 22
Roman mythology, 135
roosters, 21
rulers, queens, kings, etc., 102–103, 116
runaways, 200–201, 216
running, 209

S
sailing, 124
school buses, 30–31
school integration in the United States, 161
schools, 26–27, 29, 35, 54, 55–57, 65, 66–70, 71, 73, 74–75, 76, 77–78, 188–189, 191–192, 195, 201–202, 203, 208, 214–215, 221
science, 42–43
science fiction, 106, 113–114
scientists, 169
Scotland, 97
sea creatures, 179
seasons, 36–37, 39
self-confidence, 71–72
self-reliance, 77
September 11 Terrorist Attacks, 2001, 165–166
series, book, 9. *See also specific series*
sex role, 153

sexual subjects, 15
Shakespeare, William (1564–1616), 61–62,
    147–148
shapes, 36, 180–181
shapeshifting, 113
Shirley, Anne (fictitious character), 207–208
short stories, 134–135
Sibert Award, 11–12
silkworms, 75
single-parent families, 48–49, 50, 99, 204
sisters, 27, 37, 48–49, 50–51, 55–56, 61–62,
    63, 160–161, 198
skating, 51
slavery, 134, 148, 173
small town life, 202
social classes, 88–89
Society of Children's Book Writers
    and Illustrators, 230
soldiers, 151
space and time, 118
space exploration, 18, 113–114
spiders, 211
spies, 119, 203
sports, 209
squirrels, 89, 187
statesmen, 169
stepmothers, 156
stereotypes and prejudices, 13–14
stories of the past, 145–146
storytelling, 146, 191–192
superheroes, 187
supernatural, 97, 99, 104, 105, 106, 113,
    137, 189, 220
survival, 62, 81, 89, 92, 118–119, 122,
    203–204
swamps, 80
swans, 93

T

Taiwanese Americans, 56–57
talking animals, 21–22, 27–28, 79–80, 86,
    119–120, 128–129, 198–199
tall tales, 139, 141
teacher-student relationships, 67–68, 221
teachers, 123
technology, 175
teddy bears, 207
Texas history (19th century),
    154
text complexity, 5
theater, 56–57, 147–148

Thebes, Egypt, 122–123
thesaurus of English words and phrases, 167
Theseus (Greek mythology), 130
time travel, 29–30, 100, 122–123, 125–126,
    147–148, 151, 159
tiny people, 79–80, 88
toads, 27–28
toilets, 176
toys, 70, 82, 207
traditional tales, 127–128
transitional books, 17–18
travels and voyages, 90–91, 93–94,
    103–194, 121, 123
tree frogs, 21–22
tree houses, 29–30, 122–123
Tree of Jesse, 135–136
Trojan War, 141–142
trolls, 133
trucks, 193
true stories, 163–164
turtles, 171
Twain, Mark (1835–1910), 172–173
twins, 25, 27

U

uncles, 195
underground readers, 2
United States, folklore from, 134, 139, 141
United States history
    1912, 160–161
    Great Depression - 1929, 160,
        200–201
    1920s, 158–159
    18th century, 86
    19th century, 148, 149–150, 198
    20th century, 161
U.S. Navy, 55–56

V

vacations, 28, 48–49, 124, 149
vampire bats, 122
vampires, 190
Vermeer, Johannes (1632–1675), 216
Vermont, 48
verse, novels in, 35, 77
Vikings, 185–186
visual poetry, 36–37
volcanoes, 123
voyages and travels, 90–91, 93–94,
    103–194, 121, 123

W

Wagner, Honus (1874–1955), 151
war, 193
war on terrorism (2001–2009),
    165–166
Washington, D.C., 185
Washington (state) fiction, 153
Washington (state) history-20th century,
    154–155
Welsh folklore, 131
Welsh mythology, 112
wetland conservation, 181
wetland ecology, 181
Wheatley, Phillis (1753–1784), 173
Whittington, Richard (1354–1423), 215
wild flowers, 34
winter, 42–43
Wisconsin, 54
wishes, 100
witches, 95, 98–99, 102, 107–108, 190–191
wizards, 96, 108–109, 116

wolves, 203–204
women, 143
words, 167
words, new, 67–68
    world poetry, 39–40, 42
World War I (1914–1918), 151–152, 157
World War II (1939–1945)
    concentration camps in the United
        States, 154–155
    generally, 155
    Jews' rescue, 155–156
    United States, 157–158

Y

Yeti, 103–104
Yorkshire, Great Britain, 199

Z

Zimbabwe, 209

Author & Title Index

A

Aardema, Verna, 128
Abel's Island (Steig), 92
The Abominables (Ibbotson), 103–104
The Absent Author (Roy), 31
An Acceptable Time (L'Engle), 106
Adderson, Caroline, 66
Adler, David A., 214
Aesop's Fables (Pinkney), 128–129
Africa Is My Home: A Child of the Amistad (Edinger), 148
Alcott, Louisa May, 15, 198
Alexander, Lloyd, 112
Alice McKinley series, 15
Alice Through the Looking Glass (Carroll), 217
Alice's Adventures in Wonderland (Carroll), 216 217
All About Sam (Lowry), 58–59
All-of-a-Kind Family (Taylor), 160–161
All-of-a-Kind Family Downtown (Taylor), 161
All-of-a-Kind Family Uptown (Taylor), 161
All Stations! Distress (Brown), 166
Allergic to Birthday Parties, Science Projects, and Other Man-Made Catastrophes (Look), 72

Allergic to Camping, Hiking, and Other Natural Disasters (Look), 72
Allergic to Dead Bodies, Funerals, and Other Fatal Circumstances (Look), 72
Allergic to the Great Wall, The Forbidden Palace, and Other Tourist Attractions (Look), 72
Alligators and Crocodiles! Strange and Wonderful (Pringle), 179
Almost Zero (Grimes), 69
Alvarez, Julia, 48
Alvin Ho: Allergic to Girls, School, and Other Scary Things (Look), 71–72
Alvin's Secret Code (Hicks), 219–220
Amber Brown is Not a Crayon (Danziger), 201–202
Amber Was Brave, Essie Was Smart: The Story of Amber and Essie Told Here in Poems and Pictures (Williams), 63
Amelia Bedelia (Parish), 30
America Is under Attack: September 11, 2001: The Day the Towers Fell (Brown), 165–166
American Tall Tales (Osborne), 139
Anastasia Krupnik (Lowry), 58
Andersen, Hans Christian, 129
Anderson, M. T., 164

Angleberger, Tom, 214
The Animal Book: A Collection of the Fastest, Fiercest, Toughest, Cleverest, Shyest– and Most Surprising–Animals on Earth (Jenkins), 172
Anna Hibiscus (Atinuke), 18–19
Anne of Avonlea (Montgomery), 208
Anne of Green Gables (Montgomery), 207–208
Anne of Green Gables series, 15
Anne of Ingleside (Montgomery), 208
Anne of the Island (Montgomery), 208
Anne of Windy Poplars (Montgomery), 208
Anne's House of Dreams (Montgomery), 208
Annika Riz, Math Whiz (Mills), 74
Appelt, Kathi, 80
Ardley, Neil, 175
Armstrong, Alan, 215
Armstrong, Kelley, 113
Arnold, Tedd, 18
Arthur Spiderwick's Field Guide to the Fantastical World Around You Guide (DiTerlizzi and Black), 99
Ashley Bryan's Puppets: Making Something from Everything (Bryan), 34–35
Atinuke, 18
Attaboy, Sam! (Lowry), 59
Atwater, Florence, 184
Atwater, Richard, 184
Averill, Esther, 80
Avi, 81

B
Babbitt, Natalie, 146
Babe: The Gallant Pig (King-Smith), 85
The Bad Beginning (Snicket), 223–224
Bad News for Outlaws: The Remarkable Life of Bass Reeves, Deputy U.S. Marshall (Nelson), 178
Ballet Shoes (Streatfeild), 61–62
Balliett, Blue, 216
Bandit's Moon (Fleischman), 187
Barker, Cicely Mary, 34
Barker, Mary, 4
Barrows, Annie, 19
Baseball Saved Us (Mochizuki), 157–158
Bass, Hester, 165
The Bat-Poet (Jarrell), 84
The Battle of the Labyrinth (Riordan), 125
A Bear Called Paddington (Bond), 198–199

Because of Winn-Dixie (DiCamillo), 202
Beezus and Ramona (Cleary), 50–51
Ben and Me: A New and Astonishing Life of Benjamin Franklin as Written by His Good Mouse, Amos (Lawson), 86
Benny and Penny in the Big No-No! (Hayes), 9
Beowulf: A Hero's Tale Retold (Rumford), 140
The Best Christmas Pageant Ever (Robinson), 194
Best Friends Forever (DiCamillo and McGhee), 22
The Best Halloween Ever (Robinson), 194
The Best School Year Ever (Robinson), 194
Betsy and Tacy Go Downtown (Lovelace), 72
Betsy and Tacy Go over the Big Hill (Lovelace), 72
Betsy Tacy and Tib (Lovelace), 72
Betsy-Tacy (Lovelace), 72
The BFG (Dahl), 186
Bink and Gollie (DiCamillo and McGhee), 22
The Birchbark House (Erdrich), 149–150
Birdsall, Jeanne, 48
The Birthday Ball (Lowry), 192
Birthday Blues (English), 68
Bishop, Rudine Sims, 13
The Black Cauldron (Alexander), 112
Black, Holly, 99
Black Ships Before Troy: The Story of The Iliad (Sutcliff), 141–142
Blackwood, Sage, 96
Blizzard!:The Storm That Changed America (Murphy), 158
A Blossom Promise (Byars), 50
The Blossoming Universe of Violet Diamond (Woods), 212
The Blossoms and the Green Phantom (Byars), 50
The Blossoms Meet the Vulture Lady (Byars), 50
Bo at Ballard Creek (Hill), 152–153
The Boggart and the Monster (Cooper), 97
The Boggart (Cooper), 97
Bond, Michael, 198
The Book of Three (Alexander), 112
The Borrowers Afield (Norton), 88
The Borrowers Afloat (Norton), 88
The Borrowers Aloft (Norton), 88
The Borrowers Avenged (Norton), 88
The Borrowers (Norton), 88
Boston, L. M., 147
The Boston Tea Party (Freedman), 170

The Boxcar Children (Warner), 62
A Boy Called Slow (Bruchac), 166
Boyce, Frank Cottrell, 96, 101
Branford, Anna, 49
Brave Irene (Steig), 126
Bridge to Terabithia (Paterson), 15, 75–76
Brink, Carol Ryrie, 14
Brown, Don, 165–166
Brown, Jeff, 184
Bruchac, Joseph, 166
Bryan, Ashley, 34
Bryant, Jen, 167
Bubble in the Bathtub (Nesbø), 193
Bud, Not Buddy (Curtis), 200–201
Bugs, Bogs, Bats, and Books (Isaacs), 11, 164
Bunnicula: A Rabbit-Tale of Mystery (Howe and Howe), 190
Bunnicula Meets Edgar Allan Crow (Howe), 190
Bunnicula Strikes Again! (Howe), 190
Burnett, Frances Hodgson, 199
Busybody Nora (Hurwitz), 26
Butterworth, Oliver, 185
By the Great Horn Spoon! (Fleischman), 187–188
Byars, Betsy Cromer, 50
Byrd, Robert, 130

C
Caddie Woodlawn (Brink), 14
Caddy Ever After (McKay), 60
Caddy's World (McKay), 60
Calcutt, David, 130
The Calder Game (Balliett), 216
Caleb's Story (MacLachlan), 156
Calvin Coconut: Trouble Magnet (Salisbury), 76
Cam Jansen: The Mystery of the Stolen Diamonds (Adler), 214
Cam Jansen series, 213
Cameron, Ann, 20
Cameron, Eleanor, 113
Campbell, Sarah C., 9
Captain Underpants (Pilkey), 183
Carroll, Lewis, 216
Cartwheeling in Thunderstorms (Rundell), 209
The Case of the Stolen Sixpence (Webb), 225–226
Castle: How It Works (Macauley and Keenan), 175, 176

The Castle of Llyr (Alexander), 112
Cathedral: The Story of Its Construction (Macaulay), 174–175
Cats in the Doll Shop (McDonough), 157
Catwings (Le Guin), 86–87
Catwings Return (Le Guin), 87
The Celery Stalks at Midnight (Howe), 190
Chabon, Michael, 133
Charlie and the Chocolate Factory (Dahl), 98
Charlie and the Great Glass Elevator (Dahl), 98
Charlotte's Web (White), 211
Charmed Life (Jones), 110
Chasing Vermeer (Balliett), 216, 218
Cheng, Andrea, 66
Chickadee (Erdrich), 150
Childhood of Famous Americans series, 11
The Children of Green Knowe (Boston), 147
Children's Book-a-Day Almanac (Silvey), 229
Chimneys of Green Knowe (Boston), 147
Chin, Jason, 167–168
Chitty Chitty Bang Bang: The Magical Car (Fleming), 100–101
Chitty Chitty Bang Bang and the Race Against Time (Boyce), 97
Chitty Chitty Bang Bang Flies Again (Boyce), 96–97
Chitty Chitty Bang Bang Over the Moon (Boyce), 97
Cicadas! Strange and Wonderful (Pringle), 179
Cleary, Beverly, 50, 67, 200
Clementine: Friend of the Week (Pennypacker), 208
Clements, Andrew, 67
Collins, Suzanne, 114
Comet in Moominland (Jansson), 120
The Complete Adventures of Peter Rabbit (Potter), 90
The Complete Book of the Flower Fairies (Barker), 34
Completely Fantastical Edition (DiTerlizzi and Black), 99
Conrad's Fate (Jones), 110
Cooper, Susan, 97, 115, 131, 147
Coral Reefs (Chin), 168
Coraline (Gaiman), 118
Coville, Bruce, 51
Cowell, Cressida, 185
Cox, Judy, 21
Crazy Horse's Vision (Bruchac), 166

Creech, Sharon, 35
The Cricket in Times Square (Selden), 91
The Curious World of Calpurnia Tate (Kelly), 154
Curtis, Christopher Paul, 200
Cut from the Same Cloth: American Women of Myth, Legend, and Tall Tale (San Souci), 141

D

Dahl, Roald, 98, 186, 201
Dancing Shoes (Streatfeild), 62
Dangerous Pumpkins (Jenkins), 205
Danitra Brown Class Clown (Grimes), 204
Danitra Brown Leaves Town (Grimes), 204
Danziger, Paula, 201
Dark Emperor and Other Poems of the Night (Sidman), 43
The Dark Is Rising (Cooper), 115, 116
The Dark-Thirty: Southern Tales of the Supernatural (McKissack), 137
Darkwing (Oppel), 122
Darth Paper Strikes Back (Angleberger), 215
Darwin (McGinty), 177
Dash (Larson), 154–155
d'Aulaire, Edgar Parin, 132–133
d'Aulaire, Ingri, 132–133
d'Aulaire's Book of Greek Myths (d'Aulaire and d'Aulaire), 132
dAulaire's Book of Norse Myths (d'Aulaire and d'Aulaire), 132–133
d'Aulaire's Book of Trolls (d'Aulaire and d'Aulaire), 133
Days with Frog and Toad (Lobel), 28
Dear Whiskers (Nagda), 74–75
Deep Water Magic (Jonell), 106
Delacre, Lulu, 21
The Devil's Arithmetic (Yolen), 156
Diary of a Wimpy Kid: Greg Heffley's Journal (Kinney), 71
DiCamillo, Kate, 9, 22–23, 82, 187, 202, 211, 217
Dickenson, Emily, 39
Dinosaurs Before Dark (Osborne), 29–30
Dinosaurs (Long), 174
DiTerlizzi, Tony, 99
Doctor Proctor's Fart Powder (Nesbø), 193
Dodge, Mary Mapes, 51
The Doll People (Martin and Godwin), 87
The Doll People Set Sail (Martin and Godwin), 87

The Doll Shop Downstairs (McDonough), 157
Dory and the Real True Friend (Hanlon), 25
Dory Fantasmagory (Hanlon), 24–25
Down the Colorado: John Wesley Powell, the One-Armed Explorer (Ray), 180
Dragon Rider (Funke), 116–117
The Dragons of Blueland (Gannett), 83
du Bois, William Pène, 123
Duck for a Day (McKinlay), 29
Dumpling Days (Lin), 57

E

Eager, Edward, 14, 100
Earwig and the Witch (Jones), 190–191
Echoes for the Eye: Poems to Celebrate Patterns in Nature (Esbensen), 36
Edinger, Monica, 148
Edward Eager's Tales of Magic (Eager), 100
Ehlert, Lois, 168
Eight Days of Luke (Jones), 220
Election Madness (English), 68
Ella Enchanted (Levine), 205
Ella of All-of-a-Kind Family (Taylor), 161
Elmer and the Dragon (Gannett), 83
Emily Stew: With Some Side Dishes (Rockwell), 41–42
Emma Dilemma and the Camping Nanny (Hermes), 55
Emma Dilemma and the New Nanny (Hermes), 55
Emma Dilemma and the Soccer Nanny (Hermes), 55
Emma Dilemma and the Two Nannies (Hermes), 55
Emma Dilemma: Big Sister Poems (George), 37
Emma Dilemma, the Nanny, and the Best Horse Ever (Hermes), 55
Emma Dilemma, the Nanny, and the Secret Ferret (Hermes), 55
Emperor Pickletine Rides the Bus (Angleberger), 215
Encyclopedia Brown, Boy Detective (Sobol), 224
An Enemy at Green Knowe (Boston), 147
English, Karen, 68
The Enormous Egg (Butterworth), 185
Enright, Elizabeth, 52, 149
Eratosthenes, The Librarian Who Measured the Earth (Lasky), 173
Erdrich, Louise, 149
Ereth's Birthday (Avi), 81

Esbensen, Barbara Juster, 36
Escape from Mr. Lemoncello's Library (Grabenstein), 218
The Escape of the Deadly Dinosaur: USA (Hunt), 119
Esperanza Rising (Ryan), 160
Estes, Eleanor, 53
Everything on It (Silverstein), 43
The Evolution of Calpurnia Tate (Kelly), 154
The Extraordinary Mark Twain (According to Susy) (Kerley), 172–173
Eye: How It Works (Macauley and Keenan), 176

F

Falling Up (Silverstein), 43
A Family of Poems: My Favorite Poetry for Children (Kennedy), 39–40
A Family of Readers (Sutton and Parravano), 229
The Field Guide (DiTerlizzi and Black), 99
Firefly July: A Year of Very Short Poems (Janeczko), 39
Firewing (Oppel), 122
The Firework-Maker's Daughter (Pullman), 108
Fitzgerald, Laura Marx, 217
Fitzhugh, Louise, 203
Flat Stanley (Brown), 184–185
Fleischman, Sid, 187–188
Fleming, Ian, 100
Floca, Brian, 150
Flora & Ulysses: The Illuminated Adventures (DiCamillo), 187
Fly Away (MacLachlan), 59
Fly Guy Presents: Space (Arnold), 18
Follow, Follow (Singer), 44
Footwork: The Story of Fred and Adele Astaire (Orgill), 165
Forever Rose (McKay), 60
Fortunately, the Milk (Gaiman), 118
The Four-Story Mistake (Enright), 53
Foxlee, Karen, 116
Fradin, Dennis Brindell, 169
Franco, Betsy, 36
Freedman, Russell, 170
Frightful's Mountain (George), 119
Frindle (Clements), 67–68
Frog and Toad All Year (Lobel), 28
Frog and Toad Are Friends (Lobel), 27–28
Frog and Toad Storybook Treasury (Lobel), 28

Frog and Toad Together (Lobel), 28
From the Mixed-Up Files of Mrs. Basil E. Frankweiler (Konigsburg), 216, 218, 220–221
Funke, Cornelia, 101, 116

G

Gaiman, Neil, 117–118
The Game of Silence (Erdrich), 150
Gannett, Ruth Stiles, 82
Gantos, Jack, 188
Gardner, Sally, 102
Geisel, Theodor Seuss, 8
George, Jean Craighead, 15, 118, 203
George, Jessica Day, 102
George, Kristine O'Connell, 37
The Ghosts of Tupelo Landing (Turnage), 225
The Giant Rat of Sumatra: or, Pirates Galore (Fleischman), 187–188
Ginger Pye (Estes), 53–54
Giovanni, Nikki, 37
Gloria's Way (Cameron), 20–21
Godwin, Laura, 87
Gold! Gold from the American River! (Brown), 166
Gone-Away Lake (Enright), 149
Good Luck Anna Hibiscus! (Atinuke), 19
Gooney Bird and All Her Charms (Lowry), 192
Gooney Bird and the Room Mother (Lowry), 192
Gooney Bird Greene (Lowry), 191–192
Gooney Bird Is So Absurd (Lowry), 192
Gooney Bird on the Map (Lowry), 192
Gooney Bird the Fabulous (Lowry), 192
Grabenstein, Chris, 218
Graff, Lisa, 219
Grahame, Kenneth, 83
Grandfather's Dance (MacLachlan), 156
Grasshopper Magic (Jonell), 106
Graveyard Book (Gaiman), 118
Great Books for Boys (Odean), 229
Great Books for Girls (Odean), 229
The Great Cake Mystery: Precious Ramotswe's Very First Case (Smith), 72–73
Great-Grandpa's in the Litter Box (Greenburg), 189
Greenburg, Dan, 189
Greenwitch (Cooper), 115
Gregor and the Code of Claw (Collins), 114

Gregor and the Curse of the *Warmbloods* (Collins), 114

Gregor and the Marks of Secret (Collins), 114

Gregor and the Prophecy of Bane (Collins), 114

Gregor the Overlander (Collins), 114

The Grey King (Cooper), 115

Grimes, Nikki, 38, 69, 204

Gully's Travels (Seidler), 90–91

Gutman, Dan, 151

H

Haas, Jessie, 24

Haig, Matt, 103

Half Magic (Eager), 100

Halfway to Perfect (Grimes), 69

Hamilton, Virginia, 134

Hamster Magic (Jonell), 105–106

Handel, Who Knew What He Liked (Anderson), 164

Hanlon, Abby, 24

Hans Brinker (Coville), 51

Harper, Charise Mericle, 69

Harper, Jessica, 25

Harriet the Spy (Fitzhugh), 203

Harry Potter and the Sorcerer's Stone (Rowling), 108–109

Harry Potter series, 5, 10, 108–109

Hate That Cat (Creech), 35

Have Fun Anna Hibiscus! (Atinuke), 19

Hayes, Geoffrey, 9

He Has Shot the President (Brown), 166

Heidi (Spyri), 210

Hello, Bumblebee Bat (Lunde), 9

Hendrix, John, 151

Henkes, Kevin, 9, 54

Henry, Marguerite, 152

Henry and Beezus (Cleary), 67

Henry and Mudge and the Great Grandpas (Rylant), 32

Henry and Mudge: The First Book of Their Adventures (Rylant), 32

Henry and Ribsy (Cleary), 67

Henry and the Clubhouse (Cleary), 67

Henry and the Paper Route (Cleary), 67

Henry Huggins (Cleary), 67

Heos, Bridget, 170

Hercules (McCaughrean), 136

Hermes, Patricia, 55

The Hero and the Minotaur: The Fantastic Adventures of Theseus (Byrd), 130

Hicks, Clifford B., 219

The Hidden Gallery (Wood), 226

The High King (Alexander), 112

High Time for Heroes (Osborne), 122–123

Hill, Kirkpatrick, 152

Hip Hop Speaks to Children: A Celebration of Poetry with a Beat (Giovanni), 37–38

Holling, Holling Clancy, 171

Holm, Jennifer L., 153

Holt, Kimberly Willis, 55

A Home for Mr. Emerson (Kerley), 173

Homer Price (McCloskey), 14

Honus and Me: A Baseball Card Adventure (Gutman), 151

Hooray for Anna Hibiscus! (Atinuke), 19

The Horn Book Magazine, 229

The Horse and His Boy (Lewis), 107–108

The House at Pooh Corner (Milne), 207

How Tía Lola Came to (Visit) Stay (Alvarez), 48

How Tía Lola Ended Up Starting Over (Alvarez), 48

How Tía Lola Learned to Teach (Alvarez), 48

How Tía Lola Saved the Summer (Alvarez), 48

How to Catch a Bogle (Jinks), 105

How to Train Your Dragon (Cowell), 185–186

Howe, Deborah, 190

Howe, James, 190

Howliday Inn (Howe), 190

Hunt, Elizabeth Singer, 119

Hurwitz, Johanna, 26

I

I Barfed on Mrs. Kenley (Harper), 25

I Want My Hat Back (Klassen), 9

Ibbotson, Eva, 103–104

If the Shoe Fits: Voices from Cinderella (Whipple), 44–45

Igraine the Brave (Funke), 101

In Search of a Homeland: The Story of the Aeneid (Lively), 135

Indian Shoes (Smith), 61

Indigo's Star (McKay), 60

Inkheart (Funke), 117

An Interrupted Tale (Wood), 226

The Invention of Hugo Cabret: A Novel in Words and Pictures (Selznick), 223

Invisible Inkling (Jenkins), 204–205

The Ironwood Tree (DiTerlizzi and Black), 99

Isaacs, Kathleen T., 11

Island: A Story of the Galápagos (Chin), 167–168
Ivy + Bean (Barrows), 19
Izzy Barr, Running Star (Mills), 74

J

Jack Plank Tells Tales (Babbitt), 146
Jacques, Brian, 119
Jane on Her Own (Le Guin), 87
Janeczko, Paul B., 39
Jansson, Tove, 120
Jarrell, Randall, 84
Jasper John Dooley: Star of the Week (Adderson), 66
Jenkins, Emily, 70, 204
Jenkins, Martin, 121
Jenkins, Steve, 172
Jenny and the Cat Club: A Collection of Favorite Stories About Jenny Linsky (Averill), 80–81
The Jesse Tree (McCaughrean), 135–136
Jet Plane: How It Works (Macauley and Keenan), 176
Jinks, Catherine, 105
Jinx (Blackwood), 96
Jinx's Fire (Blackwood), 96
Jinx's Magic (Blackwood), 96
John Muir: America's First Environmentalist (Lasky), 165
Jonathan Swift's Gulliver (Jenkins), 121
Jonell, Lynne, 105
Jones, Diana Wynne, 110, 190, 220
Jo's Boys (Alcott), 198
Josephine: The Dazzling Life of Josephine Baker (Powell), 178–179
Judy Moody (McDonald), 73
Julia Gillian (and the Art of Knowing) (McGhee), 206–207
Julia Gillian (and the Dream of a Dog) (McGhee), 207
Julia Gillian (and the Quest for Joy) (McGhee), 207
Julie (George), 204
Julie of the Wolves (George), 15, 203–204
Julie's Wolf Pack (George), 204
Junie B. Jones and the Stupid Smelly Bus (Park), 30–31
Just Grace (Harper), 69–70
Just So Stories (Kipling), 5, 134–135
Juster, Norton, 191

K

Keena Ford and the Field Trip Mix-Up (Thomson), 78
Keena Ford and the Second-Grade Mix-Up (Thomson), 77–78
Keena Ford and the Secret Journal Mix-Up (Thomson), 78
Kelly, Jacqueline, 154
Kelsey Green, Reading Queen (Mills), 74
Kennedy, Caroline, 39
Kennedy, X. J., 39
Kerley, Barbara, 172
King of Shadows (Cooper), 147–148
King-Smith, Dick, 85
Kinney, Jeff, 71
Kipling, Rudyard, 5, 134
Klassen, Jon, 9
Knight's Castle (Eager), 100
Knights of the Kitchen Table (Scieszka), 125–126
Konigsburg, E. L., 213–214, 220–221

L

Lady Liberty: a Biography (Rappaport), 165
Larson, Kirby, 154
Lasky, Kathryn, 173
The Last Battle (Lewis), 108
The Last Olympian (Riordan), 125
Lawnmower Magic (Jonell), 106
Lawson, Robert, 86
Le Guin, Ursula K., 86
Lee, Milly, 155
Left Behind (Adderson), 66
L'Engle, Madeleine, 106
Leroy Ninker Saddles Up (DiCamillo), 23
Let It Begin Here (Brown), 166
Levine, Gail Carson, 205
Levy, Dana Alison, 56
Lewis, C. S., 107
A Light in the Attic (Silverstein), 43
The Lightning Thief (Riordan), 124–125
Like Bug Juice on a Burger (Sternberg), 77
Like Carrot Juice on a Cupcake (Sternberg), 77
Like Pickle Juice on a Cookie (Sternberg), 77
Lin, Grace, 9, 27, 56, 121
Lindgren, Astrid, 206
Ling & Ting: Not Exactly the Same! (Lin), 27
Ling & Ting Share a Birthday (Lin), 27
Ling & Ting: Twice as Silly (Lin), 27

The Lion, the Witch, and the Wardrobe:
    A Story for Children (Lewis), 107
Lipson, Eden Ross, 229
Little Author in the Big Woods: A Biography of
    Laura Ingalls Wilder (McDonough), 177
Little House in the Big Woods (Wilder), 162
Little Men (Alcott), 198
Little Women (Alcott), 15, 198
Lively, Penelope, 135
The Lives of Christopher Chant (Jones), 110
Lobel, Arnold, 27
Locomotive (Floca), 150
Loki's Wolves (Armstrong and Marr), 113
Long, John, 174
The Long Secret (Fitzhugh), 203
Look, Lenore, 57, 71
Louisa: The Life of Louisa May Alcott
    (McDonough), 176–177
Love That Dog (Creech), 35
Lovelace, Maud Hart, 72
Lowry, Lois, 58, 155, 191–192
Lucinda's Secret (DiTerlizzi and Black), 99
Lulu and the Brontosaurus (Viorst), 196
Lulu and the Cat in the Bag (McKay), 28
Lulu and the Dog from the Sea (McKay), 28
Lulu and the Duck in the Park (McKay), 28
Lulu and the Rabbit Next Door (McKay), 28
Lunde, Darrin, 9

M
Macaulay, David, 174–176
MacLachlan, Patricia, 59, 156
Magic by the Lake (Eager), 14, 100
Magic Tree House Fact Trackers (Osborne),
    123
The Magical Fruit (Nesbø), 193
The Magician's Nephew (Lewis),
    107–108
The Magicians of Caprona (Jones), 110
Make Way for Dyamonde Daniel (Grimes), 69
Maniac Magee: A Novel (Spinelli), 209
Many Waters (L'Engle), 106
Marr, Melissa, 113
Martin, Ann M., 87
The Marvelous Inventions of Alvin Fernald
    (Hicks), 220
Mary Poppins and the House Next Door
    (Travers), 211
Mary Poppins Comes Back (Travers), 211
Mary Poppins in Cherry Tree Lane (Travers),
    211

Mary Poppins in the Park (Travers), 211
Mary Poppins Opens the Door (Travers), 211
Mary Poppins (Travers), 13, 210–211
Mathematickles! (Franco), 36–37
Matilda (Dahl), 201
McCaughrean, Geraldine, 135–136
McCloskey, Robert, 14
McDonald, Megan, 73
McDonough, Yona Zeldis, 157, 176
The McElderry Book of Grimms' Fairy Tales
    (Pirotta), 139–140
McGhee, Alison, 9, 22, 206
McGinty, Alice B., 177
McKay, Hilary, 28, 59
McKinlay, Meg, 29
McKissack, Patricia C., 137
Meadowlands: A Wetlands Survival Story
    (Yezerski), 181
The Meanest Doll in the World (Martin and
    Godwin), 87
Meet Danitra Brown (Grimes), 204
Meow Means Mischief (Nagda), 75
Mercy Watson Fights Crime (DiCamillo), 24
Mercy Watson Goes for a Ride (DiCamillo),
    23–24
Mercy Watson: Princess in Disguise
    (DiCamillo), 24
Mercy Watson: Something Wonky This Way
    Comes (DiCamillo), 24
Mercy Watson Thinks Like a Pig (DiCamillo),
    24
Mercy Watson to the Rescue (DiCamillo),
    23–24
Merrill, Jean, 193
The Middle Moffat (Estes), 53
Mightier Than the Sword (Yolen), 143
Mikis and the Donkey (Tak), 52
Mill (Macaulay), 175
Mills, Claudia, 74
Milne, A. A., 207
Minn of the Mississippi (Holling), 171
The Miraculous Journey of Edward Tulane
    (DiCamillo), 82
Mirror Mirror: A Book of Reversible Verse
    (Singer), 44
The Misadventures of the Family Fletcher
    (Levy), 56
Misty of Chincoteague (Henry), 152
Mochizuki, Ken, 157
Moffat Museum (Estes), 53
The Moffats (Estes), 53
Montgomery, L. M., 15, 207

More All-of-a-Kind Family (Taylor), 161
More Perfect than the Moon (MacLachlan), 156
More Sideways Arithmetic from Wayside School (Sachar), 195
Mosque (Macaulay), 175
The Mouse and the Motorcycle (Cleary), 200
A Mouse Called Wolf (King-Smith), 85–86
The Mouse of Amherst (Spires), 91–92
The Mouse with the Question Mark Tail (Peck), 89
Mr. Bass's Planetoid (Cameron), 114
Mr. Popper's Penguins (Atwater and Atwater), 184
Mr. Revere and I (Lawson), 86
Mrs. Frisby and the Rats of NIMH (O'Brien), 222
Murphy, Jim, 158
My Father's Dragon (Gannett), 82–83
My Side of the Mountain (George), 118–119
Myers, Walter Dean, 35
The Mysterious Howling (Wood), 226
A Mystery for Mr. Bass (Cameron), 114
The Mystery of Meerkat Hill (Smith), 73
The Mystery of the Missing Lion (Smith), 73

N
Nagda, Ann Whitehead, 74
Napoli, Donna Jo, 137–138
Naylor, Phyllis Reynolds, 15
Nelson, Vaunda Micheaux, 178
Nesbø, Jo, 193
The New Way Things Work (Macaulay and Ardley), 175
The New York Times Parent's Guide to the Best Books for Children: 3rd Edition (Lipson), 229
The Newsy News Newsletter (English), 68
The Night Fairy (Schlitz), 109
Nighty Nightmare (Howe), 190
Nikki & Deja (English), 68
Nim and the War Effort (Lee), 155
Nora and the Texas Terror (Cox), 21
Norton, Mary, 88
Not in Love (Adderson), 66
Not One Damsel in Distress: World Folktales for Strong Girls (Yolen), 143
The Not-Just-Anybody Family (Byars), 50
Number the Stars (Lowry), 155–156
Nuts to You (Perkins), 89
Nye, Naomi Shihab, 60

O
O'Brien, Robert C., 222
Octopuses! Strange and Wonderful (Pringle), 179
Odd and the Frost Giants (Gaiman), 117
Odean, Kathleen, 229
Odin's Ravens (Armstrong and Marr), 113
Odysseus (McCaughrean), 136
On the Far Side of the Mountain (George), 119
100 Best Books for Children: A Parent's Guide to Making the Right Choices for Your Young Reader, Toddler to Preteen (Silvey), 229
Operation Bunny: The Fairy Detective Agency's First Case (Gardner), 102
Ophelia and the Marvelous Boy (Foxlee), 116
Oppel, Kenneth, 122
Osborne, Mary Pope, 29, 122, 139
Our Only May Amelia (Holm), 153
Over Sea, Under Stone (Cooper), 115–116

P
Paddle to the Sea (Holling), 171
Pagoo (Holling), 171
Parenteau, Shirley, 158
Parish, Herman, 30
Parish, Peggy, 30
Park, Barbara, 30
Park, Linda Sue, 75
Parravano, Martha V., 229
Paschen, Elise, 40
Paterson, Katherine, 15, 75
Pearce, Philippa, 159
Peck, Richard, 88
The Penderwicks: A Summer Tale of Four Sisters, Two Rabbits, and a Very Interesting Boy (Birdsall), 48–49
The Penderwicks at Point Mouette (Birdsall), 49
The Penderwicks in Spring (Birdsall), 49
The Penderwicks on Gardam Street (Birdsall), 49
Pennypacker, Sara, 208
The People Could Fly: American Black Folktales (Hamilton), 134
The People Could Fly: The Picture Book (Hamilton), 134
Perkins, Lynne Rae, 89
Permanent Rose (McKay), 60

Perseus (McCaughrean), 136
The Phantom Tollbooth (Juster), 191
Picturing the World (Isaacs), 11, 164
Pieces and Players (Balliett), 216
Pilkey, Dav, 183
Pinkney, Jerry, 128–129
Pinky Pye (Estes), 54
Piper Reed, Campfire Girl (Holt), 56
Piper Reed, Forever Friend (Holt), 56
Piper Reed Gets a Job (or . . . Party Planner)
    (Holt), 56
Piper Reed, Navy Brat (Holt), 55–56
Piper Reed, Rodeo Star (Holt), 56
Piper Reed, the Great Gypsy (Holt), 56
Pippi Longstocking (Lindgren), 206
Pirotta, Saviour, 139
A Plague of Bogles (Jinks), 105
A Pocketful of Poems (Grimes), 38
Poetry Speaks to Children (Paschen), 38, 40
A Pond Full of Ink (Schmidt), 42
Poppy and Ereth (Avi), 81
Poppy and Rye (Avi), 81
Poppy (Avi), 81
Poppy's Return (Avi), 81
The Porcupine Year (Erdrich), 150
Potter, Beatrix, 90
Powell, Patricia Hruby, 178
Prelutsky, Jack, 41
Prince Caspian (Lewis), 108
Princess Labelmaker to the Rescue!
    (Angleberger), 215
Pringle, Laurence, 179
Project Mulberry: A Novel (Park), 75
Pullman, Philip, 108
The Pushcart War (Merrill), 193
Pyramid (Macaulay), 175

R
R-T, Margaret, and the Rats of NIMH
    (O'Brien), 222
Racso and the Rats of NIMH (O'Brien), 222
Rafi and Rosi (Delacre), 21–22
Rafi and Rosi: Carnival (Delacre), 22
Ragweed (Avi), 81
Ralph S. Mouse (Cleary), 200
Ransome, Arthur, 124
Raskin, Ellen, 214, 222
Ray, Deborah Kogan, 180
Redwall (Jacques), 119–120
Redwoods (Chin), 168
The Reluctant Dragon (Grahame), 83–84

Return to Gone-Away (Enright), 149
Return to Howliday Inn (Howe), 190
Return to the Willows (Grahame), 83
Ribsy (Cleary), 67
Rich (Grimes), 69
The Right Word: Roget and His Thesaurus
    (Bryant), 167
Riordan, Rick, 124, 136
Rip-Roaring Russell (Hurwitz), 26–27
The River of Green Knowe (Boston), 147
Robin Hood (Calcutt), 130–131
Robinson, Barbara, 194
Rockwell, Thomas, 41
Rooftoppers (Rundell), 125
Ross, Catherine Sheldrick, 180
Rotten Ralph Helps Out (Gantos),
    188–189
Rowling, J. K., 108, 230
Roy, Ron, 31
Ruby Lu, Brave and True (Look), 57
Ruby Lu, Empress of Everything (Look), 57
Ruby Lu, Star of the Show (Look), 57
Rufus M (Estes), 53
Rumford, James, 140
The Runaway Dolls (Martin and Godwin), 87
Runaway Radish (Haas), 24
Runaway Ralph (Cleary), 200
Rundell, Katherine, 125, 209
Ryan, Pam Muñoz, 160
Rylant, Cynthia, 9, 32

S
Sachar, Louis, 194
Saffy's Angel (McKay), 59–60
Salisbury, Graham, 76
Samuel Blink and the Forbidden Forest (Haig),
    103
Samuel Blink and the Runaway Troll (Haig),
    103
San Souci, Robert D., 141
Sarah, Plain and Tall (MacLachlan), 156
The Saturdays (Enright), 52–53
Schertle, Alice, 39
Schlitz, Laura Amy, 109
Schmidt, Annie M. G., 42
Scieszka, Jon, 125, 229
Scorpions! Strange and Wonderful (Pringle),
    179
The Scraps Book: Notes from a Colorful Life
    (Ehlert), 168–169
The Sea of Monsters (Riordan), 125

Seabird (Holling), 171
The Secret Chicken Society (Cox), 21
The Secret Garden (Burnett), 199
The Secret of Platform 13 (Ibbotson), 104
The Secret of the Fortune Wookiee
    (Angleberger), 215
The Secret World of Walter Anderson (Bass),
    165
Secrets at Sea: A Novel (Peck), 88–89
See You Around, Sam! (Lowry), 59
The Seeing Stone (DiTerlizzi and Black), 99
Seidler, Tor, 90
Selden, George, 91
The Selkie Girl (Cooper), 131
Selznick, Brian, 223
Separate Is Never Equal: Sylvia Mendez and
    Her Family's Fight for Desegregation
    (Tonatiuh), 161
Seuss, Dr. *See* Geisel, Theodor Seuss
Shapes in Math, Science and Nature: Squares,
    Triangles and Circles (Ross), 180–181
Ship of Dolls (Parenteau), 158–159
Shooting at the Stars: The Christmas Truce of
    1914 (Hendrix), 151–152
Sideways Arithmetic from Wayside School
    (Sachar), 195
Sideways Stories from Wayside School
    (Sachar), 194–195
Sidman, Joyce, 42
The Silver Cow: A Welsh Tale (Cooper), 131
The Silver Chair (Lewis), 108
Silver on the Tree (Cooper), 115
Silverstein, Shel, 43
Silverwing (Oppel), 122
Silvey, Anita, 229
Singer, Marilyn, 44
Singh, Vandana, 195
Skating Shoes (Streatfeild), 62
Skit-Scat Raggedy Cat: Ella Fitzgerald (Orgill),
    165
Skylark (MacLachlan), 156
Smith, Alexander McCall, 72
Smith, Cynthia Leitich, 61
Snicket, Lemony, 223
Sobol, Donald J., 224
Spiderweb for Two (Enright), 53
Spinelli, Jerry, 209
Spires Elizabeth, 91
Sport (Fitzhugh), 203
Spunky Tells All (Cameron), 21
Spyri, Johanna, 210
Starry River of the Sky (Lin), 122

Steig, William, 92, 126
Sternberg, Julie, 77
The Stones of Green Knowe (Boston), 147
The Stories Julian Tells (Cameron), 20
Stormy, Misty's Foal (Henry), 152
Stowaway to the Mushroom Planet (Cameron),
    114
The Strange Case of Origami Yoda
    (Angleberger), 214–215
A Stranger at Green Knowe (Boston), 147
Streatfeild, Noel, 61
Stuart Little (White), 93–94
Substitute Trouble (English), 68
Sunwing (Oppel), 122
The Surprise Attack of Jabba the Puppett
    (Angleberger), 215
Surprise Island (Warner), 62
Sutcliff, Rosemary, 141–142
Sutton, Roger, 229
Swallowdale (Ransome), 124
Swallows and Amazons (Ransome), 124
A Swiftly Tilting Planet (L'Engle), 106
Swirl by Swirl: Spirals in Nature (Sidman), 43

T
Tak, Bibi Dumon, 52
The Tale of Benjamin Bunny (Potter), 90
The Tale of Despereaux: Being the Story of
    a Mouse, a Princess, Some Soup, and a
    Spool of Thread (DiCamillo), 217
The Tale of Mr. Tod (Potter), 90
The Tale of Peter Rabbit (Potter), 90
The Tale of the Flopsy Bunnies (Potter), 90
Tales of Dimwood Forest (Avi), 81
Tales of Hans Christian Andersen (Andersen),
    129
Tam Lin (Cooper), 131
A Tangle of Knots (Graff), 219
Taran Wanderer (Alexander), 112
Taylor, Sydney, 160
Theater Shoes (Streatfeild), 62
Then There were Five (Enright), 53
Theseus (McCaughrean), 136
The Thief Lord (Funke), 117
Thomson, Melissa, 77
Thor's Serpents (Armstrong and Marr), 113
Those Rebels, John and Tom (Kerley), 173
The Three Pickled Herrings (Gardner), 102
Three Times Lucky (Turnage), 225
Thursdays with the Crown (George), 103
Time and Mr. Bass (Cameron), 114

The Time Garden (Eager), 100
The Titan's Curse (Riordan), 125
Toilet: How It Works (Macauley and Keenan), 176
Tom's Midnight Garden (Pearce), 159
Tonatiuh, Duncan, 161
Toy Dance Party (Jenkins), 70
Toys Come Home (Jenkins), 70
Toys Go Out: Being the Adventures of a Knowledgeable Stingray, a Toughy Little Buffalo, and Someone Called Plastic (Jenkins), 70
Travers, P. L., 13, 2110
Treasure of Green Knowe (Boston), 147
Treasury of Egyptian Mythology: Classic Stories of Gods, Goddesses, Monsters & Mortals (Napoli), 138
Treasury of Greek Mythology: Classic Stories of Gods, Goddesses, Heroes & Monsters (Napoli), 137–138
Tree in the Trail (Holling), 171
The Trouble with May Amelia (Holm), 153
The True Blue Scouts of Sugar Man Swamp (Appelt), 80
The Trumpet of the Swan (White), 93
Tuesdays at the Castle (George), 102–103
Turnage, Sheila, 225
The Turtle of Oman: A Novel (Nye), 60
The 20th Century Children's Poetry Treasury (Prelutsky), 41
The Twenty-One Balloons (Du Bois), 123
Two for One (DiCamillo and McGhee), 22

U

Ubiquitous (Sidman), 43
Uh-oh, Cleo (Harper), 25
Ukulele Hayley (Cox), 21
Unbuilding (Macaulay), 175
Under the Egg (Fitzgerald), 217–218
Underpants on My Head (Harper), 25
The Unmapped Sea (Wood), 226
The Unseen Guest (Wood), 226

V

The View from Saturday (Konigsburg), 221
Violet Mackerel's Brilliant Plot (Branford), 49
Violet Mackerel's Natural Habitat (Branford), 49
Violet Mackerel's Personal Space (Branford), 49

Violet Mackerel's Possible Friend (Branford), 49
Violet Mackerel's Possible Protest (Branford), 49
Violet Mackerel's Remarkable Recovery (Branford), 49
Viorst, Judith, 196
Vision of Beauty: The Story of Sarah Breedlove Walker (Lasky), 165
A Voice of Her Own: The Story of Phillis Wheatley, Slave Poet (Lasky), 173
The Voyage of the Dawn Treader (Lewis), 108

W

The Wanderings of Odysseus:The Story of The Odyssey (Sutcliff), 142
Wanted . . . Mud Blossom (Byars), 50
Warner, Gertrude Chandler, 62
Wayside School Gets a Little Stranger (Sachar), 195
Wayside School Is Falling Down (Sachar), 195
Webb, Holly, 225
Wedding Drama (English), 68
Wednesdays in the Tower (George), 103
Welcome Home, Anna Hibiscus! (Atinuke), 19
The Westing Game (Raskin), 222–223
Whales! Strange and Wonderful (Pringle), 179
What to Do About Alice?: How Alice Roosevelt Broke the Rules, Charmed the World, and Drove Her Father Teddy Crazy! (Kerley), 173
What to Expect When You're Expecting Hatchlings: A Guide for Crocodilian Parents (and Curious Kids) (Heos), 171
What to Expect When You're Expecting Joeys: A Guide for Marsupial Parents (and Curious Kids) (Heos), 170–171
What to Expect When You're Expecting Larvae: A Guide for Insect Parents (and Curious Kids) (Heos), 171
Where the Mountain Meets the Moon (Lin), 121–122
Where the Sidewalk Ends:The Poems and Drawings of Shel Silverstein (Silverstein), 43
Where the Wild Things Are (Sendak), 7
The Whipping Boy (Fleischman), 188
Whipple, Laura, 44
White, E. B., 93, 211
Whittington (Armstrong), 215
Who Cut the Cheese? (Nesbø), 193

Who Was Ben Franklin? (Fradin), 169
Who Was? biography series, 11
The Whoopie Pie War (Jenkins), 205
Why Mosquitoes Buzz in People's Ears: A West African Tale (Aardema), 128
Wilder, Laura Ingalls, 162
Willems, Mo, 9
Williams, Vera B., 63
A Wind in the Door (L'Engle), 106
The Wind in the Willows (Grahame), 83
Winnie-the-Pooh (Milne), 207
Winter Bees & Other Poems of the Cold (Sidman), 42–43
Witch Week (Jones), 110
The Witches (Dahl), 98–99
Wolfsnail: A Backyard Predator (Campbell), 9
Wonderful Alexander and the Catwings (Le Guin), 87
The Wonderful Flight to the Mushroom Planet (Cameron), 113–114
Wood, Maryrose, 226
Woods, Brenda, 212

The Wrath of Mulgarath (DiTerlizzi and Black), 99
Wright, Richard, 39
The Wright 3 (Balliett), 216
A Wrinkle in Time (L'Engle), 106

Y
The Year of Billy Miller (Henkes), 54
The Year of the Baby (Cheng), 67
The Year of the Book (Cheng), 66–67
The Year of the Dog: A Novel (Lin), 56–57
The Year of the Rat (Lin), 57
Yezerski, Thomas F., 181
Yolen, Jane, 143, 156
Younguncle Comes to Town (Singh), 195

Z
Zooman Sam (Lowry), 59